THE MENDOLA REPORT

THE MENDOLA REPORT

A New Look at Gay Couples

MARY MENDOLA

CROWN PUBLISHERS, INC.   NEW YORK

Inquiries should be addressed to Crown Publishers, Inc.,
One Park Avenue, New York, New York 10016
Printed in the United States of America
Published simultaneously in Canada
by General Publishing Company Limited
Library of Congress Cataloging in Publication Data
Mendola, Mary.
The Mendola report.
1. Homosexuals—United States. 2. Homosexuals—
United States—Interviews. I. Title. II. Title:
Gay couples.
HQ76.3.U5M46   1980   306.7'6   80-13775
ISBN: 0-517-541394
Design by Camilla Filancia
10 9 8 7 6 5 4 3 2 1
First Edition

For Valerie,
my number one editor . . .

who worked at
making certain
our marriage
survived
the book on marriage

CONTENTS

ACKNOWLEDGMENTS

If one is going to hold down a full-time job and produce a book in thirteen months, it's best one have a lot of help! And I had it. There were people and organizations to help administer and distribute the questionnaire. There were people to help arrange for the interviews. And there were people to volunteer for whatever needed doing—whether it was stuffing envelopes or coding questionnaires.

No sexual barriers existed among the people who became involved. They were heterosexuals, homosexuals, and lesbians—men and women—who made a personal contribution to an idea. And I am grateful to them for helping me bring the reality of that idea to these pages. They are:

DAVID COHEN, PH.D.

TERRY GEARY

GEORGE AND MARY KAYLOR

TONI NARDUCCI

JOSEPH NEBGEN

THE 30 VOLUNTEER "CODERS"

SISTER JEANNINE GRAMICK, SSND, NEW WAYS MINISTRY, MT. RAINIER, MD.

BILL LABARR, GAY AND YOUNG, INC., NEW YORK CITY

JUDITH SAUNDERS

SOUTHERN CALIFORNIA WOMEN FOR UNDERSTANDING

PROLOGUE

I am a human being. I am a woman. I am a lesbian. Like other lesbians and homosexuals, I am tired of being defined in terms of my sexual behavior because my sexuality is but a part of my emotional life, is but a part of my humanity. Like other human beings, I am a whole person: I hope, I laugh, I pray, I work.

I will no longer pretend I am a heterosexual—neither to myself nor to anyone else. I will no longer participate in prolonging a perverted system of social and religious values that perpetuates itself by nurturing my self-hate. I will not cooperate in my own degradation because, as long as I remain threatened, I myself provide the weapons with which I can be threatened.

I will no longer use protective pronouns to hide an identity that should not be hidden. I will no longer use the anonymous *we*. I will no longer use the words *friend* or *roommate* to define the woman I love—the woman with whom I share my life. I will no longer accept the "language of the hidden" because it both demeans my dignity as a person and demeans my human potential to love. I will no longer be "kept in my place" because accepting "the place" to which I have been relegated serves to debase me in my own eyes. I will no longer accept my shame because there is nothing for which I am ashamed. I will attest to the fact that I am a lesbian. I will attest to my human dignity and to the positive human values in which I believe.

I will not accept less than the very best life has to offer because I am a lesbian—nor should other lesbians and homosexuals accept less than what are their rights as human beings: the right to love, the right to make a life with the partners of their choice, the right to be happy. And, also, the right to fail. If I fail in a relationship, I have failed because I am human. I will not accept the assumption that I am doomed to failure *because* I am a lesbian. As failing is part of the normal life cycle for heterosexuals, so my failings are a part of that same normal life cycle. Failing in love and failing in life are part of the human condition. Like any other person, my failures are human failures, not—because I am a lesbian—"proof" of my depravity, my instability, my worthlessness.

I will not wait for any state to give me what are my inalienable rights as a human being. No one can give me what is rightfully mine. Politicians can, in an election year, barter with what are our human rights. Legislators can negotiate what "exactly" are our rights as lesbians and homosexuals. And although I see this process as a necessary evil in securing the civil rights of *all* people, I will not wait. I will, while legislative bodies debate, design for myself a life with the woman of my choice—because, as the legislative bodies debate ad infinitum, life goes on. And as life goes on, so do all the problems and the happinesses of life that have nothing to do with the political issues. I will not permit the government to deprive me of those things that are my right to enjoy. Whether or not my person is illegal, and whether or not I am a crime in most states, I will have a home. I will have a Christmas tree and Christmas presents on Christmas morning. I will have a full life which I will share with the woman I love. We will share the warmth of a quiet evening in front of our fireplace. We will share the strain of a budget that never seems to balance. We will share the car payments and the grocery bills. Together we will worry about our aging parents—hers and mine—their health, their financial situations. We will share planning for vacations and planning for *our* old age. No law and no government can deprive me of these things. No state can sanction my life or legislate my right to love whom I choose.

I will also not wait for any church to establish my goodness in the eyes of God. Because while they spiritually dissect my lesbian soul and decide upon my everlasting whereabouts, I know God and God knows me; ours is a relationship of mutual respect. And while organized religions theologize about my life both now and in the hereafter, God has already given me the dignity and the self-respect He or She bestows upon all human beings. Whether or not this or that church decides or votes to accept me, a loving God accepts me for who I am.

I believe these things for myself as I believe them for all lesbians and homosexuals: take what is yours because it comes from within yourself—no church or any state can give you the dignity that is rightfully yours. I will nowhere and in no aspect of my life accept second-class citizenship or second-rate anything because I am a lesbian.

All these things I believe seem so arrogant, so courageous, so proud. They do not represent a militant and naive utopian philosophy—nor are they intellectual delusions. They are born of confusion and pain, rejection and self-hatred, rage and the struggle for self-acceptance. I am not unique. I am one with millions of other lesbians and homosexuals who have paid the piper for being who they are.

As a people, we will continue to pay: we will pay in religious and legislative tokenism, we will pay in degrading stereotypes, we will pay in denied civil and human rights. We will pay with our sorrow when friends, learning who we are, quietly disappear from our lives.

We cannot control the payments. We can, however, control the degree to which we permit this terrible "paying" to affect our lives and our happiness. For myself, I will no longer recoil in pain, no longer hide in shame. I will no longer accept less than what I deserve as a decent and productive human being. But by not accepting less—by refusing to yield to a society that denies me my basic rights as a human being—I accept the fact that I will continue to pay. And I am afraid. Like other human beings, I do not want to be hurt, I do not want to be rejected, I do not want those I love to experience pain because of who I am. These things frighten me terribly. However, as a lesbian, what are my alternatives: to hide, to live a lie, to deny the woman I love—to deny all that is the essence of my being?

I deeply respect and admire Radcliff Hall both as a writer and as a person. She was a woman and a lesbian of her time as I am a woman and a lesbian of my time. But, unlike Radcliff Hall, I will not accept "the well of loneliness"—I will take what is my right to life.

And now, let's get on with this book. . . .

New York City   MARY MENDOLA
April 1980

THE MENDOLA REPORT

INTRODUCTION

Most writers and creative "types" are subject to occasional delusions of grandeur. Put me behind a typewriter and I am a giant. Proposing a book to a publisher is quite different from receiving the contract to write the book you have proposed: then you have to do what you said you were going to do. In the proposal stage, when it is just you, your typewriter, and your ideas, there is nothing you cannot do. However, in the writing, or "doing," stage, you question your sanity, wondering, "How did I ever think I was going to be able to do this?"

In the proposal stage, you tell the publisher why you think the book you are proposing is important. Your proposal explains how you would, if given the opportunity, actually produce the book. A book such as I was proposing should be—I naively committed myself—based upon a nationwide questionnaire and extensive personal interviews.

The Mendola Report, I explained, would introduce lesbian and homosexual couples who are quietly living happy and full lives with the partners of their choice. No matter where they are living, whether in the suburbs, a city, or in a rural community, they are the couple next door to someone—only no one knows it.

The purpose of such a book: it is time—finally—for lesbian and homosexual couples *themselves* to define the emotional and sexual dimensions of their lives. The book would serve as an open and positive forum where lesbian and homosexual couples could explore the marital lifestyles of their peers in terms of the following premises.

ESSENCE

The essence of a committed relationship is the same whether the union is between two men, two women, or a man and a woman. The qualities of caring, dedication, and sharing are neither male

1

nor female qualities: they are human qualities. I am not "more" committed because I am a woman. And the degree of my commitment is neither diminished nor enhanced by my lesbianism. My commitment is based upon who I am as a person. As a lesbian, I am neither more nor less capable of commitment than a heterosexual woman.

Love and commitment transcend sexual orientation. They are universal experiences that are shared by all people. My ability to love is a *human* characteristic—not an exclusively heterosexual, homosexual, or lesbian characteristic.

EMOTIONAL PREFERENCE

The term "sexual preference" is ludicrous and serves only to degrade a particular minority group of which I am a member. If I ask a male heterosexual why he loves a certain woman, he will probably explain his love for her in terms of his emotional, intellectual, and sexual needs. He will not explain his love in terms of his "sexual preference." Why then should a homosexual's love be defined only in terms of his "sexual preference"? Why is the term "sexual preference" never used when discussing heterosexual relationships?

If, as a lesbian, I am defined only in terms of my "sexual preference," then for me the sex act has nothing to do with my emotional life—if the fact that I have an emotional life is even acknowledged. I am not disputing "sex for sex's sake." However, emotionless sexual experiences seem to be a healthy alternative for heterosexuals and media-created despondency for lesbians and homosexuals: our "sexual preference" seems to some to presuppose a lifetime of emotionless "same sex" experiences. (I get despondent just thinking about it.) Did you ever hear the expression "different sex relationships" used on an afternoon soap opera? Think what that could do to a television program's Nielsen rating.

Words paint pictures: if you continue to define people only in terms of their "sexual preference," the picture can become pornographic, the person's self-image debased.

SANCTION

Lesbian and homosexual couples are involved in marriages and committed relationships that are as meaningful and as valid as any heterosexual marriages sanctioned by a church or state. Churches and states do not sanction a relationship between two people. Couples themselves sanction their relationships.

As heterosexual couples ascertain the value of their relationships, so lesbian and homosexual couples determine the positive or negative impact of their relationships upon their lives. Just as a legal or a religious divorce does not in itself end the love relationship between two people, so a legal or religious ceremony does not create a love relationship between two people—whether they be two men, two women, or a man and a woman.

I personally have no need or desire for either a civil or religious ceremony to sanction my union with the woman I love: we ourselves sanction it as we live together day by day. Our marriage is as deserving of respect as any heterosexual relationship. The woman I love is not my "friend." She is my partner, my spouse— the person with whom I share my life.

Exclusive of my personal feelings on a civil or religious ceremony, I can respect those lesbian and homosexual couples who have chosen to have their relationships blessed in religious ceremonies—either in a Commitment Ceremony or in a Holy Union ceremony. Is God less present in their commitments and marriages because their ceremonies were not performed under the auspices of any institutional religion? That, in fact, is what the institutional churches would have us believe. However, if the institutional churches have decided God is not present in these committed lesbian and homosexual relationships, then institutional churches also deny God what are His or Her rights.

SIMILAR LIFE EXPERIENCES

During my first lesbian marriage, my ex-wife and I were suburban homeowners. We were the couple next door to our heterosexual neighbors—as they were the couple next door to us. The four of us shared many common problems: ever-increasing property taxes, whether or not our homes were properly insulated, crab grass. Mrs. Next Door talked to me about returning to teaching. I talked with her about my never having graduated college. Mr. Next Door had a difficult time relating to his mother-in-law. My mother complained because, as she saw it: "I raised a son and a daughter and ended up with two daughters-in-law." Mrs. Next Door's father helped Mr. Next Door lay a new roof. My father and I planted a Scotch pine in the yard one cold November afternoon. I remember one week in particular: their oil burner motor and our hot water heater "went" almost simultaneously.

As two couples, one heterosexual and one lesbian, we were good neighbors to each other. They would leave their little girl with us if they needed an evening out. We would ask them to "watch" our house while we were away. We knew they knew we were gay, and they knew we knew they knew—nothing was ever said. We discussed many personal things, realizing as two couples that we had similar communication problems with our respective partners. And, of course, all four of us had something to say about similar "who does what around the house" conflicts.

The major difference separating us as heterosexual and lesbian couples: our lesbian marriage had none of the support systems Mr. and Mrs. Next Door enjoyed. I had not had a bridal shower or a bachelor party, depending on how one looks at it. We had not had a wedding. Aunts and uncles did not come to visit and admire our home. We never received anniversary cards. As trivial as these things may seem, they represent something vitally important: heterosexual couples are encouraged to stay together. Their union is celebrated and shared with loving and supportive families and friends. If there is a serious illness, the heterosexual couple will usually receive the emotional—and, oftentimes, the financial— support they need.

Lesbian and homosexual couples have no such support systems. Rather than being encouraged to stay together, we are conditioned to believe there is no future for us as couples. And often, depending on where we live, we exist in isolation. Fear of being discovered can force a lesbian or homosexual couple to exist in an emotional and social vacuum.

Although my lesbian marriage lacked the important support systems enjoyed by the average heterosexual couple, my realization of the similar life we shared with Mr. and Mrs. Next Door began to change my perspective. There were, in fact, differences between my lover and me and the couple next door. However, those differences were sociologically based: income and educational level, ethnic and religious backgrounds, political orientation.

My lesbianism less and less separated me from a whole world of heterosexuals who were "just like me." Their lives were absorbed with many of the same things with which my life was absorbed: working hard at building a relationship, struggling to maintain a home, hoping and planning for the future.

SEARCH for a PEOPLE

I began to believe there were probably thousands—if not millions—of other committed lesbian and homosexual couples whose lives were similar to my own. But where were they? I believed they were out there—somewhere. But I also knew their lives were probably as hidden as my own. I believed that if I discussed my marriage with a lesbian or homosexual couple in Atlanta, Chicago, or San Diego together we would realize our commonality: our similar lifestyles, problems, and values. There would be differences between us, but those differences would also be sociologically based.

I did not know who these gay couples were—as they did not know me or, across the country, know of each other. But I knew that if I looked hard enough I *would* find them. If we could come to know each other, we could begin to see ourselves as a people and as a minority group—not as scattered and hidden couples with no support systems and no representation other than media-created stereotypes.

In becoming aware of each other's lives, we would realize we were not alone. We would realize that as a people we have nothing to be ashamed of—and much to be proud of.

The "SPEAK OUT" QUESTIONNAIRE

In proposing a nationwide survey of the gay community as the foundation for *The Mendola Report,* I produced for myself one six-month-long anxiety attack. I did not want to do an exclusively New York/San Francisco study. My rationale: between the East Coast and the West Coast there is a whole population that represents gay America. By continuously studying New York City and San Francisco homosexuals and lesbians, the gays in Louisville and in rural areas of California and New York State were never represented. What had emerged from New York/San Francisco studies was only a partial (and one-dimensional) view of the lifestyles of homosexuals and lesbians. If you wanted to study heterosexual marriage, you would not confine yourself to Manhattan and San Francisco. You would research couples in Brooklyn and Queens—and in Glendora and San Pedro.

Second self-destruct criterion: I did not want to distribute the questionnaires exclusively through political organizations. I *would not* distribute them in bars. Because, I contended, lesbians and homosexuals living in Vermont or Arkansas might not have political organizations they could join—let alone a local gay bar they could go to. And because a particular gay couple was not a member of an Arkansas or Vermont gay political group did not necessarily mean they were not quietly living a happy life together in either place.

My third criterion: I would not do a sexually oriented questionnaire. If you were studying heterosexual couples, you would not ask only questions pertaining to their sexual life. Why, then, in homosexual and lesbian studies were we only asked questions pertaining to our sexual life? Few have asked us how we live. What seems to sell is how we perform—or do not perform—sexually. A book on heterosexual marriage would include couples discussing the many dimensions of their relationship: finances, children, conflicts. Heterosexual couples would be asked to explain what they considered most important in a marriage. I am neither a psychiatrist nor a psychologist; I am a writer. Therefore, in developing the "Speak Out" questionnaire I sought the direction of an experienced research psychologist. Working together, we included questions on community involvement, interaction with neighbors, family relationships, etc.

A short paragraph at the beginning of the questionnaire established my terms: "The *American Heritage Dictionary* defines marriage as the legal union of a man and a woman. However, the same dictionary defines the verb *to marry* as entering into a close relationship, uniting or forming a union. In the second reference, there is no distinction made as to the sexes or the legality of the act. For the purposes of this questionnaire, the term *marriage/relationship* applies exclusively to gay couples: two men or two women committed to a permanent or ongoing relationship with each other."

Writing one "Speak Out" questionnaire was no problem. Distributing 1,500 copies of that questionnaire was, to me, monumental. Sitting in the bathtub late one February night, I thought about drowning myself. My life insurance could be used to repay Crown Publishers for the advance I had received and spent printing a questionnaire I did not know how to distribute. How do you mail questionnaires to people if you do not know who they are—or where they are? What do you say? "I'm trying to reach you because I believe you're out there?" And to whom do you say it?

I began by asking personal friends if they had friends living in states other than New York. If a friend gave me the names and addresses of two people—one in Florida and one in Texas—I wrote them explaining what I was trying to do. I asked if they would help by distributing questionnaires in their areas. And I asked them whom they knew who lived outside *their* respective states. *Every* person to whom I wrote responded positively: yes, they would distribute the questionnaires and, yes, included were the names and addresses of lesbian and homosexual friends who lived in states other than their own. One person in one state led me to another person in another state. Let no one ever underestimate the gay network that exists in this country. And let no one ever underestimate the willingness of gay Americans to become involved in an idea in which they believe. They were out there and they were ready to help—and ready to be heard.

I am sure my mailman was convinced I had succeeded in organizing a nationwide chain letter. I began receiving letters from people to whom I had *not* written: "I heard about what you are doing from a friend in St. Louis and I'd like to distribute your questionnaire here in Kansas City." The more supportive letters I received, the less scared I was. I became convinced my idea was right. A letter from a group in Canada not only made my day, it made my month. "We heard about what you're doing from someone in Washington, D.C. We'd like to be included in your study so would you please send us questionnaires." In closing, and I could feel their warmth extend right across the border: "If you run out of money doing this down there, let us know and we'll do a fund-raiser for you up here."

Fifteen hundred questionnaires were mailed to distributing individuals and nonpolitical organizations throughout the United States—and, of course, to the Canadian group. I was advised by experienced marketing research professionals that I could expect between a one percent and a 5 percent return. A 10 percent response, I was told, would be outstanding. And that was what I wanted: 10 percent, and nothing less than outstanding. But what if what I wanted was neither possible nor real? Although 1,500 questionnaires went out, there was no guarantee any would come back. I became a mailbox "freak." What if I was wrong? What if the committed gay couples I had said were out there were not out there at all—or were so small a group as to be untenable? Life revolved around the daily mail. And emotionally I swung somewhere between the despair of a one percent return and the euphoria of a 10 percent response.

Initially, the silence of an empty mailbox. And then they began to come: trickling in, steadily coming in—and then pouring in. Four percent, 7 percent, 10 percent: I had gotten my "outstanding." As the number moved up to 12 and 15 percent, I was secretly betting on a 20 percent return. When it broke 20 percent, I prayed to Our Lady of the Post Office for a 25 percent return. Beyond 25 percent, it was gravy. The final results: a 27 percent response representing 26 states, including Hawaii, plus the District of Columbia. Canadian questionnaires are included in the return, and also one questionnaire that somehow found its way to Singapore and back. Indicative of the gay network: questionnaires were returned from states to which I knew I had not mailed.

No figures on the total gay population of the United States are available. Nor is it my intent to make generalizations concerning an estimated 20 million people. "Speak Out" is a sampling of the gay population. However, the lesbians and homosexuals who responded to "Speak Out" represented every region in the United States: Pacific and Metropolitan Los Angeles; West Central and Metropolitan Chicago; Southeast; Southwest; East Central; New England and Middle Atlantic and Metropolitan New York. Of the respondents, representing every minority group: 56 percent were women, 44 percent were men.

Although a 27 percent return is exceedingly high for an attitudinal survey, the questionnaire was not sent out randomly—nor could it be, based on the unique characteristics of the gay population. Therefore I am not presuming that the data represents the values and lifestyles of the *entire* gay population. We *can* assume, though, that the people who responded to *this* questionnaire are "typical" of people who would respond to any questionnaire of this nature. This type of person is better educated and of a higher socioeconomic background than the general population.

Overall, the data shows no significant differences between homosexuals and lesbians. And where there *are* differences between homosexuals and lesbians, these differences can be attributed to normal cultural, economic, and social differences which generally exist between men and women. For instance, more lesbians seem to own things jointly with their partners than do homosexuals. However, the average salary of a homosexual might be higher than the average salary of a lesbian, thereby eliminating the need for joint ownership. The data also shows that more lesbian couples live in the suburbs than do homosexual couples. Is that a difference in the *choices* made by lesbians and homosexuals? Or is it easier for two women to live together in the suburbs than it would be for two men? Straight suburban neighbors can rationalize two women purchasing a home together for financial reasons. However, they might not be able to rationalize such a financial necessity for two men, thereby making suburban living "less comfortable" for a homosexual couple.

In terms of how gay couples perceive their relationships, based on the gay population surveyed in "Speak Out," they see their relationships as not different from heterosexual marriages. They see the similarities as internal similarities, the differences as external differences. Regarding similarities, "Speak Out" respondents believe "commitment" and the "interpersonal relationship" that exists for gay couples is the same as it is for straight couples. In terms of how the respondents perceive differences between gay couples and straight couples—overwhelmingly, the major difference is societal approval.

The homosexual and lesbian respondents to "Speak Out":

Their ages:
- 10% 18–24
- 17% 25–29
- 23% 30–34
- 19% 35–39
- 21% 40–49
- 10% 50 or over

Their occupations:
- 54% Professionals
- 12% Officials and managers
- 9% Office and clerical
- 6% Technicians
- 5% Sales personnel

How they define their marital status:
- 67% Permanently committed (married)
- 11% Living with someone
- 11% Separated (divorced)
- 10% Single
- 1% Widowed

Based upon their own definition of a marriage relationship, the number of times they had been married:
- 47% Once
- 31% Twice
- 11% Three or more times
- 11% Never

Length of their relationships:
   19%   Less than 1 year
   16%   1 year but less than 2 years
   29%   2 or more but less than 5 years
   19%   5 or more but less than 10 years
   17%   10 or more years

The "Speak Out" questionnaire included thirty-nine questions: four essay questions and the balance multiple choice. One essay question asked those responding to give their definition of what they considered a gay marriage/relationship. Two essay questions pertained to what the respondents saw as the similarities and differences between a gay marriage/relationship and a straight marriage/relationship. The fourth essay question: What do you consider to be most important in a marriage/relationship?

Sitting in my Manhattan living room, I was *with* the people I had believed were out there. As I read their questionnaires, particularly the essay questions, I was touching the lives of people everywhere from Springfield, Massachusetts, to Marina del Rey, California. What most impressed me was their openness and the degree to which they shared the intimacies of their lives. They completed the essay questions expressing their values, their lifestyles, and their pride in themselves as committed homosexuals and lesbians.

I had begun with a basic idea. The astoundingly large 27 percent return on the questionnaire proved to me that the reality of lesbian and homosexual couples was so much bigger than my own idea. Most rewarding to me were the men and women who wrote notes on the questionnaires and those who enclosed personal letters. Some people wished me good luck. Others said they would pray for me. And dozens more commented: "It's about time something like this was done." The printed questionnaire included a note from me saying, "Thank you for sharing your thoughts with me." Below it, men and women wrote: "Thank you for asking." There is no way, thank Whomever, to code the personal letters and run them through a computer.

From New Jersey a woman wrote:

I hope your book will be read and embraced by gays. Maybe those who want a permanent relationship will be heartened by the knowledge that there are more than just a few "unusual" lesbian and homosexual couples.

An older man from Chicago:

> My present relationship is now in its ninth year. Previously, I had an eighteen year relationship which ended with the death of my partner. I strongly feel you have a "side" to tell—a side that is not readily known nor very visible.

A gentleman from Georgia:

> This type of thinking is long overdue. We both want to thank you for taking the initiative on a book such as this.

A woman from Maryland:

> I appreciate what you are doing to further the cause of gay rights. Only by counteracting myths can we ever hope for public understanding and acceptance of homosexuality and lesbianism as a meaningful, valid—and yes, moral lifestyle.

The "Speak Out" questionnaire had done what, in fact, it had been intended to do: encourage people to proudly speak out. Based on the personal letters that people had enclosed, it also provided me with many of the lesbian and homosexual couple interviews for this book. No one was paid to be interviewed.

It was late spring becoming almost summer. The oil industry and the government were providing us with a gas shortage. The questionnaires were at New York City's Columbia University for a run through the computer. It was now time for me to go out and personally meet these couples. Despite the necessary structure of formal interviewing, I would share, although briefly, their homes and their tables. They would share with me their everyday lives, their concerns and their problems, and their hopes for the future.

It was a wonderful trip—from Manhattan Island out into the hinterlands—my own gay odyssey.

1

VIGNETTES
Gay Couples Discuss Their Lives

Just as there is no such thing as a "typical" Italian or a "typical" black, there is no such thing as a "typical" gay. Just as socioeconomic influences impact upon heterosexuals, those same socioeconomic influences impact upon homosexuals and lesbians. I believe these socioeconomic influences—*not* sexual preference—determine an individual's lifestyle and values.

Society does not classify a heterosexual couple by their sexual acts. A heterosexual couple engaging in anal intercourse would not be classified as a "typical anal couple." An upper-income heterosexual couple is not classified as a "typical straight couple." There is truly nothing that makes anyone typically anything. It is individual perception that determines what is or is not "typical," is or is not normal.

The individuals and couples interviewed for this book are a cross spectrum of American society. They represent all but one minority group—I could not find one gay American Indian to interview. If environment is determined by economics, then every economic group is represented in these interviews. One interview was done poolside at a palatial home, another in a humble rural household where home-grown vegetables were served for supper. I met with lesbian and homosexual couples in their city apartments and in their suburban homes. In one home I said evening prayers with the couple before we began our meal. In another we had cocktails before dinner.

The couples introduced in the following vignettes are couples you, the reader, will meet again and again throughout this book. You determine what is or what is not "typical" about them.

13

BEVERLY *and* DEBRA

It was over twenty-two years ago, but Beverly and Debra still laugh about the circumstances of their meeting. The women, both forty-two, were college students when they met in 1957. "I was married at the time," Debra says. "I had heard about this girl Beverly my brother-in-law was trying to meet. Well, he met her." Beverly reminisces: "The four of us double-dated. Deb and I played tennis together. Took the same bus to school in the morning, came home together in the afternoon."

"My marriage was wrong," Debra explains. "It was what you did: you got married because you were supposed to. And you made babies because you were supposed to. I wanted to finish college and teach. My husband and my in-laws were insisting that I drop out of college and become pregnant. The irony of it is that I didn't realize how wrong my marriage was until Bev—when we were together, I was happy. Knowing how happy I was with her made my life with my husband more unbearable."

Although Debra had had previous lesbian experiences, Beverly had not. "It was a long courtship," says Debra, winking. "It was well over two years before we became lovers. During that time, I'd left my husband, we'd graduated from college, and both of us had started teaching. The following summer we went to Europe on vacation and became lovers there."

An afternoon with Beverly and Debra is an afternoon filled with laughter and seriousness. They argue about their "pacing problems":

"Bev is very slow at doing things," Debra explains.

"I am not," Beverly retorts. "It's all because of breakfast and it's been going on for years."

"What about breakfast?" I ask, feeling I am intruding on a deep family secret.

"I make breakfast and it never fails—Bev takes so long to get dressed that it's cold by the . . ."

"Deb, I've been telling you for years—you don't have to make breakfast. It gets cold and then you try to lay this guilt trip on me about your poor eggs. And don't give me that *War and Peace* routine again."

"War and Peace?" I ask, an obvious outsider.

"I can read *War and Peace* three times while Bev is getting dressed . . ."

"That's a lie. You couldn't even read it once—all the way

through. See?" Beverly sighs, turning to me. "She gets up first, so she cooks. I feel like I'm being controlled because I have to eat . . . and I get angry. She gets angry because she's waiting for me to eat and everything is getting cold. Can't stand this *War and Peace* routine. Really, Deb, you tell that to everyone."

I am sitting there laughing at both of them as they laugh at themselves. I get the feeling that if these two women are together in fifty years they will be arguing about cold eggs and *War and Peace*. They confirm my feeling.

"Timing is a problem," Beverly explains. "We've been out of step for years."

"Yeah," interrupts Debra. "She's slow and I'm fast."

"I am not slow," Beverly laughingly yells at her.

Now, I am the writer and I am supposed to be in control of the interview. And according to my tract, when I come upon a problem in a relationship I am supposed to ask the couple what they are doing to resolve the problem. So I do my bit: "Do you two think you'll be able to work this out?" Now they are a united front against the opposition—me.

"Of course we'll never be able to work it out," answers Beverly. "Everybody moves with their own rhythm. Deb is a little bit out of tune . . . that's all."

Debra, ignoring Beverly's remark: "You can't always be at the *same* place at the *same* time with another individual—not for twenty-two years. Bev can't help it if she's slow . . . I accept it"—she grins sheepishly—"as part of her personality."

"I am not slow, Debra. That's simply not true . . ."

Beverly and Debra laugh about a lot of things—their meeting and their pacing, cold eggs, and *War and Peace*. However, there has been a great deal to be serious about during their twenty-two years together. Beverly's mother would not, for many years, accept her daughter as a lesbian. Debra, after fifteen years with Beverly, had an affair with another woman. Neither of them believes in sexual fidelity. Both of them see their relationship as the basis of their lives. They are very serious about the future—together or apart.

PHILIP *and* TODD

Philip and Todd met two years ago at Dignity, a gay religious organization. Both men are in their early thirties. Philip is a chemist; Todd, a dietician.

"I was the all-American male," explains Todd. "A career in the military. A wife and two children. I was twenty-five when I realized I was a homosexual. I rationalized what I considered my bisexuality until I was twenty-eight. But I knew I was lying to myself. I was certainly lying to my wife and my children. Then I decided to give up the game. I knew who I was and I decided to *be* who I was. It was at that point that I left the military . . . and, shortly after, left my wife."

Philip smiles as he listens to Todd discuss his "coming out" process. Later, he explains: "I was also twenty-eight when I came out. I guess you come out to yourself first . . . that's what happened to me. It was like all my life I had this secret. There was no way my religious upbringing and my homosexuality were going to come together. Then I began to realize one part of me wasn't spiritual and another part gay. It was all me and God loves me as me."

Both Philip and Todd believe there are few differences and many similarities between gay and straight marriages. "Don't tell me," Todd laughs. "I've been on both sides. No matter which side you're on, there's good times and bad times. There's peace and there's turmoil. I was married to Fran, and now I'm married to Philip. I don't particularly like the word *marriage* but I'm comfortable using it to describe our relationship. The big difference is Philip and I don't have society's approval. We can't be open and public about out relationship. We have to be careful. But other than having children, that's the only difference I see."

"We can't have children," Philip adds, "but that doesn't mean we can't raise children. If Todd's kids came to live with us we'd have the same problems raising them that Todd and his wife would've had if they'd stayed together. Other than the physical act of procreation, it's all the same. As far as societal approval, I disagree a bit with Todd. Heterosexual interracial couples don't have it, heterosexual common-law couples don't have it. We don't have a monopoly, thank God, on societal disapproval—they spread it around real good."

Philip and Todd had their relationship blessed in a religious ceremony. Both men consider themselves permanently committed: both believe they will grow into old age together. Their commitment to each other includes sexual fidelity. I asked them if sexual fidelity is always a problem for gay men. Philip answers, "No. Is it always a problem for gay women?" I smile. "Okay, your point. No, it's not always a problem for gay women." Philip continues, "We believe in sleeping only with each other. There's always the possibility something's going to happen. It's a possibility in any relationship—gay or straight."

"But," Todd comments, "it doesn't have to mean the end of the relationship. Anyone can slip up. You could always meet Robert Redford. Sexual fidelity is important to us. Infidelity as an isolated incident is one thing. As a regular occurrence—neither of us want that."

When the interview is over, Philip and Todd, my lover Valerie and I go out for dinner. We arrive at a neighborhood pub and are told we will have to wait at the bar for a table. As we order drinks we break into two separate conversations.

"You know," Philip explains to me, "my father was a homosexual. Growing up, I was told he was dead. When I was in my teens my mother told me she'd divorced him because he was involved with another woman. But doing as most teenagers do, I put the pieces together.

"After my mother divorced my father, we moved away. My father wasn't involved with another woman. My mother found him in bed with his male lover. She believed my father's family had made him a homosexual . . . so she never wanted me exposed to them or to him.

"I never knew him. But when I was in my twenties, shortly after my father had really died, a relative told me the whole story. And then I hated them both: my mother and my father. I didn't hate him because he was gay. But you see, when I realized I was a homosexual . . . if I could've had someone to turn to, especially my father, I would've never gone through the self-hate I went through."

While Philip is telling me about his father, I can see Todd showing Valerie pictures of his children: a black-and-white snap shot of a seven-year-old boy happily hanging off his father's shoulder. A studio portrait of a little girl: blond hair, blue eyes, dressed up and starched to have her picture taken. I am listening to Philip, but I can hear Todd. "When my children are old enough to understand, I want them to know who I am. If I've been a good father, I hope to God they'll love and accept me. They'll realize my gayness doesn't make any difference."

EM *and* LOUISE

The directions say, "We're right off the parkway. Make a right and then make another right." What the directions do not say is that it is about ten miles to the first right, about five miles to the second. The directions do say it is the first brown house on the left side of the road: "You can't miss it." Mile and mile of open fields and winding roads. Sociologists would call this a rural area. For someone like myself, born and raised in Brooklyn, it is the "country"—I went on summer vacation to places like this.

I pull into the driveway of the first—and only—brown house I see. Em and Louise walk out to the car, greet me, and help with my luggage. They have no doubt as to who I am—mine is probably the only New York license plate to pass down this road in a long time. The house is quiet as we sit in the living room coasting through social amenities. Louise asks if I saw their rabbits when I got out of the car. When I say I did not, she ushers me to a living room window. Em excuses herself, saying there is something she has to show me. Moments later, she returns, both her hands filled with two-week-old kittens. A big woman in her late forties, Em laughs. "These are our latest additions to the family." Louise, in her late thirties, sitting with Em on the couch explains how they had both helped deliver the kittens.

The quiet of the house is suddenly broken by what sounds like a tornado. I hear a door slam and then more than two footsteps running up the stairs. Louise, without moving from the couch, shouts: "You two come down here and introduce yourselves like gentlemen. Ya hear me?" The only answer is the sound of footsteps coming back down the stairs. Two teenage boys appear in the living room, introduce themselves, and shake hands with me.

While the two teenage boys are explaining their whereabouts of the afternoon, I notice a five-year-old boy quietly standing in the doorway.

"Here's my little fellow," shouts Em. "Come over here, you, and give your grandma a hug." Once his presence is acknowledged, the boy runs and pounces on Em. As she embraces him, she turns to me, saying, "This is my daughter's boy."

The two teenagers leave the room, heading for the refrigerator. Em's grandson plays on the floor with the kittens. "I have seven sons and one daughter." Em says proudly. Louise laughs. "Now you'd never know it to look at her, would you? Would you think this lady is a grandmother."

"My children have known I am a lesbian since 1973. Louise and I have only been together two years. I was with another woman for five years—the relationship was no good. My children rejected her because they thought she was selfish. My daughter is twenty-five, my oldest boy is twenty-three . . . old enough to understand it wasn't a good thing for their mother. But they love Louise."

I ask Louise how it feels to become involved with a woman who has eight children? "I took on a whole family is what I did," says Louise. "And I wasn't prepared for what was ahead of me. But we've all worked hard at it—me and Em and all the kids. The children didn't scare me away from wanting to become part of her life. I was married before but"—Louise frowns—"I never had any love in my marriage and I never had any children in my marriage. I knew I loved Em and I wanted a life with her. And she needed me. Together we're making a good family."

Later in the evening Em's two teenage sons take their five-year-old nephew home. The house is quiet again.

"You see," Em begins to tell me, "I was in a lonely situation before I met Louise. I needed someone I could love and someone who'd love me. It just wasn't there in my previous relationship. I'm a praying person and I prayed about it. I believe God answers prayers." She begins to laugh; her blue eyes glow. "I know this sounds crazy, but I laid out specific instructions for God. I told Him just what kind of a woman I wanted. I'm Swedish, you know. And on my knees I prayed to God to send me a good Swedish woman. I wanted her to be a dark-haired Swede, not bigger than five-foot-three because I'm a big woman"—she blushes—"and I didn't want a woman who was going to be bigger than me. A little while after I told God what I needed, He sent me Louise."

"Em and I," explains Louise, "are making a life together. Our future doesn't include the boys who are now at home because one day they'll be grown up and on their own. Our present life together is filled with love and happiness . . . a lot of hard times and working overtime to support the boys, ourselves, and this house. Love is the important ingredient in our home. We have to make sure that the love we show each other and the love we give the children will help them be good men someday."

At the time of the interview, Em is training for a license to become a tractor/trailer driver. "If I get my license I can make over four hundred dollars a week. That's more than double what I'm making now." Louise, a telegrapher, explains that the overtime money she earns is important to their financial situation. "But if Em gets her license, she could be away several days at a time. I'd have to be home at night with the boys, so we'd lose my overtime money. We don't get any support from the boys' father, so it's hard. Em and I don't have much earning power—money is tight.

There you go, Mary." She laughs at me. "That's one of the similarities between gay couples and straight couples—a lot of them are struggling to financially survive, too."

TROY *and* ED

Troy is in his mid-fifties; Ed, in his early sixties. Both are practicing psychologists. After interviewing them, I am convinced they are the forefathers of "open marriage." Not only were they "in" before it was "in," but they will be "in" after open marriage is "out."

Their open marriage began twenty-five years ago. Talking with me in his plant- and clutter-filled office, Troy explains: "I was twenty-nine and Ed was thirty-seven when we met. After four years of struggling with sexual incompatibility—call it what you will—I decided I didn't need the tension. I mean, we didn't chart it out or anything like that. But I knew I could get plenty of good sex with regulars I'd known for years. Quite simply, there was something neurotic going on in me with this monogamy thing: so I gave it up."

Ed stretches out comfortably on the living room couch. His feet are happily resting on top of a magazine-laden coffee table. "Understand," he says, "the first few years we did try to be true to each other: you know, monogamy and all that. But after a few years, we started finding other people. Certainly, at first, we were both very secretive about it. But I think we both understood and accepted the idea that there *would be* other people. In fact, when we became honest with each other about 'other people,' we had a couple of threesomes. However, we never got too far with that. Troy never liked threesomes—that is, not with me as a third.

"You're young"—Troy smiles at me—"but when you've lived with someone twenty-five years, little roots intertwine in a way that hurts if you try to pull them apart. Someone might say to you, 'Get rid of that old pair of slippers.' But *you* look at them and you think to yourself, 'They might be old, but they're mine. They're comfortable. They're an important part of me and my life. I'm simply not going to give them up.' When you love someone you can live comfortably with that person—you're not going to give him up. There are always plenty of people around to sleep with. Why"—he laughs—"I've had somewhat of a stable of men with whom I've been sleeping, some for twenty-five or thirty years. Not all at the same time, of course. But with Ed, he's the person I *live* with. It's all the things you know the other person would like or be interested in. It's the joke you wait to tell him or the question you wait to ask him. It's knowing that somebody is going to come home between five-thirty and six. That person is there—sorting out the mail, messing up the living room. You even get involved with his laundry. I mean, after twenty-five years you can instinctively recognize *his* laundry."

I ask Ed how he explains his twenty-five-year relationship with Troy. He sits there staring out the window and swinging the microphone around by the wire. The silence is deafening. I can hear buses and taxi cabs blasting their horns on the street below. Finally: "Sexual attraction seems to fade very quickly"—he sighs— "so the 'staying power,' certainly between Troy and me, had to be in terms of other things. Troy saw me through the death of my mother very early in our relationship. And I saw him through the death of his mother in 1972. We've seen each other through many major disappointments. These things all count. They make a fabric of experience with a great many threads going through it, and I can't say any one of these threads in particular has held us together. It's a whole lot of threads. We love and trust each other. We look to each other for comfort and guidance.

"If I ask Troy for advice, it's not going to take him a half hour to figure out what I want or what I'm driving at: he knows. We depend upon each other." Still staring out the window, he smiles. "Dear, it's even something better than depending upon each other: we know where we *can* depend on each other—and we know where we *cannot* depend on each other."

Both Ed and Troy define themselves as "permanently committed." They are comfortable using the word "marriage" as applied to their relationship. I talk with Ed at length about partnership agreements, wills, financial problems, and retirement. Troy discusses his thoughts on mature gay families and building support systems for one's old age and death.

ANGEL *and* TIMOTHY

If you are a reasonably smart thirty-five-year-old woman, you will not try to play disco queen with a nineteen-year-old young man. While Timothy is working as disc jockey at a Saturday night gay dance, Angel has me out on the floor for an endurance test. After ten straight minutes of music that never stops, I beg for mercy. He laughs, telling me how much he loves to dance. Finally, he takes my arm, escorting me off the floor to a nearby table. While I try to control my hyperventilation, Angel talks about his background.

"I was born in Cuba but raised in this country," he explains. "I come from a very strict religious family. And of course, with my Spanish background, I was pushed into a real 'macho' image—at ten years old you're supposed to be making out with girls. When my mother found out I was gay, she wanted to send me to a priest. When I wouldn't go, she started lighting candles. Then she went to this spiritualist who told her to sprinkle this magical potion around the house and it would make me straight. She did it—sprinkled this potion and started chanting. It didn't work."

Angel, nineteen, is no longer living at home. He and Timothy have been living together in a committed relationship for over a year. The three of us discuss their relationship, how they see themselves as homosexuals, and what they want out of life.

Timothy is a blond-haired, blue-eyed twenty-one-year-old. I ask him if, as a gay man, he believes he can have a long-term relationship.

"Absolutely," he bounces back. "I see no reason why I shouldn't be able to. I don't think it matters one way or another if you're gay or straight. Just because you're gay doesn't mean you can only have 'temporary' relationships. It depends on the two people involved, the love between them. A relationship is based on the understanding between two people: knowing the other person so well that everything fits together nicely. A good relationship is a good combination of two people, like a team. Angel and I know that we are there for each other when we need each other. We listen to each other's problems, we talk, we share everything. Our first concern is each other—that's what we're about."

We talk about the word *marriage*. Angel: "The word *marriage* to me means fear: I don't like it." Timothy: "I look at Angel and me as being married. But I don't like the word: it implies roles and we're not into roles." Angel and Timothy agree that if they had to attach words to their relationship they would call it a "bonding friendship."

In discussing the future, Angel blushes and says he has a "romantic dream." When I ask him what it is, he stammers and laughs: "You'll think I'm silly." I convince him there is nothing silly about anyone's dreams. "I never even told Tim." Timothy encourages him to tell us both.

"My dream"—Angel smiles, gazing off into space—"is for Tim and me to have a house on the beach. I want it to have big windows so we can see the ocean. A nice fireplace so we can stay home and sit in front of it on cold winter nights. Maybe we'll even drink some wine. Sometimes, when I'm daydreaming, I see us in this room. It also has one of those nice fur-skin rugs in front of the fireplace. It's our home—our place. I want us to have a nice life and a good time together. Someday I even want us to go on a cruise to Bermuda."

I ask them both, "What is your greatest fear?" Both of them look at me with somewhat confused expressions. Then they look at each other. No answers. Finally Angel says, "You first."

Timothy moans something about Angel's being unfair. Then he says, "I suppose at this point in my life my greatest fear is people automatically rejecting me because I'm gay. Not looking at me as a person: just laying some label on me. That's it. That's my greatest fear—being labeled without even being given a chance to express myself. Being rejected by people before they even know who I am."

In terms of his greatest fear, Angel talks about loneliness. "I think my greatest fear is being alone by myself. Having nobody to talk to, not knowing anybody, being lonely. I guess my biggest fear is being alone in old age."

LISA *and* MARJE

It is early Saturday evening. Lisa and I are waiting for Marje to come home from work. Marje, a nurse, has been at the hospital since seven in the morning. She finally arrives at seven-thirty in the evening, and the three of us sit down and turn on the tape recorder. Marje is a serious and soft-spoken woman. She seems strong but not aggressive. Lisa has more energy than a little league baseball team. She is intense and she is angry.

Lisa, twenty-six, explains to me what she sees as the difference between living together and being committed: "If you're committed, you feel more responsible in terms of the other person— and in terms of yourself. When you have problems you're going to try to work them out. If you're just living together and are having problems, you're going to split."

"A commitment," adds Marje, thirty-five, "is common sharing. It's emotional, physical, and spiritual bonds. My commitment to Lisa is my marriage." "What about sexual fidelity," I ask. "Is that part of your definition of marriage?" "Sexual fidelity," Marje continues, "is important, but sometimes I think we place more importance on it than it deserves. Sex is overemphasized. The important things in a relationship are the sharing and the understanding between two people. You have to understand your partner and where her feelings are coming from."

We talk extensively about my personal definition of a "mixed world": Is it better to live in an exclusively gay world or to live in a mixed world of heterosexuals, homosexuals, and lesbians? "I think," comments Lisa, "that it's much healthier to live in a mixed world of gays and straights. It's unhealthy to cut yourself off from part of the world—gays cutting off straights, straights cutting off gays, lesbian feminists cutting themselves off from gay men. All this separatism is unhealthy."

"If you live in an all-gay world," adds Marje, "you just cut yourself off." "Cut yourself off from what?" I ask. Marje answers, "Cut yourself off from a variety of options we have as people. You cut yourself off from learning and sharing. And you cut yourself off from educating straight people as to what we're about."

"Marje," I say, "it seems to me you're carrying some heavy burdens. You're a black lesbian living with a white woman. How does that all work out?" "No heavy burden . . . not at all: it's not *my* burden. I think the burden is on outsiders and how they view it . . . whether or not they can deal with it. If they can't, then it's *their* burden—not mine. I don't have to deal with their burdens and their problems. I've got enough real ones of my own." She laughs.

Lisa and Marje have been living together for three years. During those three years, Lisa's mother has not acknowledged Marje. "My mother," says Lisa angrily, "acts as if Marje doesn't exist. If she calls and Marje answers the phone, she won't even speak to her. If she's talking to me, she won't even ask how Marje is . . . and Marje is the person I'm sharing my life with."

I ask Lisa why she believes her mother is acting like this. "Supposedly, it's because Marje is black. But I'm not so sure it isn't my mother's cop-out to the whole lesbian issue. All I can do—and it's hard to do it with mothers—is let her know I'm going to live my life and if she doesn't like it—that's really too bad."

"Marje, what about you," I ask, "do you have any problems with your family because Lisa is white?"

"No, I don't get any grief from my family because Lisa is a white woman." And then she explains quite seriously: "My family background is such that we've always had interracial marriages, so they accept . . ."

Lisa and I both, almost simultaneously, break out in laughter. Marje, confused, looks at the two of us.

"What are you two hysterical about?" she asks, cocking her head.

"Don't you see what you just said?" laughs Lisa.

"No . . . what did I say?"

She thinks about it a second and then covers her mouth, giggling. "Oh, my, I suppose as a lesbian I've added another whole dimension of interracial marriage to my family. Oh, Lord . . . I mixed their world up real good."

PAUL *and* MICHAEL

I leave Lisa and Marje after nine o'clock. It is raining heavily. I have been expected at Paul and Michael's at eight for dinner. I do not have the courage to call them a second time and say I will not arrive until ten. I have called them at eight, saying I will be there at nine. The turnpike, of course, is completely unfamiliar. I am tired.

Finally, after a thirty-minute drive that takes forty-five minutes, I locate the street. While I am parking, I notice two men emerge from a doorway and walk toward the car. Paul opens the door on the driver's side: "My God, were we worried . . . you are one crazy woman." Michael grabs my suitcase and attaché case and the three of us, jumping puddles, run to the front door.

The living room of their duplex is softly lighted. The dining room table is set. Michael makes me a drink and Paul gives me a towel for my hair.

"We're serving charred turkey tonight," teases Paul, an attractive man in his mid-thirties. "But relax—we've put it back in the oven for the sixth time."

"How many interviews did you do today?" asks Michael.

"Probably too many." I laugh.

"Listen," Paul says, addressing Michael, "I don't want any writer interviewing us unless she's in good shape. All you have to do is look at her. She is not in good shape."

Michael, laughing, turns to me. "You *may* interview us tomorrow . . . after brunch."

The three of us relax in the living room. It is probably midnight before we eat our charred turkey dinner. We discuss theater, politics, and inflation. Over dinner we talk about their recent problem with Michael's daughter.

"Well," Michael explains, "I'm a middle-aged father and my daughter's involved with a guy and she's doing a number on her mother and me—playing one against the other. Our long-distance charges this month will probably equal the rent. But I think we got it straightened out. I gave her two choices: she could stay out there with her mother or come here and live with us. I made her understand that both would be equally as bad unless she got her act together. You know, it's bad enough realizing your daughter is a sixteen-year-old young woman—but then add the complications of being a long-distance father."

"Come on, Michael," Paul says, "I think everything worked out just fine. It's the first time in four years that we were able to work together as four adults with a common problem—trying to straighten out this girl."

And then, turning to me, Paul continues: "We put our heads together as four human beings—not two heterosexuals and two homosexuals. Together we could come up with the best solution for the girl. Personally, I'm sort of glad the whole thing happened. Michael and his wife have finally established some sort of rapport."

Paul and Michael have been together four years. Michael explains: "We're both at a point in our lives—and at an age—where we have entered into our second relationship or second marriage. Paul had a nineteen-year relationship with another man. I was married to my wife for eighteen years."

After a great dinner, I get a good night's sleep in a huge four-poster bed. Maybe I have been too tired to notice Paul's not drinking during the course of the evening. Maybe I have been too tired to notice Michael's tension when he discussed being a long-distance father. However, the following morning, Paul tells me he has been an alcoholic for fifteen years.

"What made you give it up?" I ask.

"Michael provided me with a whole new lifestyle. I have a happiness I never had before—and I don't want to lose it. Michael and our life together was what motivated me. He had faith in me. Drying out and staying dry has been very difficult, but we did it together."

"I nearly had a nervous breakdown when my wife decided to move halfway across the country." Michael shakes his head. "I simply could not believe I wasn't going to be able to see my children. Paul helped me a great deal. He made me see and accept the fact that there was nothing I could do about it. He promised me that together we would make the best of it. And we have. My children come to visit for extended periods of time. I fly out to see them as often as I can. We talk constantly on the phone. I could never have gotten through their leaving the state without Paul's support."

"What is it like," I ask, "to be a gay father? Do your children know you're a homosexual?"

"No"—Michael lowers his eyes sadly—"they don't. Hopefully, someday when they're a little bit older . . . we'll see."

"What do you do when they come to visit?" I ask.

Both men laugh. "That," Paul says, "is a book in itself."

CHARLOTTE *and* NANCY

Leaving Paul and Michael on Sunday afternoon, I begin my three-hour drive north. I have left Lisa and Marje in the city and then driven to Paul and Michael's suburban home. Now, I am on my way to Charlotte and Nancy, who live in a small rural community.

I arrive at their home at approximately six in the evening. It is dinnertime and the three of us sit down to a simple meal. After Nancy has put the food on the table and sat down, both women lower their heads for grace before the meal. While we are eating, Charlotte comments on the curtainless windows. "We won't cover the windows—you can see the hills and the mountains from every window in this house."

"Faith," Nancy explains over dinner, "is important to us. It's the cornerstone of our relationship. I believe it's our shared faith that has kept us together for so long. Together we share a lot of the same Christian values."

Charlotte, forty-one, and Nancy, forty, have been together thirteen years. After they had been together four years, Charlotte became ill. "The first five years of her illness were the worst," Nancy explains. "No one knew what was wrong with her. We went crazy with it until some very sophisticated testing was done at a large medical center. They found a rare blood disease."

Charlotte has been disabled and unemployed for nine years. However, she does receive state disability assistance. "The fact that I've had a long illness has definitely affected our relationship. I try not to think about the negative aspects. Positive effects: Nancy and I have been forced to grow closer together. There can't be a lot of bickering in a relationship when you've had something like this going on for nine years. We've had to create our own resources— both as a couple and as individuals."

I ask Nancy if she feels she has sacrificed herself because of Charlotte's illness. "Maybe if Charlotte hadn't been ill I might have done other things with my career. But I'm not a hundred percent sure of that. My relationship with Charlotte has been a very positive and stabilizing force in my life. Who can say that if this or that hadn't happened I might have done this . . . or that.

"Charlotte and I love each other—and that love has been the sustaining factor in our relationship. Even though we've had problems—the most serious being Charlotte's illness—we've worked them out. We worked out the problems and we've lived with the illness because through it all we didn't want to lose each other."

"Nancy and I," says Charlotte, "have a loving partnership. We were both willing, right from the beginning, to grow in a long-term committed relationship. And"—she laughs—"a committed rela- tionship is so much more interesting than promiscuity. With promiscuity you repeat the same thing over and over again. The only thing that changes is the body. In a long-term relationship it goes on like a series of lifes, deaths, and rebirths. You're forced to grow. Personally, I like the image the Indians use. Marriage or a committed relationship is like two stones that rub together and polish one another."

Charlotte's illness has not been the only serious problem in their relationship. In their earlier years Charlotte and Nancy lived as husband and wife. Charlotte was the wife; Nancy, the husband. I ask Nancy why she had assumed a male role?

"Well," Nancy explains, embarrassed, "I knew growing up I wanted to love a woman. And I thought to love a woman I had to be like a man. So I fashioned my behavior after my father. Where do we get our role models from if not our parents? My fantasy was that in order to love a woman I had to be the aggressor. Isn't that what we're taught: men are the aggressors. Therefore, if I was 'aggressed,' it was an unnatural role reversal for me. Don't look so bewildered," she teases me, "I had this all worked out in my head . . . all very together. Of course, Charlotte was ill, and I was the only one working. That solidified my role as husband: after all, wasn't I the breadwinner?"

As if listening to Nancy describe her role as husband has not left me dumbfounded enough, the two of them confuse me even more as they begin to laugh uproariously. Obviously, Nancy's breadwinner recollections have triggered in them a part of the story to which I am not privy.

"The women's liberation movement," Charlotte explains, "had a tremendous impact upon me." She laughs so hard she can hardly talk. "Well, when you're ill, disabled, not working and not earning any money, it's pretty difficult to go to your partner and say, 'Hey, you, husband, whoever you think you are, I want to liberate our relationship.'"

Charlotte and Nancy have obviously, if not painlessly, worked out their roles—or succeeded in completely abolishing the stereotypes we most often associate with heterosexual couples. In the course of their thirteen years together, they have resolved many things: Charlotte's illness, separating after nine years, their immobility—and living in an area, where, to their knowledge, they are the only lesbians "in town."

ROB *and* BOB

Rob, twenty-six, is a dancer; Bob, thirty-two, a bartender. They met approximately two years ago. Rob, at that time, had recently signed a contract with a prestigious dance company. Bob was managing a bar. Rob explains: "We met at a time when neither of us wanted any ties. I had just come out of a five-year relationship. Bob had had two relationships in two years. We had a loose relationship until it was almost time for me to leave town with the new company I'd signed with."

Bob, realizing Rob was leaving, told him he wanted to spend as much time together as possible. "And we did spend a lot of time together," Bob recalls. "But then he was gone. I had let him go because of my own fears. We then started spending all of our time on the phone and traveling back and forth to see each other."

"Actually," Rob says, "it was my director who helped me make the decision. All he said was, 'Sometimes in life you have to make a choice and stick to it.' I broke my contract and left the dance company. What I did was choose Bob and the life I believe we can have together. As a professional dancer, there's nothing for me in this city. It's just too small. Eventually, I would like to teach dance here . . . but that's as close as I can come to my career."

"I think people look at us in awe," Bob laughs. "On my nights off we go to the bar where I work. We love to dance, we love the music. I can have a good time and be as frivolous as anybody. Yet I can be mature and responsible. I see loving Rob and being aware of his needs as a responsibility. All it comes down to is thinking about *us* instead of thinking about him or me—thinking of us together as a married unit."

"There's always a better body or a better face," Rob concedes. "I personally lived the life described in the book *Faggot. I* know I can be promiscuous—but can I be loyal?" Both Rob and Bob believe in a sexually exclusive or monogamous relationship. "Our commitment," says Bob, "is to love each other and build our lives together. If Rob decided he wanted to have sex with someone else, well, he'd have to come to grips with that. But it would be for me to figure out why he had to go to someone else. I'd have to ask myself why I wasn't pleasing him."

Although both men are comfortable using the word *marriage* to define their relationship, Bob feels no one has the right to actually marry them. "Nobody has the right to do that to me," he states. "A piece of paper is worthless. What is viable and valuable is the bond—the commitment two people have to each other. And if that's lost, no piece of paper is going to do anything to keep it together. Love is there or love isn't there. If Rob should no longer love me, a legal marriage isn't going to do anything to keep us together."

"Look," Rob explains, "we're married and that's it. My relationship with Bob is a relationship of love. Call it husband and husband if you have to call it something. I want our home and our dog and our garden. The difficult thing for us now," Rob admits, "is to work out what are our career problems. I can't just stay home and play housewife or househusband. It doesn't work that way for either of us. We talk about a lot of different things: maybe I could try to start my own small dance company—Bob could manage it. Or we'd both enjoy owning a bar. We've got to work it out . . ."

Although I interview Bob and Rob in a small city, both men live in Bob's home in the suburbs. They talk affectionately about their elderly tenants. "If they do know"—Bob smiles—"they don't say anything. They're an old Irish-Catholic couple, beautiful people. We try to take care of them, help them when we can."

As a committed homosexual couple, Bob and Rob are doing well in suburbia. Both men see few differences and many similarities between gay and straight couples. In planning to grow into old age together, Rob and Bob believe their relationship will change a great deal. "It would have to," Bob says, "we're still young." Rob, holding Bob's hand, laughs. "This is a hot man I've got here. We've got to take real good care of what we have. We've both been around . . . it took us a while to get here." Trinka, their white Labrador retriever, as if in assent, barks into the microphone and officially ends the interview.

ANN *and* KATE

Ann and Kate met twelve years ago at what both of them describe as "one of those nice little all-girls' colleges." "Ann," Kate says, "was an adorable underclassman. We were on the basketball team together when we became friends. About eight months later we became lovers." Although they attended the same college, Ann and Kate come from different socioeconomic backgrounds. "Kate," Ann explains, " had a strict middle-class upbringing. I, fortunately, had a lower-class upbringing—it doesn't do as much damage. The difference between Irish and Italian is that, as a hot-blooded Italian, I like my animal instincts. She's had all these sexual hang-ups . . . and I really love sex. We've been working it out for years." Kate, retaliating: "Ann was a hood from Hoboken. Don't know how they ever accepted her into a private *women's* college."

I ask Kate to describe her relationship with Ann—and then am sorry I have. "Everything is enhanced," Kate explains. "It's exponential rather than logarithmic." "It's what?" I ask. "It's simple," she continues. "It goes beyond two times two. Exponentially, two times two equals four; four times four equals sixteen; sixteen times sixteen equals . . . ? What does sixteen times sixteen equal?" Ann, looking at her in total dismay, answers, "Who the hell cares?" "Okay," Kate goes on, "we're not an addition: you don't add her to me or me to her. It's an extrapolation all the way up. We don't qualify our relationship as a portion or a fraction of our life. It's our whole life." Ann smirks and says, "See what a college education can do for you?"

Ann, thirty, is a guidance counselor in a school for problem children. Kate, in her early thirties, works in cancer research at a major medical center. They live in an apartment in a large city, own land together, and recently purchased a vacation home in a beach resort area. Both women define themselves as permanently committed. Neither woman believes in sexual fidelity.

"Originally," Kate says, "I thought sexual fidelity was important.

Now I feel sex is only a small facet of a person's life. Why should it then become a major part in a relationship between two people? I wonder how many heterosexual couples engage in frequent sex after ten or fifteen years of marriage? Sex creates a certain manipulative tension between two people. Sex is used as power over another person. The partner that is being forced to be sexually faithful feels as though it's a favor done for the other partner. In the end it causes resentment among both of them. We had all these sexual struggles during our earlier years. Now we're free of it—there is so much more in our relationship that's more important than sex."

"The sexual dimension of our relationship ended," explains Ann, "after the first time I got involved with another woman. Kate and I had a good sex life together all through college. When Kate graduated, there was a physical separation, and I got sexually involved with someone else at school. It didn't in any way alter my love for Kate."

I ask Ann her definition of love. "I can't define it." She laughs. "I'm no poet. It's everything I share with Kate. It's the trust, the warmth, the communication—our total concern for each other."

"It's like a balloon," Kate adds.

"A balloon, Kate?" I ask. "You going to start again with me?"

She laughs. "No, this is simple. You see this very beautiful balloon, right? You want to see what's inside. So you make an incision . . . and you destroy everything. Leave love be—don't try to dissect it. You destroy the whole thing."

Ann was eighteen and Kate was nineteen when they first met. Although it was Kate's first relationship with either a man or a woman, it was not Ann's first relationship. Over the years each has had relationships with other women. Both discusss the sustaining factors in their relationship: trust in the love they share, communication, total honesty. "Without those things," Ann says, "it would have ended so many times."

CHARLES *and* RICHARD

"Charles and I," explains Richard, "began 'dating' in April 1971. We went together until October: dinner, dancing, the theater. Believe it or not, we didn't have sex until we decided to live together in October. When we had made a commitment to each other and were living together in our own apartment, we began living as two married people." I smile, asking him if it was because they did not believe in premarital sex. Both of them laugh at *me*, Richard answering, "Yes, that was it . . . that was exactly it."

Charles, who earns his living in management, is in his late forties. Richard, who is permanently disabled and unemployed, is in his late thirties. Both men define themselves as permanently committed. Richard, based on his own definition of marriage, considers himself to have been married three times. Charles defines his relationship with Richard as his second marriage. They concur— their decision to live together included a permanent commitment. A psychiatrist recently told me he believes a bit of conflict is healthy for any relationship—gay or straight. After an eight-year relationship, Charles and Richard still have their share of conflicts. Charles does not like the word *marriage* used to define his relationship with Richard. Richard, on the other hand, is comfortable with the word *marriage*. As regards sex, Charles has sex mostly with Richard, but does have occasional sexual affairs outside the relationship. Richard has sex exclusively with Charles.

Both men believe civil marriage is important for homosexual couples. "There's absolutely no protection for us," Richard explains. "A couple can spend many years together working and building, and should one of them die, there are inheritance problems. Even if the couple should break up, there's no protection for either of them." I ask Richard about a religious ceremony. "It's not important," he answers, "but *it is* nice. Charles and I had a religious ceremony in 1973. We decided we wanted to make a public commitment to each other among our friends. We wanted everyone to know where we stood. We stand committed to each other for better or for worse. It was a 'drag' wedding and over a hundred of our friends attended."

"You know"—Charles laughs, reminiscing—"a lot of my straight friends and business associates didn't know I was gay until I invited them to our Holy Union Ceremony. They accepted the invitation not knowing exactly what they were being invited to. Everyone was thrown in together—gay men, lesbians, straights, transsexuals. It worked out marvelously. Everyone had a chance to see people just being people."

I ask Charles if he feels the almost ten-year age difference between himself and Richard presents a problem. "Richard and I," he answers, "plan to grow into old age together. The difference in our ages hasn't caused us any problems . . . and I don't foresee it causing us problems in the future."

"What if," I ask, "when you reach your late fifties, you're no longer interested in sex. Charles would be in his late forties. Would your relationship with him be sustained without a sexual dimension?"

"Sex," he answers, "isn't what has sustained our relationship for the past eight years. What has sustained it is our compatibility, our love for each other, our trust in each other. We're *not* building a sexual relationship with each other. We're making a life together. We have many happy sexual years ahead of us. When and if it totally goes, it is only one small aspect of our total life together."

"Do you think you and Charles are unique?" I ask. Both men find my question absurd. Says Richard, "There are a vast number of homosexual couples like ourselves. This is a small city and there are plenty here."

Charles interrupts sarcastically: "We don't get any media coverage. No one is going to make any movies about us: we don't base our lives or our relationship on sex."

Richard, gently educating me: "Look, we have elderly homosexual friends—couples. These men have been together fifteen—some twenty—years. They're couples like us who have made a good life and a good home together. You'll see them at private house parties, for dinner somewhere . . . at the theater. You won't find them—as you won't find us—in bars."

JOAN, PAT, CHRISTINE, *and* STEVEN

Joan and Pat have attached a personal letter to their completed questionnaires volunteering to be interviewed. They include their last names, their address, and their telephone number. I am interested in interviewing the two women because Pat is the mother of two children—Christine, twelve, and Steven, nine. The women, who have lived together with the children for five years, define themselves as a "family unit."

Several weeks after the arrangements have been made, Joan telephones me. "Listen," she explains, "we have two children, as you know." Wrongly, I assume the children present a problem. "We don't have to do the interview in your home," I say. She laughs. "No, that's not the problem. We told the kids about being interviewed for your book. And they told us if you want to know about gay families, you ought to interview the whole family. Chrisie told her mother if you're going to interview us, you have to interview her. Stevie is walking around the house saying he doesn't want to be left out of the book. So would you mind? It's either all four of us or none of us."

Although I have two weeks to prepare the interview, I cannot develop the questions for the children. I leave for the trip without having written the children's interviews. It is a nine-hour drive to Joan and Pat's suburban home. I am truly nervous because I am unprepared to interview Christine and Steven. What do you ask two children of a lesbian marriage? After driving for five hours, my own gay "crazies" crash down on my head. "You jerk, you're all wrong. What would you ask two children of a heterosexual marriage? That wouldn't be a heavy. *You're* the one that's making this a heavy. Ask them questions you'd ask any other kids." Pulling off the turnpike, I write the questions for the children. Both Joan and Pat review and approve the children's questions before we turn on the tape recorder.

"The children could tell there were secrets," Pat explains. "Joan wasn't just a friend who lived with us. By explaining our lesbian relationship to the kids, we've made them more comfortable because now they understand what's going on. Joan has established her place in their lives. We function as a family—two adults and two children. We've all had to work hard at building family unity, but it's coming. We want to become a family—and grow to love and accept each other as members of a family."

"The main problem," Joan concedes, "is my attitude toward children. I knew I loved Pat and I wanted to make a life with her, but there was no way I wanted the responsibility of being a parent. If I hadn't been able to accept these two"—she screws up her face at Christine and Steven—"I would have lost Pat. I would never put her into a position of having to make a choice. She'd choose these monsters. It's been a fight and I'm still fighting—some wins and some losses. The kids have put up with a lot from me, and I've put up with a lot from them. And there's Pat—she's put up with a lot from all three of us."

I ask Christine her definition of a family. "A family is like us," she answers. "We all clean the house together, we work in the yard. If I didn't have my mother and Joan and my brother, I'd be scared because then I'd be all alone." Christine discusses her relationship with her father. She also talks about her uncomfortableness explaining Joan to her classmates at school. For a twelve-year-old girl, Christine has some very serious and very real fears about her family's lifestyle.

Steven confides in me and discusses his position as the only man in the house. "Well"—he shrugs—"it has some advantages and some disadvantages. I don't have to go through all the trouble they do just to go to the bathroom. They're always in the bathroom so long. And then sometimes I think they know things I don't know." I ask him, specifically, what things they know that he does not. And I should *not* have asked him. "Cleo, our cat"—he giggles—"was in heat. Chrisie said I was the only one that could help her because I was the only boy in the house." "Stevie," Pat barks threateningly. "But, Mom," he continues forthrightly, "I don't understand how I could make love to a cat." Looking at me forlornly, he sighs. "The three of them laugh at me. See, they're laughing at me now, and I still don't know how a boy can make love to a cat."

It is an afternoon of family jokes, problems, and stories. We discuss their interacting as a family with the local school system. Pat and Joan talk about their heterosexual neighbors and *their* children. There is a lot of laughter throughout this Saturday interview, but also a lot of tears and a lot of pain. Coming out is enough of a problem for lesbians and homosexuals. Coming out to your children is a whole other dimension. And knowing your children will also eventually have to "come out" because of who *you* are is an awesome burden for parents.

"Chrisie and Stevie learned the word *lesie* from their own father," Pat bitterly explains. "When he sees them he has to allude to the fact that their mother is a 'lesie.' Can you understand? We *had* to talk to them about our relationship and help them see that the love we have for each other is a *good love.*"

ROBERT *and* BOB

Robert and Bob have been committed to each other for four years. Both men consider this their second marriage; both of their respective first marriages lasted seven years. Robert, a traffic manager, is in his early thirties. Bob, in his mid-thirties, is a project manager in a company personnel department. Together they own a large suburban house; each has life insurance naming the other as beneficiary, and both have wills bequeathing each other their common properties.

"I don't think there's that much difference between gay and straight marriages," Bob states. "I'm in personnel work and I often end up playing psychiatrist. Of course, I'm dealing primarily with straights, listening to them talk about their marital problems. Not only do the same type of problems come up, but the *reasons* for those problems are even the same. I don't see any differences. Faith and hope and love and understanding are the priorities in any relationship—gay or straight. You don't have them, you're not going to make it—gay or straight."

"The big difference between gay and straight marriages," says Robert, "is the legal aspect. Our home is in both our names, and, should one of us die, no will is going to guarantee that a family won't create problems. We couldn't get mortgage insurance when we bought our house in 1977: we were two men and we weren't related or married. Then we decided we'd each get life insurance naming the other as beneficiary. In the event one of us died, the other would have money to help pay the mortgage alone. We were told we couldn't name each other as beneficiaries because we weren't related or married. We each had to name someone in our family as beneficiary on the life insurance. When we did that, the insurance company agreed to issue us the policies. We waited a couple of months, and then we changed the names of the family beneficiaries and named each other. There is no getting around it: legal marriage protects you."

Robert and Bob both have some thoughts on roles and stereotypes. "We mix things up pretty well," Robert explains. "We both repair our own cars. We both do the yard work. We both enjoy cooking so we both cook. I hate to vacuum, so he vacuums. I clean the bathroom but he does the tub." "People," Bob says adamantly, "stereotype people. Straights stereotype gays and gays stereotype straights. We stereotype on the basis of behavior. No one ever thinks I'm gay, and that's because they *know* how gay men act. It's funny, but sometimes gays don't even know I'm gay. See, we even stereotype ourselves. I just try to act like myself—what's normal behavior for me. I can't help it if someone then, observing my behavior, accuses me of being straight."

Neither Robert nor Bob believe in extramarital relations. Both believe sexual fidelity is important to a relationship. As Robert explains it, "When you've been with somebody you love for years and then you switch to another bed partner, the intimacy, the touching, the kissing and being held—it's not there. And that's something I don't *want* to get used to."

JILL *and* DOLLY

I ask Jill what has held her marriage with Dolly together for twelve years. "Nothing," she says, grinning. "If you *have* to hold something together, then you have nothing to begin with. We want to be together and that's what's held it together. If you want to be together bad enough, you don't have to have anything to hold it together."

"Love," adds Dolly, "is what has held us together. We honestly love each other." "What is love?" I ask her. "Love"—she smiles—"is when you go out camping and shut out the whole world. You're happy to be there at the campsite—just the two of you alone. Love is when you finally realize you don't have to run to the bars on a Saturday night, you're having more fun at home, sitting in front of the fireplace together. Love is being with each other and knowing you honestly care about each other."

Jill and Dolly, both in their late thirties, have lived in their suburban home for almost ten years. I ask them how long their neighbors have known they are a lesbian couple. "Probably"—Dolly laughs—"two days after we moved in. We certainly didn't try to hide it and we didn't flaunt it. I just think that they surmised it—and that was that." "One of our women neighbors," Jill adds, laughing, "keeps telling us she can't wait to die and be reincarnated gay because we treat each other better than her husband treats her."

Jill and Dolly talk extensively about Tom and Clara, their next-door neighbors. "When they go Christmas shopping," Dolly explains, "they leave the children at home with *our* phone number. Now that's got nothing to do with gay or straight. Tom and Clara see us as people; they know we're responsible and they know we care about the kids."

"Okay," I say, "they see you as *people,* but do they respect you as a *couple?*" "I'm sure they do," Dolly answers. "They celebrated our seventh anniversary with us." Jill sits back, smiling. "You know what was great about their having dinner with us that night? Afterward, they insisted we all go to a gay club because, they said, they wanted us to celebrate our anniversary with them in *our* world, not theirs." And then, smirking at me, she says, "We're not like *some* people we know: we don't have gay restaurants where we live. . . ."

"There's 'their world' and 'your world.' How do you compare the two?" I ask Jill. "Why compare them?" she quickly answers. "The only thing different is the plumbing . . . but don't put that in your book because I don't want anyone else to know. Seriously"—she laughs—"why compare them? If you love somebody and want to be with that person, what the hell difference does sex, race, or any of that have to do with loving someone? Society compares them and as gays we get the raw end of the deal because we don't have that little piece of paper—the marriage certificate. All a marriage license does is make it hard to get out. That's the one advantage we as gays have over straights—we don't have a legal contract holding us together. *We* hold us together. I refuse to compare my marriage to a straight marriage: why, that's downright insulting. If they need some comparisons, let them compare straight marriages to gay marriages."

At the time of this interview, Jill is seriously ill. In less than one year she has been hospitalized six times for severe asthma. I ask Dolly about the effects of Jill's illness on their lives. "In many ways," Dolly explains, "her illness has brought us even closer together. A house, jobs, family, and friends all become second class. I've watched her deteriorate in the past year . . . I'll do anything we have to do to keep her breathing. I'm so scared . . . I don't want to lose her."

2

COUPLING / MARRYING

As human beings, we have been walking two by two since we first left the cave. Most everyone remembers their grammar school history books. There they were, Clara and Clyde Neanderfolk, timidly setting forth from the cave. For cave people they were modest—his groin and her whole body, including her breasts, were covered with animal skins. As a child, I never understood where they got the animal skins, if this was their first trip out of the cave.

Anyway, Clara and Clyde were a lovely couple. However, their children—and all Neanderthal children—were bastards. Clara and Clyde were "living together"—they were not "married." Mr. and Mrs. Neanderfolk's nudity was not the only thing the history books covered up. Actually, Clara and Clyde left the cave *after* Bill and Harry. And behind Clara and Clyde were Mildred and Shirley. No one wanted to go out and face the elements alone, so they did it in couples—much the same as we need supportive relationships to survive today.

A few millennia later, civil and religious laws institutionalized hetero sapien coupling and renamed it "marriage." Children were also legitimated and classified "offspring." There was no need to legitimate Harry and Bill and Mildred and Shirley because they did not produce "offspring." With all this in order, civilization moved forward.

As one century ran into another, people forgot that "marriage" had its historical origins in coupling. Heterosexuals, a subcategory of Homo sapiens, continued to structure and restructure marriage. Homosexuals and lesbians, another subcategory of Homo sapiens, continued "to couple," since they had never been legitimated.

With one out of three marriages ending in divorce, institutionalized marriage does seem to be declining. However, no one should panic—we simply seem to be returning to coupling. In June 1979, the Census Bureau reported that the number of unmarried couples living together more than doubled in the first eight years of this decade: *cohabitation,* to use the Census Bureau word, has increased by 117 percent.*

Throughout history homosexuals and lesbians have been coupling and cohabitating. Adapting to the vernacular, some homosexuals and lesbians have defined their coupling process as a "commitment" or a "primary relationship"; others have simply adopted the word *marriage.* In responding to the "Speak Out" questionnaire, 56 percent of the lesbian and homosexual population that responded said they were comfortable with the use of the word *marriage* as applied to permanent gay relationships and 44 percent said they were *not* comfortable with the word *marriage.*

No matter what you call it, however, all subcategories of Homo sapiens do it: cohabitate and copulate. But while all forms of modern science have studied the many dimensions of heterosexual coupling, the emotional dimension of homosexual and lesbian coupling has been sorely neglected.

Attribute it to a fluke of history, but homosexual and lesbian couples have never been institutionalized. As a result, our contribution to civilization has been the perpetuation of the basic tenets of coupling. And although we have never been legitimated, recognized, or validated, we are alive and well and living in America—and in the rest of the world.

WHERE DO GAY COUPLES MEET?

Gay couples seem to meet in many of the same places straight couples meet. Twenty-one (21) percent of the lesbians and homosexuals who responded to the questionnaire met their partners through mutual friends, 13 percent met in business, and 13 percent met at school. Bars, whether gay or straight singles bars, are constantly attacked by the general population. However, 18 percent of those questioned met their partners in bars. This was one of the few areas where there was a difference between gay men and gay women. Only 11 percent of the women met their partners in a bar, while 27 percent of the men met their partners in bars.

The following is not intended as a dating/mating guide for lesbians and homosexuals. However, it is interesting to review the differences between gay men and women in terms of where they

* The *New York Times,* June 27, 1979, p. 12.

met their partners. For example, 19 percent of the women but only 5 percent of the men "met someone" in business. Are businessmen, then, more threatened than businesswomen? Or is it that lesbians, even in business, are less threatening than homosexuals—therefore less likely to be fired if they are discovered? Are homosexuals more threatened because of the higher economic stakes? Only 6 percent of the men said they met their partners at school. However, 18 percent of the women met their partners in high school or on a college campus somewhere. If young lesbians are freer to develop relationships in school, what is happening to young homosexuals? Is their development as persons being thwarted because they are not representative of the college jock-macho-football player image? And how much damage is caused to a young man by this type of estrangement and isolation?

Fifteen (15) percent of the men but only 5 percent of the women said they met their partners at a religious organization—and I will not touch *that one* with a ten-foot pole. One (1) percent of the total population surveyed met through professional organizations. And 1 percent—and I am a happy member of this group—met their partners through family relations.

DATING and DECISIONS

Undocumented common knowledge seems to attest to the instability of gay relationships. Several untruths: gays jump out of one relationship and into another with remarkable speed; gays tend to spend one night together and the next morning over breakfast decide to spend their lives together; lack of a marriage license decreases the seriousness with which gays approach relationships.

The data we collected contradicts these negative assumptions. We asked people how long they knew their partner before they began living together. Of the total female and male population surveyed, 19 percent knew their partners less than three months; 24 percent, three but less than six months; 21 percent, six months but less than one year; and 35 percent, one year or longer. The only statistical difference between the men and the women seems to be in the one-year-or-longer category: 42 percent of the women and 26 percent of the men knew their partners one year or more before living together.

A national magazine conducted a reader survey entitled, "Would Two Perfectly Happy People Throw Over Living Together for

Marriage?" * The questionnaire was, of course, directed to hetero-sexual couples. Among the 44 percent of married couples respond-ing: from the West, 44 percent shared a household before marriage; from the South, 42 percent did likewise; and from the East, over 30 percent lived together before their trip to city hall for a marriage license. The average time spent living together before the legal step: approximately one year.

Lesbian and homosexual couples have no "legal step" to legiti-mate, make public, or solidify their relationships. The step, it seems, is taken privately when two gay people make a commitment to each other. Pietropinto and Simenauer state in their book, *A Nationwide Survey of Marriage:* "It is reasonable to assume that virtually all couples enter a marriage wanting it to be permanent and successful."† Is it not, then, fair to assume that gay people, having made a commitment to each other, want it to be a permanent and successful relationship?

The "Speak Out" questionnaire asked those surveyed whether the decision to live together included an agreement to live together on a trial basis, to live together permanently, or whether it just evolved. Twelve (12) percent of the respondents said they and their partners had decided to live together on a trial basis; 32 percent said the decision was to live together on a permanent basis; and 56 percent said the decision to live together just evolved. Gay couples simply do not have neat and orderly structures upon which to base their relationships. It is normal for a heterosexual couple to mark their commitment to each other as the date they took that "legal step"—and a small fortune is spent on anniversary cards. However, for gay couples as well as for heterosexual common-law couples, it is a calendar of intimate and personal events that marks their union as two persons.

CIVIL and RELIGIOUS CEREMONIES

There is no way of determining what pressures are placed upon a heterosexual couple in terms of living together versus legal mar-riage. However, whatever the reasons, most do take some form of

---

* "Would Two Perfectly Happy People Throw Over Living Together for Marriage?" *Apartment Life,* February 1979, p. 12. (Hereinafter referred to as *Apartment Life.*)

† Anthony Pietropinto, M.D., and Jacqueline Simenauer, *Husbands and Wives, A Nationwide Survey of Marriage* (New York: Times Books, 1979), p. xvii. (Hereinafter referred to as Pietropinto/Simenauer, *Husbands and Wives.*)

ceremonial step. A national magazine survey reports: "Thirty-five percent of those responding had themselves or knew of couples who had a traditional religious ceremony. Another 27 percent opted for a quick trip to city hall."* Heterosexual common-law couples have chosen not to take either a civil or religious matrimonial step—for whatever are *their* reasons. There is no civil matrimonial step for lesbian and homosexual couples—hence, no choice. Although religious commitment ceremonies are available to gay couples on a limited basis, such ceremonies are often determined by where one lives and by one's religious orientation.

My questionnaire asked lesbians and homosexuals if, given a choice, they would choose to be married in a civil ceremony, a religious ceremony, or not to be married in any type of ceremony. The total responses of both men and women—*if given a choice:* 9 percent would be married in a civil ceremony; 33 percent in a religious ceremony; 1 percent in both a civil and religious ceremony; and 55 percent would choose not to be married in any type of ceremony.

• • •

Robert and Bob share the same religion. "I guess," says Robert, "we would like to have a wedding within our own church. But could you imagine bringing the question of gay marriage to the Pope?" I asked them about the Roman Catholic-oriented Dignity Holy Union Ceremony. "When we made our commitment to each other," Bob explains, "we didn't know such a thing existed. The nearest Dignity branch to us is pretty far away. We have a big house and a lot of work; we're lucky if we make it to our own church on Sunday." Robert says he would like to become involved in local church activities. "However, I do block the whole thing because of the church's stand on homosexuality . . . I'd feel hypocritical."

Ann sums up the ceremonial question in six sentences: "Legal marriage isn't important to me. I don't care what society says because society is pretty confused anyway. And I don't buy religion. It's a man-made thing people need to survive in this jungle. It's something outside of themselves they can call upon. I want to call upon what's inside of me—and I don't need religion to do it." Kate sarcastically adds: "Now wouldn't my life be perfect if Ann were a man. Then I could legally marry her and I'd do it in a second. But Ann is *not* a man. And even if the laws changed and I

Apartment Life.

could marry her as a woman, I couldn't do it: I don't have the stamina it would take to buck the system that much. If I could legally marry Ann without pressure from society and rejection from my family, I'd do it. But no law can guarantee me that. As far as a religious ceremony, I think most religions are a lot of hypocrisy and people who perpetuate them are hypocrites. I see no reason to indulge religious hypocrites or to indulge myself in religion. It's more important to be honest with yourself than to be honest with some invisible God."

In discussing religion with the lesbians and homosexuals interviewed, there does seem to be a separation between what is institutional religion and the individual's spiritual life. Discussing their feelings on it, Rob and Bob state they would not be interested in a civil or religious ceremony. "A legal marriage," said Rob, "isn't going to keep us together. I think a legal marriage is ludicrous. Quite simply, I couldn't—wouldn't—be bothered." Religion, according to Bob, is archaic: "I don't believe in God, but if there is a God, our marriage is recognized in His or Her eyes. A priest, minister, or rabbi reciting a few words means nothing. It's the vows between the two people that count. For me spirituality is another thing. I can see two people having a religious ceremony if they want to express their devotion to each other in front of God and their friends. Rob and I do that in our daily lives . . . we don't need any ceremony."

Joan and Pat had a Dignity Holy Union Ceremony that was attended by both their families and friends. Christine and Steven also attended the ceremony. "They're my children," Pat says, "of course they were there." Christine and Steven gave Joan and Pat flowers the morning of their Holy Union Ceremony. The children attached a note to the flowers: "Dear Mom and Joan, Have a nice wedding even though it's kind of a secret. . . . Love, Chris and Stevie." When I ask Joan and Pat about the children's use of the word *secret,* both of them laugh. "You don't know Stevie"—Joan smiles—"he was so excited about it, he would've told the whole neighborhood. Their mother was getting married, they were happy about it, and they wanted to tell everyone." "It was hard," Pat adds, "to try to tell kids that even though they're happy about something, and even though we were proud of what we were doing, they couldn't tell anyone. I told them some people might not understand or might say something to them about it that would hurt them. Chrisie got the message—she's twelve. Stevie kept saying he didn't understand. He believes if something is good and happy you should be able to tell everyone. Try to tell a nine-year-old you don't want him to be hurt, don't want some callous person to take away his happiness or his excitement. . . ."

Although Charlotte and Nancy are spiritually oriented people, neither of them would have a religious ceremony. "For us," Nancy explains, "any type of ceremony comes too close to heterosexual marriage. And heterosexual marriage has too many negatives. I don't want to emulate a heterosexual relationship. We don't need what they need to make their relationship valid: *we* make our relationship valid." Charlotte does not regard her relationship with Nancy as a marriage. "I look at it as a loving partnership. We are Christians and faith is the basis of our life together. But that has nothing to do with having a religious ceremony." Nancy wants nothing to do with heterosexual structures: "We've had enough problems with roles in our relationship: me being the husband; Charlotte, the wife. It took us a long time to work through that and we got *that* from the heterosexual molds we were raised in. I don't want anything to do with it. . . ."

• • •

I had, throughout the course of the interviews, met men and women who are in spiritual pain. Their suffering is caused by any and all of the traditional religions in which we were all raised. Listening to gays discuss their religious and spiritual problems, I would think to myself: "Why do they even bother? Give it up for your spiritual survival. Why do they care? I don't care. . . ." The fact that I no longer care is not important; the fact that they care *is*. It seems their pain is not in their estrangement from the particular institutional church or religion in which they were raised. Their pain is caused by the spiritual separation they experience. Because they have been ostracized by their various religions, they feel they have lost God. And if they have lost God and have been excluded from their religions, to whom do they pray, where do they go? They want to reclaim their relationships with God. They want their marriages and relationships blessed by God.

This "wanting" constitutes the spiritual void experienced by many religious lesbians and homosexuals. To them, being accepted by their respective religions would mean God had accepted them as persons and had accepted the holiness of their relationships. Until that happens, they have lost God. If a church rejects a person who is divorced, it is rejecting that person because of something that person has *done*. When religions reject lesbians and homosexuals, they are rejecting them based on who they *are*. Such rejection is phenomenally destructive to gay people who see their spiritual lives in terms of a particular church or religion.

I spent an evening with Bishop Robert M. Clement and the Right Reverend John Noble at the Church of the Beloved Disciple in New York City. Both men are ordained Eucharistic Catholic priests. At this point in my life, I would have to define myself as irreligious. I was not, therefore, overanxious to spend an evening discussing religion. When I finally left at almost midnight, I had *not* been converted. However, I knew I would use the interview in my book.

"I want lesbians and homosexuals to stop suffocating in the spiritual closets of the institutional churches," said Bishop Robert. "Love is of God and God is love. Those who have a religious nature and who realize their own love must be aware that God is a part of that love. They are a part of the love of God."

It was in July 1970 that the first Holy Union Ceremony was performed at the Church of the Beloved Disciple. "The essence of the Holy Union Ceremony," said Father John, "is in its catholicism." "Our ceremony," added Bishop Robert, "is between the two persons and their God. If as individuals they believe God is important in their lives, then they are involving God in their relationship. In a Holy Union Ceremony, the two people bring the love they have found to the church and the priest formally blesses it. Declaring your love openly in a church and having the church's assurance of God's blessing is a tremendous strengthening for lesbian and homosexual couples."

"Understand," Bishop Robert continued, "a Holy Union Ceremony between either two men or two women is not a parody of heterosexual marriage. Gay people can be free of the institutional churches' interpretation of marriage. By being gay one has a chance to freely explore what is meant by coming together in a bonding relationship of consequence and importance in a person's life. The institutional churches are all too casual about heterosexual marriage. Here people are free to explore the real value of their relationship *for themselves*. Here people are free to explore the real religious dimension of the commitment they are making to each other."

"We feel that marriage, in the culture of the moment, is a travesty of true marriage," Father John explained. "It's obviously breaking down. There are heterosexual couples who go from the church to the divorce courts—almost instantly. Gay people have no standards to live by, except their parents' standards. Marriage today is not what it should be. Why should we 'ape' heterosexual marriages when we have something very positive to work with? Gay standards concerning marriage should be new positive standards. We feel that heterosexual standards concerning marriage are negative standards. Why then should gay unions 'ape' crumbling heterosexual unions? We're free to find decent standards of our own. A true marriage is what our Holy Union is—the coming together of two minds and two hearts . . . openly and lovingly. And I don't think any other considerations are important."

• • •

GAYS DEFINE THEIR MARRIAGES / RELATIONSHIPS

Debra and Beverly debate each other's answers to every question I ask. However, when I ask them to define their relationship, a certain quiet settles in among the three of us. "It's twenty-two years now," Debra says, "and it's still good. When the honeymoon wears off, we'll find something else to do."

"What's 'good' mean?" I ask. "Good," Debra answers, grinning at Beverly. "Good is when we can be with other people or be alone. Good is when we're both reading, we haven't talked for an hour, we're on separate ends of the sofa, and our toes are touching. Reading like that, we're together and we're not together, but we each know the other is there.

"You can't do certain things with just anybody. I can go to the theater with anybody who enjoys theater—and that's okay. But there are certain things I can only do with Beverly." I do not know if I should, but I ask anyway, "What can you do with Beverly that you can't do with anyone else?"

"Nonsense things," Debra answers, beginning to deliver her thesis on nonsense. "When you're talking about nonsense, you're talking about things you can only do with someone you love. I can only watch fireworks with Beverly. Another nonsense thing, an organized walk on the beach for an express purpose. 'Today,' we say, 'we are looking for small white rocks: they must be flat. Not blue rocks or pink rocks: today they must be small, white, flat rocks.' See, I can't do that with anyone but Beverly. And she can't do it with anyone but me. Of course, sometimes Bev brings me presents: a piece of exquisite and well-done green or brown beach glass.

"That's nonsense, Mary. It's ours: mine and Beverly's. No one has defined it and no one has told us we *should* be enjoying it. That's what makes *our* nonsense so special. No one has critiqued it and said this or that is good or bad. It's good for us, it's what we like . . . and that's all that matters."

"There's nothing I could or would add to that," Beverly says, winking at me. "I don't believe that," I say, and the three of us laugh.

Neither Angel nor Timothy likes the word *marriage*. "Okay, Tim," I say, "what then have you two got going?" "Everything is between us: problems, joys, sorrows," he answers. "We don't keep secrets from each other . . . except my surprise birthday party, which Angel planned and I found out about. We have disagreements, but we know where each other is coming from. If we try to handle them intelligently and if we don't *expect* to agree on everything, then we work the disagreements out and we're okay."

"Give me a name for it," I laughingly demand of Angel. "I can't"—he giggles—"I really can't. I see it, or us, as a serious relationship . . . that's the only thing I can think of." "Then," I ask, backing him against the proverbial wall, "tell me what a serious relationship is." "You're a hard woman," he sneers at me. "Tell me," I demand threateningly.

"A serious relationship is what Tim and I have. Okay, okay . . . don't hit me. A serious relationship is living with the person, not just seeing him a couple of times a week. It's dealing with the whole person, what he likes or doesn't like, what he thinks and feels. When it's a serious relationship, you want to spend the rest of your life with that person. You understand each other, you accept each other. I don't want any roles. I guess I want what me and Tim have—an equal relationship—we treat each other as equals. We love each other and we're friends."

"I am a man," says Bob, "and then I am a gay man. I love Rob. Together we're making what is a marriage to us. What it comes down to for me is thinking of us as a unit. We have a commitment to our relationship. And that commitment is to love each other and build our lives together. We have a healthy relationship. I don't expect it to be like a straight marriage, or like another gay marriage. Marriages are as different as the people in them."

"We're husband and husband," Rob adds, enjoying his play on

words. "To me, my homosexuality is an emotional need. I need this masculine love. I need a man's love and I have that with Bob. And it's a man I want to love, but I love him as a man. Loving Bob as a man is my emotional preference, which involves my sexuality as well. I've had sex with many women; I was twelve when I started to make it with the little girls in the neighborhood. That sounds terrible, but I was a little boy then and they were all older than me. I was eighteen when I experienced *love* for the first time and it was with a man. This is who I am: I am a man who loves other men. That love is expressed in my sexuality. That's the foundation of my marriage to Bob."

I ask Dolly if she is comfortable with the word *marriage.* "I'm as comfortable with the word *marriage* as I am in these old dungarees I'm wearing. A marriage is two people who are very much in love, who don't cheat on each other, who enjoy being together. It's sitting down at the end of the day and telling each other all the things that happened during the day when you weren't together. It's when you have each other and that's all you really need. Other people—family, friends—they pass through your life, you share it with them, and that's fine. As long as you're together—as long as Jill and I are together—that's all that really counts."

"My turn," Jill says, perking up. "I don't have any definition for marriage—mine or anyone else's. There's no definition for marriage, you just live it. You don't think about it—most often you don't have time to think about it. You love each other, you respect each other, you stand by each other. You just live it . . . you do what comes naturally—and it does come naturally if you love the person you're with."

"What makes a house a home?" I ask Jill. "A little Waterford, a little stained glass, a little china," she answers, laughing. "Dolly makes my house a home. If I weren't there, it would just be a house for her. We make it a home for each other. It's a place where you feel comfortable. Hey, when you're in trouble, you don't go *house*— you go *home.* First, you share it with the person you love. From there, if it's your *home*—you share it with friends. Like around the holidays, we just open our home to everybody. If you've got love there, that's what makes a house a home. That's what Dolly and I have. We're proud of it and we want to share it. Even you can come if you don't bring this goddamned machine."

When I ask Richard and Charles to define their relationship, Richard responds first. "Each partner in the relationship is committed to the other person. You share everything—your personal life, your sexual life . . . expenses." He laughs. "A gay relationship," adds Charles, "is the same as a straight relationship: it's a commitment between two people. It's a trust and it's compatibility. What is *natural* to a gay relationship is *natural* to a straight relationship."

"Our marriage," says Todd, "is sharing a single dream from two different perspectives. And that dream is to build a life together. What you do when you marry or when you make a commitment to someone is you take life from an individual perspective and you start living it and dealing with it as a couple. We work together, we rely on each other. That's how I explain my marriage to Philip. That's how I would have also explained my marriage to my wife if I were still with her. It's the same and it doesn't matter whether you're gay or straight."

"My marriage to Todd," explains Philip, "is a permanent commitment. If I were just 'living with' him, I could walk out the door anytime I wanted to. That permanent commitment means I want it to be permanent. Permanence involves a person's willing it to be permanent. Then you use that *will* to work out the problems and make it permanent. I'm a religious person and I wouldn't live with a person—I wouldn't live with Todd—unless I were committed to him."

"I will *not*"—Kate balks at me—"define my relationship with Ann as a marriage. It is a commitment. It's a relationship of total trust. I've never loved or shared so much with someone in my whole life. And I *will not* demean our relationship by calling it a marriage."

"Call it what you want," I say. "Don't call it or name it anything—I don't care. Just talk into the mike and tell me what it's about. Just don't give me that exponential and extrapolation stuff again." "Yeah," Ann chimes in, "don't start that crap again."

"Okay"—Kate snickers—"if you two can't look at things mathematically, I'll just have to deal with that. Seriously, my relationship with Ann—my commitment to her—puts everything else in perspective. It helps me to see what is or isn't important. Our relationship is not my total life, but I look at everything in relationship to our commitment. When you love someone and have a good life together, it makes the garbage in life easier to identify. Our relationship makes me happy. Ann is *the* person I share everything with. And things are so much better when you share them with someone who cares about you, who reinforces you. It gives you more value as a person.

"I guess to me sharing is the most important part of our relationship. I share everything with Ann. When you share, the potential is tremendous. You see things through someone else's eyes. You see things you might not ordinarily see for yourself. And what you see, once you share it, is so much more meaningful. When someone you love and respect loves you, it makes you feel special."

"She thinks I'm *simply* great," Ann glibly interrupts, "and she *is* really fortunate to be committed to someone of my stature."

"Okay, hot-blooded Italian," I say, "we've heard about your lust and your passion, now let's hear about your emotional life."

"How can one Italian ask another Italian to separate them?" Ann asks. "For me, our commitment . . ." "Is based on your ability to make pasta," I interrupt. "Come on," Ann says, "I was just about to get serious." "Okay, Ann," I concede, "get serious."

"For me, our commitment is based on trust and communication. Total trust is being able to risk—saying something you've got to say to your partner knowing what it is you *have* to say could possibly end the relationship. I trust in the fact I can say anything to Kate and it'll be all right. She loves me so much and I love her so much that I can say anything to her."

"What's communication, Ann?" I ask. "Now don't rush me," she mutters, "I'm thinking carefully about everything I say because it's being taped. I'm coming to it . . .

"Communication is the ability to express to each other whatever it is you're feeling or thinking. It can be verbal or nonverbal communication—or a combination of both. It's talking, crying, laughing, holding, touching. I love the touching part"—she coquettishly wiggles—"that's delightful. I really turn on to communicating that way."

"What's love?" I ask, "And I don't want to hear Kate's balloon story from *you.*"

"I love Kate"—Ann smiles—"that's what love is. And before you ask me to explain it, I'll explain. What it comes down to is the deepest concern I've ever felt for anyone. It's the ability to put someone before yourself, their needs ahead of yours. To think of them before you think of yourself. Understand where I'm coming from in my definition of love. I believe whenever we do something in some way we're meeting our own needs whether it be our altruistic needs or our expectations concerning the 'return' on the love we're investing. I need to love Kate, I need to do for her. I need her to love me and to do for me. We're just an *adorable* couple . . . running around doing for each other, loving each other all over the place."

• • •

The feelings and thoughts expressed by the lesbians and homosexuals in this chapter are not unique. Their comments are representative of the hundreds of people who completed the essay questions in the "Speak Out" questionnaire.

Fifty-three (53) percent of the respondents believe marriage is a commitment between two people; 12 percent defined a gay marriage/relationship as an interpersonal relationship between two men or two women; 19 percent believe it is companionship; and 12 percent feel a gay marriage/relationship is based upon the self-actualization of both people within the relationship.

"Speak Out" asked: "What do you consider most important in a gay marriage/relationship?" Forty-nine (49) percent of the men and women said it is the interpersonal relationship existing between two people; 26 percent felt commitment was most important; 12 percent felt companionship the most important element; and to another 12 percent self-actualization is most important.

People who responded to "Speak Out" are as real as the people in this chapter. However, not only can you not include all their personal comments, you also cannot—via questionnaire—go further with them in discussing the issues. Many of the gay couples I interviewed have *years* behind them. Their problems with children, alcoholism, sexual fidelity, careers, and illness are as much a part of their lives as the love they share for each other. They *all* have problems, but they are all working to resolve those problems. Nobody's marriage—gay or straight—is made in heaven. Some are made in the hells we ourselves create. However, as I learned from the couples I interviewed, it is what you do to resolve those problems that is important. The commitment of both partners to their relationship can make the problems surmountable—and make the relationship more important and more valuable.

There are also relationships where, after a period of years, a couple is unable to either resolve or accept their differences. One or both of the partners loses hope. With the loss of hope seems to come the loss of a willingness to try to resolve problems. Quite simply, and I base this on comments made during the interviews, you do not believe, anymore, that things can be worked out. And no one but the two people involved can determine—or judge—whether this loss of hope is justified.

My mother always told me: "When two people are between the sheets . . . no one *knows* but those two people." This little proverb *does* sound much more erotic and much more musical in the Sicilian dialect. But, you know, when I think about it, all those years she kept telling me that, she never really specified the genders of the two people between the sheets.

3

TO HAVE AND TO HOLD

SEX and COMMITMENT

"Male promiscuity," Rob gently explains to me, "is a matter of upbringing. Male children are raised to be promiscuous. No one actually tells us but it *is* implied: sexually, we're boys and we can do anything we want. We know we can't become pregnant so we don't have to be afraid of that. As far as getting someone pregnant: well, just don't get caught at it. As little boys, we knew we could have all the sex we wanted. As a teenager, sex with the girls in the neighborhood was part of my life. All little boys grow up and become men. Some discover they're homosexuals; others pursue their heterosexuality. But the *orientation* hasn't changed. You've been programmed with a lot of societal data that says you're a man—you can go out and have sex all you want. The promiscuity is inbred in all boy children, and since most boy children don't find out they're gay until later in life, their promiscuity has nothing to do with their gayness. It has to do with their *male*ness and male orientation begins in childhood."

Without warning, Rob turns the interview around on me. "What did your mother tell you when you were a girl growing up?" "That's not fair, this is my book." I laugh. "Come on," he says, "what did she tell you?" "She told me," I confess, "I should never let a boy get above my knees." Now I *am* embarrassed. "What else did she tell you?" he insists, teasing me. "Spill it." I again remind him that *I* am supposed to be asking the questions. Bob, supporting Rob, says, "You can't ask us all these questions and not expect we're going to ask you some. We've never really talked openly with a lesbian." "Well," I say, yielding, "she told me I should never have sex with a man unless I loved him—and only after I married him. She never really told me anything about sex with women, though."

"See?" Rob laughs. "You're proving everything I'm saying. The challenge to me as a young boy, as alluded to by my old man, was

55

to get above any and every girl's knee I could. As far as sex and love—no one ever mentioned love to me."

"Rob and I," explains Bob, "have both had the male sex scene. When we came together, we decided we wanted a monogamous relationship because we'd both had everything else. This whole big thing over sexual fidelity, I don't think, has anything to do with sex. As far as sex outside the primary relationship, what it comes down to is jealousy and insecurity—not sex. If Rob had sex with someone else, I might be jealous. I might become afraid I was going to lose him. So if I did a big number, it wouldn't be because of the sexual act. It would be because I was jealous and scared of losing him."

"What you're saying," I continue, "is that you and Rob have decided upon a sexually exclusive relationship?"

"Right. We've both been in relationships where outside sexual activity was just fine—and it *doesn't* work."

"So," I continue, "if, after your monogamy agreement with Rob, he had sex with someone else and you found out about it, it would make you jealous and insecure." "Probably," Bob answers.

"But if you and Rob had agreed to outside sex, it wouldn't make you jealous and insecure?" "How could something I agreed to," he answers, "make me jealous and insecure?"

"Sexual fidelity," explains Michael, "is what Paul and I expect of each other. It's as important to me in my marriage to Paul as it was when I was married to my wife. I feel if you've committed yourself to a marriage, this is expected of you. If you're not ready to live up to these expectations, you wouldn't be in the relationship."

"We're together in our heads on the subject of sexual fidelity," says Paul. "Michael told me when we first got together, 'If I ever say I love you, I will mean it, and I will be totally bound. You'll never have to worry about my being unfaithful because when I tell you I love you I am also, at that point, giving you my word that I will be faithful.' There's simply no conflict in this area for us."

"You're both healthy and virile men right now." I address Paul. "What would happen if Michael were to suddenly become ill and could no longer have sex?"

"We're very compatible sexually," Paul answers, "and we have a great time and I hope it continues. I care for Michael more than I ever cared for anyone or anything in my whole life. If his health failed it wouldn't change anything. I feel everything we have together is of more importance and of more value than sex."

"Would you take another lover if Michael became seriously ill?" I ask.

"No," Paul answers. "I don't think so. Our feelings toward each other are much more serious and much deeper than sex. I don't think I would go out and pursue sex with someone else. I think I'd be able to satisfy myself . . . if you know what I mean. I was in a relationship for many years and the sexual thing failed. I had no alternative but to go outside and have sex since I wasn't having sex at home. It was the eventual destruction of that relationship. So if Michael were to become ill and unable to have sex, I would take care of myself and be totally happy within my relationship with him. I think any outside sexual activity would only hinder our relationship."

•　•　•

There were moments during many of the interviews when, as I listened to people discuss their relationships, I felt as if something holy were being said. The beauty and depth of what they were saying was so personal and so intimate my tape recorder seemed almost sacrilegious.

•　•　•

Paul continues: "Mary, if Michael were to become seriously ill and bedridden, I would take care of him until he died. I love him in every way that it is possible to love another human being. No matter what happened to him, I would be his and he would be mine. I love him."

I am sitting across the table from Paul and Michael. Michael's eyes have been fixed on Paul as he is speaking. Paul is so intense as he talks that when he stops he looks at Michael—whose hand he is holding—and seems almost surprised to see him sitting there.

"There's only one way to break this heaviness," I tease, "what about sex in old age?"

"Emotionally," says Michael, "we both understand that with old age comes less of an interest in sex. But we'll wait it out and see what happens." "Go away," laughs Paul, "we'll be sexually active for the duration—that's the only thing I want to understand emotionally or intellectually."

"Kate and I don't have sex together," Ann explains. "We haven't for years." "We do have a tremendous physical relationship," adds Kate. "What," I ask, "is a physical relationship without *sex*?"

Kate laughs. "We hug, we kiss, we touch. We sleep together nude. It's a wonderful warmth that transcends sex. A lot more communication and a lot less games. It's amazing how all the other qualities in a relationship come to the forefront when sex takes a back seat. We simply don't have sex with each other and we've been doing just fine without it for nine years. So if we don't have sex with each other, there's no other alternative but to enjoy sex with other people. No one can question our approach—it has evolved over twelve years of trial and error. What we've both come to is a compromise. Because the relationship is more important to us than whether or not we enjoy sex together, we've gotten rid of sex, we've eliminated the problems it causes."

"Our sexual relationship only lasted three years," Ann says. "And at the time I was twenty-one and I wanted a sexual life. So I pursued it with other people. In terms of getting seriously involved with people I might have sex with, that only happened twice. But even then, it did not take away from the love I have for Kate. I loved her as deeply when I was involved with these other women as I love her now. Oh, by the way, I wasn't involved with those other two women at the same time . . . the affairs were spaced or staggered or whatever."

"Originally," Kate explains, "I thought sexual fidelity was really important. Experience has showed me that it's not. When I think about it now, I think it was more my own insecurities and my own fear of being betrayed that made me so adamant about sexual fidelity. I felt if Ann had sex with someone else it meant she was going to leave me. Well, she has had sex with other people and she's still here. So I guess I was wrong. Or else I just can't get rid of her."

"Kate and I are both free to have sex with other people. It's not my problem if she doesn't exercise that freedom. It's her choice. She has a totally different upbringing than I do; her values are different. We've worked all this out over the years by talking about it—but *honestly* talking about it. In a way I'm glad our sexual relationship ended when I got involved with someone else in college. I found out years later, when we talked about it, that she'd never really been sexually satisfied in the first three years of our campus affair. She was faking it. *That* really upset me because I've had very satisfying sexual relationships with other people and I thought I was satisfying her. I wasn't. She was just acting. And so that ended the sex . . . but we went forward from there and made a life together."

I ask Em and Louise if they believe their relationship would be sustained without a sexual dimension. Louise laughs and blushes. "We don't have a 'constant' sexual relationship now. Yes, I absolutely believe our relationship would be sustained without sex—it's sustained on a day-to-day basis without sex. You see—we work real hard—a lot of overtime. We're involved with the boys. We have to take care of the house . . . sometimes it just doesn't happen—we're too tired."

Em believes sex is important in a relationship. "But," she explains, "if Louise was sick and couldn't have sex, I would wait until she got better. I don't believe in cheating or satisfying your sexual desires with somebody else. She's the person I am committed to, and that's that. I would wait a very long time for her to get better and I wouldn't have sex with no one else but her.

"Sexual fidelity is important to me because Louise is the one I'm committed to—she's the one I'm in love with. And I don't believe in lust—I believe in making love."

When I ask Em to define *lust* she gives me a suspicious look. "You know what lust is," she says. I answer, "I know what lust is for me. But what's lust for you?" "Lust for me," she explains, "is having sex with anyone who comes along. But love is making love. It's a deeper expression of your feelings with the person you're in love with."

"Let's forget about Louise's possibly becoming ill," I say. "Let's just say for some reason she decides she doesn't want to have sex anymore. What would you do then?"

Now Em—this grandmother and mother of eight—is blushing. "Well," she says, looking at Louise out of the corner of her eye, "I would simply have to try to get her to change her mind." And then, giggling: "I bet I could get her to change her mind."

"If either of us were to get involved sexually with someone else," Beverly explains, "it would be okay. But there's not enough time or energy for anyone else. We developed this understanding between us as a result of Debra's getting involved with another woman seven years ago. That affair forced us to sit down and start talking about this whole thing of sexual fidelity."

I ask Debra if she would talk about her affair. "Sure," she says, "it's something we've already gotten through. There were a lot of years before it and there will be a lot of years after it. What happened was I met this woman playing tennis and sparks were flying. It was the first time it had happened to me since meeting Beverly—and fifteen years is a long wait for sparks.

"I had to pursue it—there was no question in my mind that there was something there. I've never felt guilty about what I'm doing. I'm doing what I have to do, and there's no sense being guilty about it. What I did feel guilty about was being dishonest with Beverly. So I told her, and at that point we were fortunate in that we were living in an apartment with two bedrooms."

Beverly and Debra spent five months living together as roommates while Debra pursued an affair with another woman. "It ended," Debra explains, "and it should have ended a lot earlier. It should have been nothing more than the excitement of an affair. At the time, Beverly and I were having problems with our relationship—which is probably why I got involved with this other woman."

I ask Beverly why she had waited out Debra's affair. "Because," Beverly answers with a great deal of certainty, "I still loved Debbie. She never told me she didn't love me during this affair she was having, she never said she wanted to move out and end our relationship. She kept telling me she wasn't sure what she wanted, and although she was involved with someone else, she wasn't saying she didn't want me.

"I knew our relationship had some problems neither of us were facing. We'd been having problems for about three years before Debra met this woman. So I figured in all probability I had contributed to half the problems. It was just that Debra had found someone else to get involved with and I hadn't. I really couldn't say that she was all wrong or that I was an innocent party. I decided to give it time and see what happened. And seven years later . . . here we are."

"This affair happened after you two were together fifteen years, and it happened seven years ago. You both agree you feel this outside involvement happened because of the problems both of you were having—but not facing—in your own relationship. But where are you now on the issue of sexual fidelity? You first, Beverly."

"I couldn't handle a relationship where my partner was constantly getting involved with other people. Basically, I prefer a monogamous relationship. But even within a monogamous relationship, if something were to happen, it wouldn't break up the relationship. If Debra were to get sexually involved with someone right now, I don't think it would end our relationship. It would only end our relationship if it were a *love* affair. If either one of us saw someone and was sexually attracted to her, and decided to get a little involved but not fall in love—that would be okay with me."

"I would have to agree with Beverly," Debra explains. "Sexual fidelity is not important to me. But that's mainly an intellectual answer because it hasn't happened since my now historical affair of seven years ago. Neither of us has been involved with anyone else since that time. But it's not because we believe it's something 'you're not supposed to do.' Neither of us has been sexually involved with anyone else because we just haven't wanted to, or because neither of us has met someone we might be sexually attracted to—the opportunity simply hasn't presented itself."

"Sex is not the basis of our relationship," explains Richard. "However, we don't believe in swapping or switching partners. A relationship won't hold together if the partners are out with other people. I think a relationship has a greater chance of success if the partners are basically monogamous and live with each other on a totally one-to-one basis." Charles adds, "Sex has a very low rating in terms of our relationship. Yes, we have a good sex life and, yes, we enjoy it. But so many other things are more important than sex."

"What would happen," I ask, "if one or the other of you were unfaithful?" Charles answers. "There's always the possibility of cheating. But even if one of us had a one-night stand, it would not end the relationship. If you have a good and solid relationship, an isolated incident of cheating is not going to end the relationship. However, if that isolated incident should become something serious, and should your lover leave you for another person—then I don't believe the relationship was strong enough to be held together beyond one lover's isolated sexual adventure."

Jill and Dolly insist that sexual fidelity is number one in their marriage: there is no room for cheating. When I ask them what "cheating" is, Dolly answers: "Cheating isn't necessarily jumping in the sack with someone else. Cheating is when you find the need to lie to your partner about something as simple as stopping to have a drink with someone. If it's kept under the lid, then it's cheating. Most people cheat in one form or another because they're unhappy and they haven't got the guts to come out and say goodbye. A commitment to me is the same as putting your hand on the Bible and swearing your faithfulness in the eyes of God. A commitment is a commitment and there's no room for cheating and lying."

"We've had our share of fights in all the years we've been

together," Jill explains. "But what I do is try to get away from her after a fight, walk around the block a few times, take a ride down by the river. Before I got sick, I used to jog my ass off for a few hours. But in a fit of anger, there's no such thing as going to a gay bar for either of us. Or going to spend the night at someone else's house. Because there's no way in the world you can come home and make up after you do a number like that. You have a fight and then you've got to put space between the two of you—space, not somebody else's body, not getting smashed in a gay bar. When you do a number like that, it's harder to make up. You don't have to then just make up about the fight you had—you have to make up about the spree one of you went on."

The three of us talk about Jill and Dolly's sex life in relationship to Jill's illness. "Has it affected your sex life?" I ask. Jill says, "Who said we had a sex life in the first place? Since we only had sex once every six months before I got sick, nothing has changed." "Be serious," Dolly laughs. "Okay," Jill says, "I'll be serious. When you work forty or fifty hours a week, go to school, cut the grass, clean the house, take care of the dogs—how much time do you think that leaves the average human being to have sex? It's not a question of time. It's a matter of being completely exhausted. The secret, though, is we're never too tired for hugging and kissing and holding each other. We can work that in when we're cleaning the house. Can't seem to work it in at school, though. That kind of behavior just simply isn't accepted in women our age. Were we younger or older, it would be okay . . . but not at our age."

I ask Dolly if their sex life has changed over the years. "We have had our sexual ups and downs—figuratively speaking, of course. When we first got together, it was sex for breakfast, sex after dinner, sex when we went to bed at night. At that point, we both used to get thirty minutes for lunch. We'd jump in the car, rush home, have sex and rush back to work. Now we've gotten a little older and that has tapered and it's a good thing. Had we kept it up, it would have killed us.

"Now we run home to eat dinner or shop or whatever. If there's energy for sex before the big light in the sky goes out, then we enjoy it together. If we don't have the energy, we kiss each other good night and dream about it. Sex," Dolly explains, "has a place in 'the time' of a relationship. It's important in our relationship, but it's not the most important thing; it doesn't even rate in third or fourth place. It's not even in the top ten. The most important things are understanding each other, caring about each other, doing for each other."

"No," says Timothy, "sexual fidelity is not that important in our relationship. I see sex as a vital part of our relationship, but I don't see it as *the* relationship. Sex is one of the rewards of a relationship but it isn't of primary importance to me. Angel and I have an understanding about it—but we've never promised each other to be sexually faithful."

"What's the 'understanding' between the two of you?" I ask Angel. "Well, like I told you before, I don't like the word *marriage*. But even though I don't like it, from the way I was brought up, that's what Tim and I have. And because of the way I was brought up, it should just be the two people, the two lovers: you don't have sex with other people. Now that's the way I was brought up and that's what I believe. But I don't know if what I believe is really possible. It scares me sometimes. So I guess our understanding is that either of us might go astray or be tempted to have sex with someone else—but neither of us want that to be happening all the time. See, if Tim were sleeping with other people, I wouldn't feel that important to him anymore—I wouldn't under-stand: if we are lovers and if we're a team, how he could keep having sex with other people. It's just the way I feel . . . I guess it's the wrong attitude to have." He shrugs shyly.

"If it's your attitude, I don't think there can be a right or wrong," I say, smiling at him. "You really believe that?" he asks. "Yeah, I do," I tell him. "People have different beliefs about different things: Who can say one is right and one is wrong?" "See"—Timothy laughs, hugging Angel—"it doesn't matter if we disagree . . . as long as we accept each other, try to understand and respect where the other guy is coming from." Angel's eyes could melt a middle-aged lesbian. He smiles at me, saying, "You guys make me feel a lot better."

"An affair," says Todd, "is based on sex—and it's great. A committed relationship is based on a lot more than just sex. Sex is important in a committed relationship, but it is not the most important thing." Both Philip and Todd believe in sexual fidelity. As Philip explains, "If our relationship were based on sex, we wouldn't be together. Sexually, we're at a different pace—so we have to work with that. Sex, to me, is the ultimate act of love and that's a 'wonderful' attitude to have. But then there's the reality of being human: either one of us could go off. And sure, there would be hurt . . . but you work it out: you don't end a relationship because of a casual incident of infidelity."

"There have been times," Charlotte says, "when because of my illness we simply could not have sex. Sex is a very important part of a loving partnership—which is what we have. However, when an illness like mine comes along, you aren't always able to have sex. But with a loving partnership, there are a lot of other things— communication, intimacy, growing together."

I ask Nancy whether during Charlotte's illness she considered having sex with an outside lover. "No," she answers, "I can honestly say I didn't. But then, I'm convinced there's not one other lesbian in this town—maybe out on one of the farms. Seriously, though, Charlotte and I are committed to each other and that commitment includes sexual fidelity."

"Why," I ask Nancy, "is sexual fidelity important to you?" Nancy explains it based on her own perspective of a relationship between two people. "If two people have a relationship and one of them gets involved with someone else, then it's three people in the relationship. The third person then enters into what was the exclusively shared life of the couple. And the third person is encroaching on what was the intimacy of the two primary partners. It creates another dimension in the relationship which can interfere with the intimacy and the privacy of the two original partners, possibly ending the relationship of the two original partners."

Robert and Bob base their commitment on sexual exclusivity. "Sexual fidelity," Robert explains, "is important to us because we believe one of the most important things we can give each other as partners is our fidelity. When you're married (and we consider ourselves married), you pledge to keep yourself just for the other person. That's how I was brought up and that's the way I believe it should be. That's the way we live. I don't feel like I'm losing out on anything. Hey, I've 'been there.' I'm not missing anything at all."

"Fidelity," says Bob, "can't be bought or sold. It must be given. We have all sorts of material things we've bought. Some will get old and we'll throw them out. Fidelity, a sexual life together—it's a gift of love you give to your partner. We simply don't believe in extramarital sex. We've both been in relationships that failed. What happens is people start having problems and they think outside sex is going to help those problems. Wrong. Once a couple mutually decides to go outside for sex as part of their lifestyle, it's all downhill from that point on. It happened to Robert in his previous relationship. We have seen other people take this course of action: it doesn't work."

My lover, Valerie, and I have the sexual fidelity discussion with Joan and Pat. In the finest of American traditions, the children are not present. Both Joan and Pat believe in sexual fidelity within the context of their marriage. "What do you think, Mary?" Joan asks. I gulp, because I know in conversations like this there is no way I am going to win.

I swallow hard and quickly answer, "I believe in sexual fidelity. But I think it would be dishonest of me to promise Valerie that I'm never going to have sex with anyone else."

Both Joan and Pat look to Valerie for some sort of reaction. "I," Valerie says confidently, "believe in sexual fidelity."

"Look," I explain, "I don't even like the expression *sexual fidelity*. Just using the word *fidelity* implies that if you have sex with someone else you're being 'unfaithful' to your partner. Right away we put the good old Judeo-Christian value judgment on it. What about fidelity to your partner's needs? What about fidelity to what should be shared responsibility? What about fidelity to your common future? A relationship can be emotionally and psychologically destructive to both partners, but as long as they're sexually faithful to each other it's okay. Sometimes I think we distract ourselves with sexual fidelity so we don't have to look at anything else. You ever hear anyone talk about emotional fidelity? What if I'm sexually faithful to Valerie and ignore her emotional needs? Does that mean we have a good relationship?"

Pat looks at Valerie half confused and half sympathetic. "Do you know where she's coming from?" Valerie smiles and says, "That's my poet." At this point in the conversation I am happy Valerie is still smiling—because in our previous discussions of sexual fidelity she has not always been smiling.

"Mary and I have been together about two years," Valerie says. "Yeah," I interrupt, "this is my second marriage and Val married late in life." "When I first met her," Valerie continues, "sexual fidelity was of primary importance to me: it was what I was raised to believe, it was all I knew. I'd never read or heard anything to the contrary. I accepted it as 'the way it was.' Neither Mary nor I want a relationship where one or both of us is constantly sleeping with other people. I do understand, even though I might not like, what Mary is saying. What she is saying is far more broad based; it makes more sense because it's more realistic."

"What is Mary saying?" asks Pat. "Yeah, Mary," Joan says, "what are you saying?"

"I guess what I am saying is I know myself. And to me an isolated sexual experience is permissible. You can get into a situation where you're truly erotically attracted to someone. And knowing me as I do, I would probably pursue it. It has nothing to do with the love I have for Valerie. It has nothing to do with the sexual intimacy we share. It has nothing to do with anything except me and what I consider my right to privacy and my right to good old-fashioned lust."

"To Mary," Valerie explains, "it's a permissible isolated human event—hers. To me, it's an offense. A couple of years ago I would have considered it the worst thing that could possibly happen. I no longer feel quite that way. I wouldn't like it, but it wouldn't end our relationship because I know where she's coming from. It would be something we would have to work out; I still see it as an offense, but it's now an excusable offense to me. I would still be very angry and very hurt. I would be terribly jealous. I'm also very possessive, so my ego would be involved."

"Where does that leave *you?*" Joan asks, looking at me.

"It leaves me being very careful," I say. "Now if I had a case of the 'hots' for someone, it would have to be a raging fire. Seriously, Valerie and I have talked and argued about this—shed some tears. But if I hadn't been honest with her, I would never have known what her reaction would be nor to what extent it would hurt her. Knowing now how much it would hurt her, I wouldn't be quite so casual about it. But I still will not promise her that I will never have sex with anyone else. I don't now, and I probably won't. But I can't honestly say I will definitely not ever have sex with someone else. I'm too aware of my human potential and of my own 'crazies.' I guess I believe you can have *sex* with anyone. For me, sexual intimacy can only be experienced with someone I love: Valerie. It doesn't take much to have an orgasm. It takes a lot of time to build sexual intimacy. Way back when, I was once involved with a very fine man. He told me you judge a relationship between what happens before orgasm and what happens after orgasm. He said, 'If you have your orgasm and roll over and go to sleep, you just had a sexual experience.' He was right. Besides"—I laugh, trying to ease what seems to be their astonishment—"sexual infidelity is always terrible and always inconceivable—if you'll excuse the pun—when someone else is doing it. But when you find yourself *in* the situation, you might feel guilty but *you* can understand what you're doing and why. You rationalize it . . . but it's always justified."

•   •   •

The opposite of fidelity is infidelity. Inherent in the word *infidelity* is a battery of negative "isms" which automatically establish what, to me, is a system of invalid value judgments. The person who does not believe in sexual fidelity is neither a bad person nor an infidel. An individual exercises his or her right to freedom of choice regarding sexual behavior. The choice is based upon that individual's system of values. The Pietropinto/Simenauer nationwide study of heterosexual husbands and wives states: "From the data presented here, it should be apparent that extramarital sexual involvement, although widely practiced, is not close to being accepted as part of the American system of marriage." * However, it should be noted that throughout their study, Pietropinto/ Simenauer also refer to extramarital sexual involvement as "cheating" and "infidelity." Have they not made a judgment on the values and lifestyles of those who responded to their study? And *isn't it wonderful* that a *value* everyone attests to is not practiced? Everyone believes in sexual fidelity, but what is the choice: to define oneself as either a cheat or an infidel? I find that American society reserves that type of destructive evaluation for its lesbians and homosexuals: lay it on "them" because at least we give lip service to the values we do not practice.

Hence and therefore—this particular writer does not accept the expression *sexual fidelity* because the word *fidelity* is in itself a value judgment. The "Speak Out" questionnaire addressed the issue of sexual exclusivity.

The men and women responded as follows:

64% have sex exclusively with their partners
29% have sex mostly with their partners, but have occasional outside affairs
4% have sex both in their relationship and outside of their relationship on a regular basis
3% live together without a sexual relationship and each partner is free to have sex outside the marriage.

*Pietropinto/Simenauer, *Husbands and Wives*, p. 390.

MALE MYTHS and UNTRUTHS: "POOR PRESS"

I personally believe male homosexuals are exploited, slandered and victimized by the media and the press. Society's constant capitalizing on the myth of homosexual promiscuity is not only a tremendous moneymaker, but also a splendid diversionary tactic.

Sixty-three (63) percent of the male homosexuals defined themselves as being permanently committed (married). The male respondents to the sexual exclusivity question answered as follows:

49%   have sex mostly with their partners, but have occasional
       outside affairs
37%   have sex exclusively with their partners
8%   have sex both in their relationships and outside of their
       relationships on a regular basis
6%   live together without a sexual relationship and each
       partner is free to have sex outside the marriage.

Pietropinto/Simenauer write: "In our previous study for the book *Beyond the Male Myth,* where we asked men if they had ever cheated on their wives or their steady girl friends, 43% of our currently married sample had not been always faithful, whereas currently divorced men had cheated in 61% of cases. . . . Of the husbands who had cheated, only one in six had ever been involved with an outside partner for over one year."*

Forty-nine (49) percent of the homosexuals in my study said they had sex mostly with their partners but had occasional outside affairs. Are they really any different from Pietropinto/Simenauer's 43 percent of heterosexual males who had not always been faithful? Are not the expressions "Had not always been" and "occasional outside" somewhat similar? "Only one in six," Pietropinto/Simenauer report, "who has cheated had ever been involved with an outside partner for over one year." Such a statement, to me, implies "occasional" extramarital sex. Is this group of heterosexual males any different from the population of homosexuals who responded to "Speak Out"?

Although Pietropinto/Simenauer chose to use the word *cheating* in relationship to their respondents, I would not use that particular word regarding the men who responded to "Speak Out." The word I would use is *honesty*—since, if the interviews in this book are representative of the homosexuals who responded to "Speak Out," male homosexual couples are more honest than heterosexual

---

* Pietropinto/Simenauer, *Husbands and Wives,* p. 279.

males. The question of sexual exclusivity seems to be openly discussed between male homosexual couples. I wonder how many of Pietropinto/Simenauer's 43 percent of heterosexual men who had not always been faithful discussed it with their wives and steady girl friends?

Another Pietropinto/Simenauer piece of data: "Ten (10) percent of husbands would readily respond to an affair that promised to be brief and casual."* However, in a *New York* magazine interview with the noted psychiatrist Dr. C. A. Tripp, Tripp was asked: "Are male homosexuals more promiscuous than heterosexual males?" Tripp answered: "Yes, but there's nothing to suggest that promiscuity is any higher for homosexual than for heterosexual males when they're faced with equal opportunity."† I have met men in business who will sacrifice anything for a business trip—and I do not believe it is because of their burning desire to watch "their" favorite television program on a Holiday Inn "boob tube." Several years ago I had the unique distinction of being on a five-day business trip with approximately fifty men, all of whom were attending a company training seminar. In less than three days, I was sexually propositioned by at least twenty of those men. One of them did not understand why I did not see his offer as a *compliment* (his word). He was the type who did not give up easily. Finally, annoyed, I said, "You decide 'to get some' while you're away from home, and I'm supposed to see it as a compliment." He was enraged by my remark. "Has anyone ever punched you in the mouth?" he asked me. "No." I smiled coyly. "You mean not yet," he said, and walked away.

Interestingly enough, *certain* studies of homosexuals do not seem to get much media coverage, publicity, et cetera. *Christopher Street* magazine reported extensively on the Spada Report—*Gay Male Sexuality and Relationships.*‡ Who has ever heard of the Spada Report?

Christopher Street writes: "Ninety percent of the men in the survey state they prefer affection to accompany sex. Most men indicated that to them, 'having sex' is at least an act of sharing and affection, at best an act of love."**

Also from the Spada Report: "While sexual considerations seem

---

*Pietropinto/Simenauer, *Husbands and Wives*, p. 288.

†Nobile, Philip, "An Interview with Dr. C. A. Tripp," *New York* magazine, June 25, 1979 (hereinafter referred to as Nobile, "Tripp"), p. 40.

‡"The Spada Report," review of *Gay Male Sexuality and Relationships* by James Spada, *Christopher Street*, May 1979, p. 30.

**Ibid., p. 30.

relatively unimportant as reasons for enduring gay relationships, sex is an important part of gay men's lives. Perhaps the area in which gay relationships differ the most from heterosexual ones is 'open marriage.' Seventy-four percent of the men who have lovers state that they, their lovers, or both of them have sex outside their relationship."* Perhaps it is not "open marriage" that is the difference between heterosexual relationships and homosexual relationships—perhaps it is honesty. Has anyone ever tried to determine how many heterosexual women are living—unbeknownst to them—in "open marriages"?

"Nearly a quarter of the men who are involved in open relationships are unhappy about them," the Spada Report also reveals. "Most of these, and others who have been in such relationships, view outside sexual activity as destructive to a primary relationship."†

The Spada questionnaire asked: "Would you like a lover?" "Eighty-eight percent of the respondents who did not have a lover answered 'Yes' to this question. Sharing their lives with another man is clearly very important to gay men, and quite independent of their sexual views. Men who enjoy one-night stands and sexual variety as well as those who prefer to have sex only with someone they love would like to have a primary relationship with one man."‡

New York magazine asked Dr. Tripp: "Are fetishism, S & M, and other paraphilias more common among homosexual males than others?" Tripp's answer: "Undoubtedly so. It's much easier for males to find these interests among males than among females. This situation is well-shown in prostitution: A call girl who charges $100 expects several times this amount for mildly kinky sex; the rate may reach $800 an hour for less mild participations. Not so with the call boy. His rate is less than $100 and it is unusual for 'special requests' to cost much if anything extra. Remember that these differences reflect the contrast between the sexes rather than whether the sex itself is homosexual or heterosexual."** So then, based on Dr. Tripp's thoughts: Is male sexual behavior determined more by economics or sexual orientation? When discussing male sexual behavior, one must consider both the cost of living and the rate of

---

*"The Spada Report," review of *Gay Male Sexuality and Relationships* by James Spada, *Christopher Street*, May 1979, p. 41.
†Ibid., p. 42.
‡Ibid., p. 43.
**Nobile, "Tripp."

inflation: What middle-class man supporting a family and paying a mortgage can afford sexual fetishism? The average middle-class heterosexual man simply cannot be a "good provider" for his family and at the same time be sexually kinky. Alas, another economic reality.

THE LESBIAN PUT-DOWN—ANONYMITY

When, during his 1979 visit to the United States, the Pope condemned homosexuality, he did not even have the decency to condemn lesbianism. As both a lesbian and a one-time Catholic, I find that insulting. Are lesbians, as women, so inconsequential as to not even rate condemnation? If I telephoned the Vatican to clarify the situation, I would probably be told that lesbianism is implied and included in the Catholic Church's position on homosexuality. If, as a lesbian, I am immoral, I demand to be recognized as such. I refuse to be subjugated under the umbrella of male immorality. I want to be judged as immoral based upon my own merits. Homosexuals are a supposed threat to society. Women, however, have so little impact and power that even if they are lesbians they are simply not threatening. A homosexual is perceived as a pathological pervert; a lesbian, a confused woman who has not met "the right man."

In the "Speak Out" questionnaire, 70 percent of the lesbians defined themselves as permanently committed (married). Of the women respondents to the sexual exclusivity question:

83%   have sex exclusively with their partners
14%   have sex mostly with their partners, but have occasional outside affairs
2%   live together without a sexual relationship and each partner is free to have sex outside the marriage
1%   have sex both in their relationships and outside of their relationships on a regular basis.

Some of the Pietropinto/Simenauer data on women who responded to their questionnaire: 42 percent of the wives were strongly opposed to extramarital affairs;* 4 percent of the wives would readily respond to an affair that promised to be brief and casual.† How *really* different are these heterosexual wives from the

* Pietropinto/Simenauer, *Husbands and Wives*, p. 279.
† Ibid., p. 388.

lesbians who responded to the "Speak Out" questionnaire? Are the 42 percent of the wives who are opposed to extramarital affairs any different from 83 percent of the "Speak Out" lesbians who live in sexually exclusive relationships? The 4 percent of married women who would readily respond to an affair—are not their values possibly similar to the 1 percent of lesbians in the "Speak Out" survey who said they had sex both within and outside of their primary relationship?

How really different, then, are lesbians from heterosexual women? And if we are different: what is the difference? Is not the difference merely sexual preference? Are not all women struggling to free themselves of the economic, sexual, and social codes that have been imposed on them by a male-dominated society? Have not religious and sociopolitical influences had the same negative effects on lesbians as they have had on heterosexual women? Are not all women struggling to establish their identity as persons? As women, we are all striving to create for *ourselves* a system of values based upon our beliefs—not upon our *gender*. As a lesbian, I believe the women's liberation movement has had as much of an impact upon my life as it has had upon the lives of heterosexual women.

I was so late "coming out" as a lesbian, had I waited much longer, I would have been into my menopause. However, I started out as most lesbian and heterosexual women start out—as a "little girl"—therefore, someone's daughter. As Rob and Bob informed me during their interview: a homosexual is a little boy long before he is an active homosexual. Just as homosexuals are raised as boys who will eventually become men, lesbians are raised as girls who will eventually become women. The irony of the situation is that probably 99 percent of lesbians and homosexuals are raised in heterosexual homes—we, too, are someone's children.

From *The Hite Report:* "Almost all the women who answered these questionnaires had been brought up to be 'good girls.' And those still living at home were, for the most part, still being taught to be 'good girls.' Girls are still being kept from finding out about, exploring and discovering, their own sexuality—and called 'bad girls' when they try. At puberty, girls are given information about their reproductive organs and menstruation, but rarely told about their clitoris. The unspoken message is still that female sexuality is bad." *

* Shere Hite, *The Hite Report* (New York: Dell Publishing, 1976), p. 472.

Not only are we taught that female sexuality is bad, it is absolutely defunct without the presence of a penis in a woman's life. Therefore, worse than being a woman is being a lesbian—you cannot justify your existence because there is no penis actively present in your life. At least, for the heterosexual woman, there is hope. Eventually, there *will be* a penis present in her life: her womanhood will be validated. However, when talking with some married women friends, I have thought, "What she needs is a good woman in her life." I find the burdens of heterosexual married women phenomenal. It does not seem to matter what professional status they have achieved: they are still wives and mothers. And they are expected to fulfill the obligations of these roles whether or not they are earning high salaries or working longer hours than their husbands. As a lesbian, I believe I have been spared many of the problems and anxieties these women suffer. Somehow, in the whole scheme of things, my life as a woman is much fuller and richer *because* I am a lesbian.

I am not denying or ignoring the burdens of the male role, the servitude of boys who are raised to be the always responsible and always strong "good providers." Perhaps these burdens are exactly what male homosexuals do not experience. Many of the women who oppose the Equal Rights Amendment (ERA) are not backward or even uninformed: they are bright and shrewd. Without the ERA, their position of "servitude" is guaranteed. However, within the context of servitude they do not have to be concerned with responsibility for their own lives. They do not have to be concerned with providing for themselves. They can make a decision to divorce their husbands without having to be burdened with the financial consequences of their decision.

I believe men who oppose the ERA are both economically and psychologically threatened. It is definitely sexual politics and the stakes are high: the male ego. How can a man be assured of his continuing to be a "good provider" if he has to compete with women for salary increases? What happens to his ego if his wife is earning more? Are not family domestic matters influenced by who is earning more? How does a man define himself if it is not in terms of his ability to "take care of a woman." Men are as shackled by society's role stereotyping as women are. And when can we expect a men's liberation movement? It is long overdue.

I believe lesbians and homosexuals, both as individuals and as couples, are free—although not completely—of the burdens of roles. And because we are somewhat ahead of our heterosexual peers, I believe we can make a contribution to ending this economically and socially based sexual warfare. As men and women—homosexuals and lesbians—we are all victims of our upbringing. Would there not be less disharmony within the gay liberation movement if we saw ourselves as persons and not as genders? If I, as a lesbian, want homosexuals to understand what has been my burden as a woman, I must be prepared to understand what has been the homosexual's orientation as a little boy growing up in America. Just as I have been raised to believe in my subservient role, the homosexual has been raised to believe that I, as a woman, *am subservient.* If I expect a homosexual to understand where I'm "coming from," I must be prepared to understand where he's "coming from." And we are all coming from *the same place*—a system of shackles and role stereotypes that emotionally and psychologically deprive individuals of their rights to personhood. Because our sexual egos are not at stake, I believe we can be more sensitive to each other's gender orientation, realizing we have been victimized by the same society.

In doing this book, I asked other lesbians about their feelings as women.

• • •

"I never felt more like a woman in my whole life," Kate explains. "Who could know a woman better than another woman? It's a shared basic identity. Feeling like a woman is feeling good about yourself and sex is incidental."

Debra: "I've never seen myself as less of a woman because I am a lesbian. It's difficult for a straight woman to be competent, successful, and aggressive—to achieve in a male-dominated society. The first thing society says to you is there's something wrong with you if you *want* to achieve or succeed. You *should be* content to be attached to a successful man. I've rejected the stereotype of a woman. I've rejected the stereotype sex roles—and I reject society's telling me I should be heterosexual. I am what I am."

"I've been married straight and now I'm married gay," says Em. "In my gay marriage I have the right to be my own person. I don't feel that I'm being dominated. I can be me and I'm happier when I'm me. Louise allows me to be myself and I want her to be herself. That's the difference between a gay marriage and a straight marriage—in a gay marriage you can be who you are."

• • •

As a society, we are just beginning to discuss female sexuality.

Women have, within the past ten years, become free to say they actually enjoy sex—without having centuries of guilt heaped upon them. Many women are now finding the courage to openly state they do not want to be mothers. Personally, I believe it will take decades before lesbianism is studied—not as an aberration of homosexuality or womanhood—but as a healthy and natural variety of life experience. I believe my accepting my lesbianism contributed to my self-actualization as a woman. Prior to "coming out" to myself, I had spent years of self-hate because, somehow, I never seemed able to be what I was "supposed to be." I "knew" there was something *wrong* with me because I never wanted those things, as a woman, I was "supposed to want." Once acknowledged, my lesbianism served as a catalyst in my growth process. I was free: all those things I was "supposed to be" because I was a woman no longer applied. Free, then, of the shackles of womanhood, I was free to be the person I wanted to be. While society and the researchers avoid dealing with lesbianism, lesbians are fending and fighting for themselves. But I think we are doing so with many advantages not enjoyed by our heterosexual sisters.

From *The Hite Report:* "A positive attitude toward our own bodies and toward touching ourselves and toward any physical contact that might naturally develop with another woman is essential to self-love and accepting our own bodies as good and beautiful. As Jill Johnston has written, '. . . until women see in each other the possibility of a primal commitment which includes sexual love they will be denying themselves the love and the value they readily accord to men, thus affirming their own second-class status.'" *

WE ALL COME from SOMEWHERE

If it is a Sunday afternoon and I smell tomato sauce, I know I must be in Brooklyn having dinner with my parents. I am sitting at the kitchen table drinking wine and eating cheese and olives. My father is outside working in the yard. My mother is at the stove stirring the spaghetti. She is staring into the pot. Then, looking at me, she says, "I don't understand." By the tone of her voice and the tilt of her head, I know this is going to be a "heavy."

*Shere Hite, *The Hite Report* (New York: Dell Publishing, 1976) p. 416.

I spit an olive pit into the ashtray, because I know by the look on her face that if I do not get it out of my mouth I am going to choke on it. She is still stirring the spaghetti. I "casually" cross my legs, brace myself, and say: "What don't you understand, Mom?"

"We find out you're a lesbian. So you're our daughter and you're a lesbian: What can we do? Then you tell us you and Paula were married for nine years but now you're divorced. So your father and I say, 'Okay, she's a divorced lesbian.' But I talk to you on the phone last week, you tell me you went away for the weekend, *overnight,* with this woman—another lesbian. I get upset when you tell me you go away overnight with a woman you're not married to. I say to you, 'You didn't do it with her, did you? You didn't have sex, did you?' And what do you tell me? How does my only daughter answer me on the telephone? She tells me, 'I don't ask you about your sex life, don't ask me about mine.' What a thing to say to a mother. If I ever talked to my mother like that, may she rest in peace, she would've killed me."

I cannot laugh because I know she is serious: "Mom, look, I'm well over twenty-one. I'm a woman. What I do *is* my own business. I have a right to my privacy. Don't worry about it, I'm responsible for my own life."

"Just because you're a lesbian"—she is now churning the spaghetti—"doesn't mean you just sleep with any woman that comes along."

"Mom, I do not sleep with every woman that comes along. And I'm sorry about the phone conversation, but you're not going to lay all this shit on . . ."

No sooner does the word *shit* spill from my lips than my father walks into the kitchen. "Hey," he says, "you don't say 'shit' to your mother . . . you don't say 'shit' in my house. What'sa matter? What are you two fighting about now?"

My mother points the long spaghetti fork at me. I can see the steam rolling off the tips of the prongs. "She thinks," she says to my father, "that just because she's a lesbian, she . . ."

"She what?" my father says firmly. "Don't point no hot fork at anybody. What does she think?"

"She thinks because she's a lesbian she can sleep with someone without loving them or being married to them."

My father has the most astonished expression on his face I have ever seen on any human face in my whole life. He just stands there with his mouth open. After a few seconds, he says, "Well, at least she's not a nun anymore."

"What a stupid thing to say," she yells, plunging the fork back into the pot. "What"—she is now beating the spaghetti—"does that have to do with anything?"

Sitting down, he moans: "You cried when she was in the convent because she had no one. You cried when she came out of the convent because you thought she was having sex with a man she wasn't married to. Then you cried when you found out she's a lesbian. Now you're crying because she's having sex with women she's not married to. Hey, she's older than you were when you had her. Leave her alone . . . it's none of your business."

I am now waiting for the pot, the hot water, the spaghetti, and the fork to come flying across the kitchen. I do not dare laugh. She slowly walks toward him, one hand on her hip, the fork in the other. She is now standing next to him and she is looking down at him. He is *not* looking up at her. "I'm warning you," he says patiently, "don't point that fork at me. You know I don't like that in my house."

She just stands there staring but *not* pointing the fork at him. Finally, she hisses in total disgust: "That's the way a father talks about his only daughter. I should've known you'd be like this. . . ."

Now *he* is laughing. "What do you mean, 'I'd be like this . . . I should've known?' Do you want me to tell her she can't have sex again until she marries another woman? You crazy . . . *Where* she gonna go and get married? Hey, when are we going to eat?"

The look in my mother's eyes says she is now going in for the kill: she is going for "blood." The anticipation is destroying me. Sauntering back to the stove, she says to him over her shoulder, "Why don't you tell your daughter about that other girl you went out with before you went out with me? Go ahead, tell her. Tell her how you were breaking your poor mother's heart, may her soul rest in peace."

"Fifty years later," he moans, "you gotta start this."

"Your mother *knew* what she was—she wore lipstick and rouge."

"Come on," my father argues. "My mother didn't like her because she wasn't Italian." And then to me: "In those days you didn't marry nothing but another Italian." He then turns to my mother, almost pleading. "Can we stop this? When are we gonna eat?"

"That's all I'm good for." She's hissing again. "Cook, wash clothes, clean . . . and the other thing."

"Yeah"—he grins at me—"the other thing. Don't give me that. I had to go out with her for four months before I could kiss her good night. The night we got married, five times around Central Park in one of those hansom carriages before she'd go into the hotel. We stayed in the Hotel New Yorker the night we got married. . . ."

"Yeah"—she laughs, reminiscing—"remember the guy jumped out the window and everybody was teasing you the next day saying it was you because you gave up on me. What did I know, I was so innocent. I was stupid, I was so innocent. It's not like today."

Somehow, through it all—and as always—the spaghetti survives. It makes its way out of the pot to meet the tomato sauce, and finally the three of us eat Sunday dinner together. Later, over espresso, I tease the two of them: "Listen, don't get divorced now. I don't want either one of you ending up with me." I joke with my father about their current sex life: "Listen, at seventy you're doing better than the national average for thirty-year-olds." My mother reminds me *he* is seventy, *she* is sixty-seven. She also reminds me I should not talk to my father about sex.

I get ready to leave. My mother kisses me goodbye at the door. "Well, at least I don't have to worry about you getting pregnant anymore. Think of the money I save on candles. . . ."

My father walks me to the subway. "Listen," he says, "I know you're a good girl, but do me a favor—don't talk to your mother anymore about sex. Just be careful what you do . . . don't get hurt. Try to remember to ring the phone once when you get home. She worries, she drives me crazy . . . forty-seven years she's been driving me crazy."

We are, all of us—gay or straight—coming from somewhere. We all have a "background"—and background is a montage of culture, religion, experience, and exposure. As adults, we either embrace or adapt the values of our upbringing or we reject the values of our past and create our own. I do not believe values are adapted, embraced, or rejected on the basis of sexual orientation. I believe they are adapted, embraced, or rejected on the basis of life orientation. Life is myriad experiences. My response to those experiences is not determined by my lesbianism. My response to life is the response of a human being who, like other human beings, has believed and lost faith, has been wise and has been foolish, has been happy and has been hurt, has succeeded and has failed, has been brave and has been frightened. And all those "has beens" have created who I am today.

4

FOR BETTER OR
FOR WORSE
Every Couple Has Problems

BEVERLY *and* DEBRA: *An* AFFAIR . . . *and the* IN-LAWS

"Beverly," Debra says, "likes the center of the baked potato, and I like the skin—that's what's held us together for over twenty years."

"According to Beverly," I say, "she has stayed with you—amazing as it seems—because she loves you."

"Well, that's true," answers Debra, "but she had to keep me around because her feet are always cold in the winter and this body of mine is always warm."

In addition to potatoes and cold winters, Beverly and Debra have also had serious problems during their twenty-two-year relationship. The two most serious: Debra's affair with another woman and Beverly's relationship with her mother.

We discuss "the affair" first. Debra explains: "We were into roles. It was my role to take care of Beverly and I'd begun to rebel against it. The role I'd gotten myself into was a heavy trip and I didn't know how to get out of it. Along comes this other woman, and, of course, I'm having problems at home and I'm more vulnerable to getting involved."

"At the same time," Beverly adds, "while she was rejecting taking care of me, I began rejecting my dependency on her. I wanted to be my own person—but I had to *learn* to become independent of her. As I said before, Deb was having the affair, but I knew I'd contributed to fifty percent of the problems."

"I felt," Debra explains, "Bev was not meeting enough of *my* needs, and maybe someone else could meet more of my needs. One of my complaints was that I was the initiator. It was difficult to get Bev to move or to risk. I always felt I was pushing her into things and, also, that I was responsible for making sure everything worked

79

out okay—making sure she didn't get hurt. What I wanted was someone who was willing to test things with me, willing to risk with me whether or not it turned out well."

"Shortly after Debbie got involved with this other woman," Beverly continues, "I decided to go into therapy to save our relationship because I thought it was all my fault. The first thing the therapist said to me was, 'If you want to change, it won't be to save the relationship.' The therapist was willing to work with me to help me change the things I wanted to change about myself, but there was no guarantee there would be a relationship with Debbie afterward."

"A new relationship is exciting," says Debra, smiling. "It's all the learning and playing and finding out. Then, inevitably, it gets down to basic day-in-and-day-out living together—who does the dishes, who takes out the garbage. When you're dating, it's all fine. But when you get down to living together: Do you like this person enough to spend all of your time together? For me, as regards the woman I was involved with, the answer was no. The only person I can see really spending that much time with was—and is—Beverly. So it's not that my affair was bad or wrong. But it made me realize how much I was giving up with Beverly—Bev and I have a life together."

"Before this affair started," Beverly says, "we'd made plans to buy a condominium. It was being built. I decided if we could get ourselves straightened out and get the relationship going again— but not the way it had been—I'd move into the condominium with Debbie. If the relationship couldn't be changed or if we couldn't break out of the roles we were into, no way was I moving into this condominium with her. If Debbie had walked out or told me she didn't love me anymore, I would have had to face up to the possibility there wasn't going to be *any* relationship. She never told me those things and it wasn't in my head to end our relationship. I didn't like our relationship the way it was but I wasn't interested in ending it, either. It was a matter of could we work it out so it would be the kind of relationship both of us wanted."

"We talked," Debra remembers, "through my entire affair. We were talking about *our* relationship and what was wrong with it— where it was going in terms of where both of us wanted it to go. I didn't want to take care of Bev anymore and she didn't want to be dependent on me anymore—we were going in the same direction."

"It was crazy," Beverly laughs, "but during those five months we were living in the same apartment and sleeping in different bedrooms. But we never stopped talking to each other. Debra would spend one weekend with me and one with the other woman. And during the week we'd try to have some sort of relationship. I can remember our going to a Mexican restaurant one night—*during the week.* Deb asked me not to push her into a decision. She said if I didn't push her, she'd work it out. But if I pushed her into a decision, it might be the wrong one. I knew if I could hold out and not push her, she'd figure out where she was going, and then we would most likely end up together."

"Together" is how Beverly and Debra resolved their marital problems. And "together" is how they resolved Beverly's problems with her mother. "My mother said I was always welcome in her home," says Beverly, "but Debbie was dead—our life together as a lesbian couple didn't exist to her. She'd never come to visit us, she'd have nothing to do with *us:* this went on for almost ten years."

"It was a terribly heavy trip for Beverly," Debra adds. "She was caught in between her family and me. I didn't pressure her to make a choice between me and her parents. All I could do was try to encourage her to see what was going on; her mother wasn't going to change. Her mother would call every Tuesday night. Bev would be nervous before her mother called; and after, she'd be angry with herself because she felt like a child and because she knew her mother was controlling her long distance. And so every Tuesday night, *our* relationship was under strain because of this outside factor. I knew Bev had to stand up to her mother."

"And I finally did," says Beverly. "I told my parents they were either going to come and visit me and accept my life with Debra— or forget me *altogether.* That threw my mother. My father said he would definitely come with or without my mother. In the end, my mother came with him to visit us. Since then, she's been more accepting. But it's as good as it's ever going to be."

"SPEAK OUT": SOURCES of CONFLICT in a MARRIAGE / RELATIONSHIP

The "Speak Out" questionnaire stated: "There are many sources of conflict in a marriage/relationship." We then asked people to check as many areas as are applicable where they and their partners have conflicts.

Of the total number of men and women responding, 45 percent

said communication is a source of problems within their relationships. Approximately one-third of the people also cited sexual
problems, job/career responsibilities, and financial problems as
sources of conflict within their relationships. Finally, lesbians and
homosexuals seem to have more problems with in-laws than they
do with daily adjustment conflicts: 14 percent as opposed to 9
percent, respectively.

Role-identification problems and jealousy ranked quite low as
sources of conflict for gay couples: 2 percent and 3 percent,
respectively. However, 71 percent of the women, as opposed to 29
percent of the men, are having problems with role identification.
Only 9 percent of the men responding cited jealousy as a source of
conflict, while 91 percent of the women were having problems with
jealousy within their relationships.

HEALTH, JOBS, and PERSONAL STYLE

According to Richard, the biggest problem in his relationship with
Charles was, when, for a period of one year, Charles was working
in another state. "It was like being married on weekends," explains
Richard. "We *had* to talk about it. What it got down to was either I
was going to move to the state where he was working, which meant
we would give up everything we had here, or he was going to find a
job closer to home. He decided to move back home on a full-time
basis, and luckily enough for both of us, he found a good job here."

"Changing jobs is a lot simpler than changing styles," says
Charles. "Our biggest ongoing problem has been that Richard is a
very outgoing person, and I'm a very private person. This definitely
creates problems for us. I don't like meeting people, and he enjoys
constantly meeting new people." When I ask what they have done
to try to resolve their different "styles," Charles says, "Tried to be
a little more sensitive to each other. He knows what I don't like,
and I know what he likes. Basically, what it gets down to is I try to
be a little more public and he tries to be a little more private."

Illness has been the problem that Robert and Bob have had to
face together. "We've had to alter our lifestyle a little bit," explains
Robert, "because of several illnesses I've had in the past few years.
Bob hasn't complained. Even when we were trying to find out what
was wrong with me, he was very supportive and patient." Bob
adds, "I love him—of course I want him to be well. We want to be
happy together, and to be happy together we both have to be

healthy. So together we've got to work on his being healthy and staying healthy."

JILL *and* DOLLY: ILLNESS *and* INSECURITIES

Although Dolly feels Jill's illness has been the biggest problem in their relationship, Jill sees her personal insecurity as the most constant and pressing problem they have had. "I know," Jill explains, "that someday Dolly is going to walk out on me. Now all of my 'crazies' have nothing to do with Dolly. She's never given me any reason to doubt her or to doubt our relationship. But I *know* she's going to leave me. It's an emotional fear and it's based on my childhood. If, when I get into one of my crazy fits, I can remember to look deep and hard inside myself, I know she won't leave me. . . . But I can't help being afraid that someday she will. It's got nothing to do with her, it's got nothing to do with being gay—it's me. And I also realize there's nothing she can do about it. Because when you've got somebody that's into the bag I'm into, a partner can turn the world upside down and not be able to convince the insecure person they're not going to leave."

"If anything has contributed to Jill's insecurities," admits Dolly, "it's her illness. Now more than ever she's afraid I'm going to leave her. She's more dependent on me than she ever was before. It's hard for me to deal with. We've been through a lot during the years we've been together. But you know the expression 'For better or for worse'? Her illness has become our *worst.*"

• • •

The two major problems for Charlotte and Nancy: Charlotte's illness and the role-playing upon which they had based their relationship. Lisa and Marje's main problem: Lisa's mother's inability to accept her daughter's black lesbian partner. For Rob and Bob: Rob had to give up his career as a dancer and both men had to decide whether they wanted an "open marriage" or a sexually exclusive relationship. Ann and Kate: the years it took them to develop a committed relationship exclusive of a shared sexual life.

SOMEONE to TALK TO

The "Speak Out" questionnaire asked: "If you were having marital/relationship problems," with whom would you consider discussing them? Respondents could check as many areas as were applicable. Eighty-five (85) percent of the men and women responding said they would discuss such problems with gay friends. Fifty-three (53) percent would seek professional help (psychiatrist, psychologist, social worker). Interestingly enough, 35 percent would discuss their marital/relationship problems with straight friends. However, lesbians seem more open than homosexuals to confiding in straight friends: 61 percent of the lesbians as opposed to only 39 percent of the homosexuals. Twenty-three (23) percent of the men and women would discuss their problems with a member of the clergy. Fourteen (14) percent would talk with a brother or sister, and 8 percent would discuss such problems with their parents. Dozens upon dozens of people added a category the questionnaire had not included: "My partner *first.*"

HOMOSEXUAL FATHERS

Seventeen (17) percent of the men who responded to the "Speak Out" questionnaire said that either they or their partners have children. Of this 17 percent, 50 percent said the children are their own; 37 percent said the children are their partner's; and 13 percent said both partners are fathers. In only 3 percent of the homosexual relationships where there are children involved do those children live with their fathers. An additional 3 percent said the children live with them less than half of the time. Fifty-three (53) percent said the children do not live with them but visit in their homes; another 7 percent said the children visit with their fathers only outside the father's home. Thirty-three (33) percent do not see their children at all.

MICHAEL'S CHILDREN . . . and PAUL'S ALCOHOLISM

Michael and Paul have discussed the problems Michael had when Michael's ex-wife relocated, with his children, to another state. I ask Michael if he feels his role as a divorced father is more difficult because he is a homosexual. "Definitely yes," he answers. "Even when my children visit, it puts a terrible strain on our relationship. Paul and I pretend to lead a 'normal life.' We pretend we're two buddies just living together. Paul even goes out several nights on 'dates' while they're here."

"Do you think," I ask, "that this situation is unique to gay fathers?" He answers, "I don't know if it's more unique to homosexuals than it is to lesbians. But what I do know is it's difficult being a divorced man with children. It's difficult being a long-distance father. And right now I don't want my children to know I'm a homosexual. They're at an age where I don't think they could handle it. I love my children and I want to remain as close to them as possible. That's difficult enough as a divorced long-distance father. Fathers lose a certain amount of ground in their relationships with their children after a divorce. I want the relationship I have with them now to continue."

"If if were possible, would you have your children living with you?" I ask. Paul responds: "They're Michael's offspring, and because I love him I see them as a part of our relationship. And to answer your question, yes, if it were possible and if it were what Michael wanted and *could have,* his children would be living with us."

"We'd do anything we had to do," Michael says, "to help them become better people. There's nothing I won't do for my children, and I know whatever it was I had to do, Paul would help me."

"We want to buy a house," Paul explains, "but should Michael's children decide to go to college, we'll handle that financial responsibility together. I'd love to see his kids living with us. And, yes, I know it would be a tremendous burden. But it would make Michael happier, so we'd deal with the burden it would present."

"Do you think," I ask Michael, "as a homosexual father you could properly raise your two teenage children?" His eyes are begging for mercy. Paul angrily responds: "As two people, I think it would be better for Michael's children if they *were* living with us. We're decent people, we're intelligent and knowledgeable: we could provide them with a great deal. I'm not talking about material things, either. We could show them a great deal that would be beneficial to them when they become adults. We could educate them. Life can be very common and I believe the lifestyle we could provide would keep them from becoming common. Michael was a good father for eighteen years—he'd continue to be a good father if his children were living with us *now.* I'm a decent man and I want the very best for his children *because* they are so important to him. Homosexuality has nothing to do with it."

"I love my children." Michael sighs, his eyes sad. "I miss them terribly. I want them with me, but I *can't* have that. And so I'm doing the best I can to be a good father within the situation. I want them to grow up to be happy people—I'll do whatever I have to do in any situation so they can have a good future. I'm a homosexual, but I'm a parent—a father. I love my children."

"There are things you *can* do something about," says Paul, "and there are some things you simply *can't* do anything about. The situation with Michael's children is something we can't do anything about—we have to work together within the situation as it exists."

"The problem we could and *had* to do something about," continues Michael, "was Paul's drinking problem."

"Whether I wanted to admit it to myself or not," Paul explains, "I'd been an alcoholic for over fifteen years. Of course, I didn't want Michael to know. But as innocent and naive as he sometimes is, even he couldn't miss it. Actually, it was his innocence that helped me to admit to myself I was, in fact, an alcoholic."

"I was so frightened," Michael tells me. "I'd never been involved in drugs or drinking because I'd always been afraid of anything where I wasn't in total control. What terrified me was that Paul got so drunk he'd black out. The next day he wouldn't remember some of the things that had happened. I didn't like his drinking because he's a borderline diabetic. But then, when I saw to what extent he got drunk, I was really frightened."

"I'd done such a bad drinking number one night, I completely blacked out and had absolutely no idea of any of my 'activities' of the previous evening. All Michael said to me was he was afraid he was going to lose me to alcohol. The depth of his fear was such that I was hit with the reality of what he was saying: it *was* a real possibility. But if Michael was going to lose me because of my alcoholism, it only followed that *I* would lose *him* because of my alcoholism. That scared the hell out of me. It didn't scare me into sobriety. But it scared me enough for me to promise both Michael and myself I was going to give it up."

"We worked together on 'fulfilling' his promise," says Michael. "And it was a long uphill climb. It was for me to learn to understand the problem of alcoholism, which was difficult because I've never been a heavy drinker. He had to tell me what was going on. We had to constantly keep talking: I had to keep asking questions and he had to keep answering them. I had faith in him and I believed he was sincere when he said he would give it up. But we were going to have to work at his 'giving it up' and it took a long period of time."

I ask Paul if he would mind discussing his alcoholism at length. "No," he says, smiling. "It's behind me now.

"I'd spent many unhappy years," Paul explains, "and I was into heavy drinking. Even when my previous relationship ended, I just had another reason for drinking. Then Michael and I met and fell in love. I was very happy. So there went my unhappiness excuse. I had deluded myself for fifteen years with this unhappiness excuse and I knew I was deluding myself. Now that I was happy, I had to admit to myself I was hooked. And I still fooled with it. But once I knew I was threatening my relationship with Michael—frightening him and making him very unhappy—I couldn't continue drinking. I knew I was going to 'pay' in trying to give it up, but I also knew our life together was worth whatever it would be that I'd have to pay. It wasn't Michael's faith in me so much that helped me to do it. His faith in me made me have more faith in myself than I'd ever had before. Michael didn't pressure me or threaten me. The decision was completely my own. I knew it was going to be hard to accomplish, but I knew I had to do it if I was going to have a future with him. I was choosing a future with him instead of a future in the gutter, which is where most alcoholics end up eventually. I gave up drinking, but I think it's one of the hardest things a person can go through. I persevered and Michael persevered with me."

I ask Paul if he feels homosexuals are more vulnerable to alcoholism. "Yes," he answers. "I feel that as homosexuals we are put into a situation whereby to associate with people we have to be in bars. And if you're in a bar, you're going to be drinking. And if bars are the only place you can go to be free, to be yourself, then you're going to go a lot and you're going to drink a lot. I'm a homosexual, so of course my whole life has been spent with homosexuals. There is a sadness and it's that sadness that makes people drink."

"What is this homosexual sadness?" I ask Paul.

"We're society's outcasts and, what's worse, we lead a double life. We're heterosexuals during the business day and we're homosexuals at night. And we go to bars to meet other homosexuals who are suffering from the same double life we're suffering from. I think a large number of homosexuals don't have any direction in their lives because they're without partners. No matter how good-looking we are, no matter how successful we are in business, we're still alone. Once you have a person in your life who loves you and cares for you, it's a whole new approach to life. Because society is the way it is, I feel it's harder for homosexuals to have a good and happy relationship. The only place we can go to be ourselves is the bars. But everyone in the bars has sad and hungry eyes. Their hunger is for someone with whom they can have a home—someone to do things with, someone to share with. This hunger and this sadness causes people to drink, and drinking just makes it worse. It's a terrible cycle. I'm so lucky that by meeting Michael I was able to break out. Meeting him took me out of the bars. Living with him got me out of drinking. None of it has been easy. I love him, we have a good present and good future together: that's what's made the difference in my life. God put me on earth as I am for His own reasons. I've tried to cope with the life that had been given me in the best way I could. When God has made you who you are and society doesn't accept you, you're more likely to turn to alcohol. Alcohol only increases the sadness and the loneliness of being an outcast in society. I could not let alcohol rob me of Michael, who had ended my sadness and my loneliness."

PARENTS, CHILDREN, and CONFLICTS

Twenty-one (21) percent of the men and women who answered the questionnaire are parents. Of the women respondents, 25 percent are parents; of the men respondents, 17 percent are parents. However, 58 percent of the women as contrasted with only 3 percent of the men have their children living with them on a regular basis. As in the heterosexual culture, when men and women divorce, the children live with their mothers more often than with their fathers.

EM *and* LOUISE: RAISING THREE TEENAGE BOYS

"I think the biggest problem in my relationship with Louise," says Em, "has been my children. There are the financial demands of supporting three growing boys, but we share them. The other problem is between my ex-husband and me, which Louise inherited by association. You see, my boys lived with their father awhile, and their father is simply not a disciplinarian. He doesn't care whether they listen or not. And he never taught them they should respect other people. Louise and I have been fighting this battle with the boys for over two years. They have to mind what we tell them to do whether or not they like it. I don't know how far we're getting in raising them right, but it's a problem we share. It's our biggest problem, but we help each other."

"From what I've heard from the boys," Louise says, laughing, "they call me The Warden. I may be smaller than their mother, but I have a firmer hand. I have certain restrictions. They're not 'requested' to abide by these restrictions: they don't have a choice. Sure, they're Em's children, but they're *our* responsibility. With three teenage boys, we have to work together and we have to help each other in handling them. We both want them to grow up to be fine and good men—that takes a lot of doing on both our parts. But because I love her, and they are part of her, they're also a part of me."

JOAN *and* PAT: MAKING *a* HOME *for* CHRISTINE *and* STEVEN

My interview with Joan and Pat and the children is, I think, going to be a standard family interview. After all, have I not resolved my conflict about the children's interviews during my long drive to their home? And since Joan and Pat have reviewed the questions prior to beginning, I feel perfectly comfortable handling the interview I have prepared.

I begin by asking Pat if she, as a lesbian mother, had been hesitant about entering a relationship with another woman. "No," she answers, "I wasn't hesitant at all because of the children. I thought my *having* a permanent relationship would be better for them and for me. I needed a stable home life as much as the children did."

"What's stability?" I ask.

"Stability is knowing you're loved, knowing you have a place to go when you need it. It's a home you can go to whether you're right or whether you're wrong. Stability is knowing that no matter what you do there's someone there who loves you. I think everybody needs a stable home environment: myself, as an adult, and my children. They have to know they've got somebody to turn to with their problems. And if I'm not here, Joan is here to give Chrisie and Stevie a hand. They need my having a stable relationship and a stable home. When you're growing up, you need to be 'coming from' some sort of stability."

"What makes a home?" I ask Pat.

"Well," she says, "I was married to my husband for ten years and it wasn't a home. I was miserable; he was miserable; the kids were miserable. A home is the people in it. A home can be a house or an apartment, but unless there's love and respect for all the people in it, it's not a home. It has to be a place where everybody's needs are being met."

Throughout his mother's interview, Stevie is fidgeting. I know he is anxious to get his hands on the microphone. "Okay, Stevie," I say when Pat is finished, "your turn, you're on." Stevie tells me all sorts of things. "I want to be a doctor, a scientist, and a baseball player when I grow up. I want to be a doctor and a scientist first, then a baseball player. After I become a baseball player, then I want to become a fireman."

Stevie likes Christmas better than his birthday because, as he explains: "On Christmas, we all take turns opening our presents and it's fun. Especially when someone opens one of your presents and you know they really like it. But I don't like it when everyone opens presents at the same time. I like it better when we open presents one at a time." And then for the sake of the record, Stevie adds, "You know, Joan didn't come to church with us last Christmas." "Thanks, Stevie," Joan says. "I just wanted her [me] to know," he says. "She had to do something, probably some work. So Mom and Chrisie and I went without her."

Stevie then defines a "family gift." He explains, "A family gift is everybody's. The TV game is a family gift—we got it for Christmas. We don't play every night, maybe three times a week. My mother usually wins. When we don't play games at night, we have to talk about all the things we're supposed to be doing around the house. See, sometimes Chrisie and I don't do them. Or sometimes we do them wrong. Then we have to sit down and talk about them."

"No way," Joan explains, "was there any room in my life for kids. It was hard for me when I realized I was in love with a woman who had two children. I was accustomed to making decisions for *myself.* Now I'm in a position where I must think about other people. I've had to adapt my thinking to multiple choices as opposed to a single choice. I've given up a tremendous amount of what used to be my time for myself. Now it's time that is spent on Pat and the children."

Joan confesses she has a bad temper and, also, that she is impatient with the children. As is the case with children, things do not always go as planned—things are not always as they should be. I ask her about her degree of involvement with the children. "My degree of involvement is one hundred percent." It strikes me that Joan never does anything with less than a 100 percent involvement. She continues: "There is no way you can take on a family without putting yourself into it wholeheartedly. You have to make a complete effort."

"You sound like you're suffering so much," I tease her. "There must be some rewards." Her expression changes from stern to warm. "Yeah"—she smiles, looking at the children—"they're there. Like Mother's Day morning when you wake up and find out they've weeded the backyard as your Mother's Day present. And then Pat and I got breakfast in bed: burnt toast and cold eggs. The happinesses are there. They almost come out of nowhere when you least expect them. It's the joy of seeing things you've accomplished with the children. Watching them change from the kids they were when I first met them. Knowing in one way or another you've contributed to that change, knowing you're contributing to their growth. And hopefully you're contributing to making them a better person."

It is now Christine's turn to be interviewed. She has been shyly sitting in the corner of the room intensely watching this whole process. She is now sitting directly opposite me. Pat and Stevie are sitting on the floor behind her; Joan is sitting at an angle with only a profile view of Christine.

"Are you afraid of this microphone," I ask her. "No"—she giggles—"I can do this. I thought about it. I want to do it." We talk about the house for a while. "We have to clean it upstairs and downstairs and inside and outside. We all have stuff to do . . . chores, I guess you call them. I like it better when we do chores together, then it seems like fun."

I ask her if she would prefer going to a boarding school. "No," she answers, "I like it right here. I don't want to go to any boarding school because I'm happy where I am." She tells me she has recently had a problem in school because of a poor English grade. "I didn't get in trouble because of the grade, I got into trouble because I didn't tell my mom or Joan. I didn't want them to know. But my English teacher called and Joan answered the phone. My mom was working. But Joan told my mom. It was worse than the bad grade. Next time I guess I'll tell them before someone calls."

We then discuss her school life. I ask her how she would feel if her school friends knew her mother and Joan are a lesbian couple. "I think some of my friends in school already know about Mom and Joan," she says casually. "I think they know because of the way I never talk about my father. They always ask me who Joan is."

I am now getting nervous because she is getting more intense.

"Are you okay? Or are you going to hit me with my microphone?" "No"—she struggles to smile—"I'm fine. See, one day it was raining and Joan dropped me off at school. Some of my friends saw her and wanted to know who she was. I said she was just a friend who lives with us." Joan interrupts. "Chrisie," she says affectionately, "it doesn't matter if you stop." "No," Christine answers, "I can tell her."

She is now painfully staring at me but her voice is calm and confident. "Anyway, I think they know because I don't talk about my father. I say Joan's a friend and she just lives with us and stuff like that." Her eyes are now filled with tears and so are mine. She is talking to me as if there is no one else present in the room—or present on the face of the earth. Her voice is very low, almost inaudible. "If some of the kids in school started picking on me because of my mother and Joan's relationship I would feel scared, because what if somebody I really liked as a friend found out about Mom and Joan and if I really like them and they . . ."

"Chrisie," I say, "why don't you give me the microphone?" She hesitates and then gently hands me the microphone. The tears, unseen by anyone else in the room, are now streaming down both our faces. She will not look away from me, and I do not know if I can look at her pain much longer. "That's enough"—I stroke her face—"the interview is over." Christine begins to sob and runs to Joan. I turn off the tape recorder. Joan holds Christine as she cries it out. Comforting her, she says, "You're going to have enough pressures with just growing up. You don't have to apologize for your Mom and me. You don't have to defend us. We'll try to protect you as much as we can but we can't be everyplace with you all the time. We don't want you to get hurt, but God, we can't stop it."

Christine is crying. Joan is crying. Pat, now standing with them, is crying. And I, the biggest marshmallow in the world, am crying. Stevie is looking at the four of us like we are mad. He walks over to his mother, Joan, and Christine. He is on his toes patting his sister's head. He then turns to me, "Ya see, *I* don't know why they're crying. I never understand anything. Girls? They never tell me anything. I don't understand what happened. *Why* are they all crying?" Then, very annoyed with all of us, standing there with his hands on his hips: "See, *I* never know what's going on around this house and it's because I'm a boy."

Steven provides us with the levity we all need. The women in the room, including Christine, begin to laugh. "See? Why are you all laughing now? I don't understand. *Girls* always have secrets."

Joan turns to me, saying, "It all started with this picture Chrisie had to draw for school." I interrupt asking if they would mind putting this on tape. Joan and Pat agree on recording it, and Joan continues.

"Chrisie had to draw this picture of her house for school. She had to put all the people who lived in the house in the picture. Chrisie wouldn't put me in the picture and Stevie threatened to tell her teacher she'd left someone out. The two of them are fighting and Pat and I have no idea what's going on. Stevie told us Chrisie wasn't going to put me into this picture.

"I talked to her about it and I told her I understood. She didn't have to put me in the picture until she was ready to put me there. When and if she ever put me in her picture it would be because she'd made up her own mind and would be ready to take whatever people dished out because of my relationship with her mother."

Joan has told me during her interview that she has a bad temper. I am now sitting there watching and listening to her rage. "Whatever comes down on me because I love Pat, I can live with. My only sorrow is that it's going to rub off on these kids. I don't like the idea that they're going to be punished a hell of a lot more than Pat and I are going to be punished. The people who will attack and hurt them because of Pat and me are people who don't have the guts to confront us to our faces. I don't want Chrisie and Stevie to be hurt for something we're doing. I know it's going to happen and we can only try to soften it. I didn't choose to fall in love with their mother—it happened. And I can't choose to give up the happiness I feel. Pat and I are as much entitled to happiness as anyone else.

"We're doing a good job of raising our children. We're living a clean life. And there's a lot more to the question than simply saying it's right or wrong. What's right for one person is definitely wrong for another. This is definitely right for Pat and me because we love each other and we're happy. We're not doing anything harmful to anyone. We're not child abusers or child seducers. I'm as honest today as I was before I even knew I was gay. I'm as sincere, as moral, and as ethical as I was before I knew I was gay. Nothing has changed except all the love I couldn't express before I can express now. And I am expressing my love for this woman and to her children. I told Pat when we came together: 'I will be with you a lifetime, if that's what I'm allowed to do—if God gives me the years, I will spend a whole lifetime with you.'

"There are people who criticize us because we're gay. They ignore our backgrounds and our hard work—our back-breaking efforts to raise these kids and give them a good and decent home. We do the same things everyone else does—we fight with the lawn mower to get it working, we do laundry, we eat, we sleep, we pay our taxes, and we go to the goddamn school when the kids are in trouble. We do everything everyone else does except for one thing—we're lesbians and we love each other. That makes us unacceptable. We're not taking the accepted course of loving a man. And God, do I resent the idea that these kids are going to be punished, even by their own father, for the love that Pat and I have for each other.

"We send Chrisie and Stevie out to school, out to that big world. That's where they're going to hear that their mother and I are immoral. All we can do is hope they come home to us and tell us what they've heard—because we're here waiting for them and they know we love them."

At about the time I am getting ready to leave Joan and Pat's home, the children are getting ready for bed. I go upstairs to go to the bathroom. When I come out, Chrisie is standing there in a cotton nightgown and bathrobe.

"Are you leaving now?" she asks.

"Yes," I answer, "everything's packed up. Chrisie, I'm sorry I . . .''

"Don't be sorry, Mary. It's not your fault: you didn't make me cry. Will you come back?"

"You sure you want me to?"

"Yeah," she says, grinning, "it would be nice."

"Okay, I promise I will try to come back. No questions, though, and no tape recorder—I promise."

She puts her arms around me, pressing her face against my shoulder. She holds me tightly for a few seconds. And then, without letting go of me, she says, "It's not your fault—you didn't make me cry. Don't worry, you'll see: everything will be okay. I'll be okay, and Stevie and Mom and Joan. We'll all be okay."

I warm up the car a few seconds before putting it into drive. The children are at the front door; Joan and Pat are standing behind them. I hit the horn and wave. Stevie blows me kisses. I drive away and I can see the four of them waving me goodbyes in my rearview mirror.

5

"O SAY! CAN YOU SEE..."

Imagine, if you will, what would happen to the American educational system if all gay teachers were fired. What would happen to medical care on a nationwide basis if all gay doctors, nurses, and technicians were discharged? What would happen to the banks in *any* state if all gay people were to refuse to pay their mortgages or their cooperative and condominium loans? A gay rent strike? There is probably a lesbian in every ladies' room; a homosexual in every men's room. We are everywhere, only no one knows it but us.

Unlike other minority groups, once you let us into a neighborhood, no one can tell if we're "spreading." While racial minorities are easily defined and stereotyped by their "looks," gays are defined and stereotyped by their sexuality. We are sexual deviants. However, the only way to establish a couple's "deviance" is to be deviant enough to look into their bedroom window. If one really wanted a nationwide purge of gays, one would have to train an army of peeping Toms. Would lesbians and homosexuals be as threatening to the heterosexual population if heterosexuals realized that not only are they working with us every day but they are living next door to us? And while the heterosexual world might not be relating positively to our presence, we are functioning within and relating to the whole straight world around us. Of the total population surveyed in "Speak Out," 39 percent live in the suburbs, 7 percent live in rural areas, and 54 percent live in cities. Now all these people have to be living next door to *someone*.

"Speak Out" asked respondents to indicate organizations in which they are actively involved. Sixteen (16) percent are involved in charitable organizations; 26 percent in political organizations; 14 percent in citizen's committees; 5 percent in community health and welfare organizations; 13 percent in professional organizations; 3 percent in parent/teacher associations; 2 percent in scouting, and 1 percent in Little League. Nine (9) percent of those responding

95

stated they are involved in what was specifically listed as "gay service organizations." Gays are actively involved in the world around them, and it is *not* an exclusively gay world. How many heterosexuals are actively involved in gay service organizations?

Not only are gays very much a part of the proverbial "mainstream of life," but those rivers that fill the lives of heterosexual people are very much the same rivers that fill our lives. We, too, have parents and families. We, too, must work to support ourselves. And we also play.

LIVING in a "MIXED WORLD"

I ask Robert and Bob about living in a mixed world of gays and straights. Bob, laughing, says, "There's a lot more mixing than straight people would believe. So many gays are in the closet, so the straights don't even know they're mixing with us. I do think, as many of the barriers come down, there'll be a lot more 'open' socializing between gays and straights."

Richard and Charles cannot imagine living in a totally gay world. Charles elaborates: "Our social life is mostly gay. However, we *live* in a mixed world. Maybe if more straights saw us, they would see how *we* live and realize it's no different from how they live."

"We don't reject the straight world," Jill says. "They want to reject us, that's their problem. Of course we live in a mixed world." Dolly adds, "I'm still the same, my values are still the same. The only thing different is that I love a woman instead of a man. I'm as gay as anyone else marching on Gay Pride Day. But I don't reject the straight world. My parents are straight; my brothers, their wives, and their kids are straight; the people I work with are straight. I don't reject them. We live in a mixed world of all sorts of people."

•   •   •

Of the men and women responding to "Speak Out," only 2 percent said they socialize exclusively with gay people. Fifty-eight (58) percent socialize with both gay and straight people. And 37 percent said they socialize mostly with gay people. If "mostly" implies "most of the time," then it is safe to assume that some time is spent socializing with straights. Three (3) percent of those responding socialize mostly with straight people.

When my ex-lover and I bought our home, I decided if my

straight friends came to visit they would come knowing it was *our* home. This was no roommate situation, nor was this a financial partnership—and I was not renting Paula a room. My straight friends could either accept our relationship or reject it; but I would not live a double life in my own home because at that point in time I was living it in too many other places.

Such bravado! It was a comfortable stand to take since none of my straight friends knew I was gay. And since I was not about to tell them, no one was ever invited to the house. I played this absurd game for about six months. Two couples in particular knew I had bought a home and patiently waited to be invited. I could not, based on the ground rules I had myself established, invite them: they did not know I was gay.

I had met George in business in 1970. Over the years, our friendship expanded beyond our business relationship. I had been invited to his home. He and his wife, Mary, have six children: five daughters and one son, ranging in age from eight to twenty-five. They were very open with me, sharing a great deal of their personal lives. I am an ex-nun and George is a staunch Catholic; we had many theological arguments over many glasses of wine over many years.

George is blunt. And, six months after I had bought the house, he was saying things like: "Are we ever going to be invited to see this house? I don't believe you really bought a house." Finally, the day of reckoning. I told him I wanted to have lunch with him because I had something to tell him. It is a three-block walk from my office to the pub where I was supposed to meet him. It was one of the longest walks I ever took in my life. I was terrified. Sitting at the table alone, I had my first drink before he even arrived. I *knew* what was going to happen—all his Catholicism was going to come down on my gay head.

He arrived, sat down, looked at me, and said: "You look terrible—what kind of trouble are you in? You get fired? You sick?"

"I want to talk to you about the house, George."

"What house?" he teased. "The one we haven't been invited to?"

"George, knock it off!" I was crumbling. "I live with someone in the house—that's why I haven't invited you."

"You're living with someone you're not married to and you think that's going to bother Mary and me? Hey, dummy, as long as you love him and you're happy, that's all that matters to us."

"Her," I said.

"Her what?" He looked confused.

"I'm living with *her* and I'm not married to *her*. *I* didn't buy a house; *we* bought a home." And then the words stuck in my throat. "I'm gay, George, I have been for years."

"Is that why you look so terrible? You were afraid to tell me you're gay? You fool. I've known Mary Mendola for years and my wife and I have loved and respected her. Whenever I've had problems, I called Mary Mendola. When I couldn't relate to one of my crazy daughters, I called you. You think I'm going to reject you now because you're telling me you were gay all those years and I didn't know it? Okay, who is she? Where did you meet her?"

Now I really died. "In the convent."

"Well," he said. "I feel a little better knowing she is *at least* Catholic. Mary will be pleased, too. Now, what do you want for a housewarming gift and when the hell are you going to invite us?"

Doris and I had met in business in 1966. She met me after she had met Michael, whom she married in 1967. I remember their wedding, their getting their first apartment, their buying their home. Susie was born, then Noel. I celebrated with them the earliest beginnings of the family they wanted to build. I had shared a great deal of their life with them, but had withheld so much of my own. They said goodbye to me when I went into the convent and welcomed me back when I came out of the convent. All three of us had grown up in Brooklyn: they, in a Jewish neighborhood; I, in an Italian neighborhood. I was talking with Doris on the phone one day.

"Ah, Mary," she said, "you going to invite us to this house you bought? We've waited over ten years to give you a housewarming gift and we figure it's time. Like you got a mortgage now, so you won't be moving once a year anymore."

I begged off. "I'll get back to you—we'll set a date."

That night I went home and wrote to Doris and Michael. In the letter I told them I was gay. I told them that, as I had shared their life with them for many years, I now wanted them to share mine. I told them that, as I had respected their marriage, I wanted them to respect mine. And, of course, I would understand if they could not accept my lifestyle.

The following week, Doris called me at the office.

"Mary Mendola," I said, picking up the call.

"You gotta write, you can't talk all of a sudden?"

"Hi, Doris," I said.

"Vell, listen." She went into her Brooklyn Jewish routine. "Ve got your letter. Ve talked about it. There's just one thing we want ta know. Is the girl at least Jewish?"

When I said the "girl" was not Jewish, Doris said, "Vell, vat can you say, it happens in the best of families. Michael said you should send directions. He said *good* directions so ve shouldn't get lost trying to find the vay. We're coming in two weeks, on a Saturday, and we're bringing the kids, unless you tell us not to."

Two out of two is not a bad average for a kid just coming out. I went for three—and lost. The third person was an older woman I had known since I was seventeen. She had been one of my high school teachers and the first person in my life to treat me as an adult. In an all-girls private Catholic academy, she had not encouraged my dissent, but she had encouraged and influenced my dissenting mind. Beyond high school, and in the twelve years that followed, we developed a friendship as two women. Over all those years my relationship with her was vitally important to both my intellectual and spiritual development. I wrote her telling her I was gay and inviting her to my home. She never responded.

There were other losses, but also other wins. I came to see my closeted life as a tremendous injustice to my straight friends. By living a double life in my relationships with them, I was protecting myself by never giving them an opportunity to reject me. However, I never trusted them enough to believe they would accept me—that was the injustice. I had shared the intimacies of their lives while remaining aloof and evasive about my own. By automatically assuming they would reject me if they knew I was gay, I never allowed them the benefit of the doubt. I had boxed and stereotyped both them and their reactions just as I, as a lesbian, was boxed and stereotyped. I had committed the same injustice against them I accused the heterosexual world of committing against me. It took the majority of my straight friends less time to accept me than it had taken me to accept myself.

In a *Gaysweek* article, David Rothenberg wrote: "It is clear to me that one of our major political/activist stumbling blocks is our inability to accept acceptance. We have become so enmeshed with negative views of ourselves that rejection becomes our paramour. Ron Gold told me years ago, in an accurate prophecy: 'When you come out, the people who love you don't love you less. They begin to change their minds about what being gay is, as they relate to you.'" *

---

* David Rothenberg, "Another Voice—Time and Time Again," *Gaysweek*, April 1979, p. 13.

An aunt telephoned me one afternoon. "Who is this Anita Bryant? I was just watching her on television. If she comes to New York, will you lose your job? Will they be able to throw you out of your apartment?" When someone loves a person who they *know* is gay, antigay politics becomes a very personal matter. It is no longer, "These gays, what do they want?" Suddenly, "these gays" are a son or a daughter, a niece or a nephew, a sister or a brother—a friend. For heterosexual families and friends, someone they love is being threatened. They understand the gay issues.

SURVIVING in SUBURBIA

"Can a gay family survive in suburbia?" Pat laughs. "We're doing a lot more than surviving, we're living. We're a family that happens to be gay and we happen to be living in suburbia. Our neighbors don't know we're gay. But we know we do the same things they do—pay our taxes, fight the schools, watch Little League games, and go to swimming meets. We lead very much the same lives as our neighbors." I ask Pat if she is sure their neighbors do not know. "We haven't felt any hostility from the neighbors. They're friendly. Steve and Chris play with their children. Our neighbors seem like normal neighbors."

Joan's viewpoint on neighbors is not quite as relaxed as Pat's. "One of these days," Joan says, "our neighbors will know for sure that we're gay. Then we'll really find out what kind of people they are. I don't have very much faith that we'll be allowed to continue living here peacefully once they know for *sure*. They all have kids and they don't want us rubbing off on their children—that's what people are afraid of."

"Our neighbors know Rob and I are a homosexual couple," says Bob. "We're not overtly affectionate on the streets, but this is our home and within it we're free. Our neighbor next door is a carpenter—he's done some work for us. We don't have any qualms about showing affection in front of him when he's doing a job in *our* home. We may touch each other outside the house when we're working around. But it's not embracing; it's more roughing it up as most men do. I think our hugging each other on the lawn *would* upset the neighbors. We try to make a conscious effort not to do it. But exclusive of embracing in the front yard, if they lose respect for us because we're homosexuals, then they're losing respect for themselves. There's much more to me as a man than my sexuality.

If their respect for me as a person is based only on the sexual dimension of my life, then they're doing something to themselves."

INTERACTING with NEIGHBORS

Regarding urban, suburban, or rural neighbors, "Speak Out" asked the men and women responding to describe their interactions with their neighbors, checking as many choices as were applicable. The men and women responded as follows:

48%   do not care whether or not their neighbors know they are a gay couple

31%   their neighbors treat their relationships as simply two friends living together with no commitment

30%   their neighbors are not aware that they are a gay couple

29%   do not socialize with their neighbors by choice

26%   their neighbors accept their gay relationships (e.g., treating them and their partners as couples)

12%   are careful to make certain their neighbors do not know they are a gay couple

3%   their neighbors either deny or ignore their relationships

1%   their neighbors refuse to have anything to do with them because they know they are gay.

GAYS HAVE PARENTS; GAY COUPLES, IN-LAWS

"I could've absolutely died," Jill says. "Dolly's parents had invited us for dinner. They always invite us for dinner but we got the feeling this was something special. When we got there, Dolly's mother wanted me to sit with her: she wanted to know if it was all right for them to put my name in the family Bible. When I said it was, she went right to it.

"Everything was going good—my name, where I was born. Then we got to the part where it was supposed to say what relationship I am to which member of the family. She kept staring at the line. I didn't dare laugh, but then she started laughing. So I got up and got her and me a beer and we sat there laughing together. I told her I could see how she might find that part confusing. What was she going to write—'my gay daughter-in-law'? So, according to the family Bible, I am their daughter—period."

"It happens every time we go out with my folks," Dolly says. "My father has to introduce his two sons and his daughter to everyone in whatever restaurant we happen to be in. I can always see it coming. A friend of his drops by the table and he does his routine. 'This is my son——and his wife. This is my son——and his wife. And this is my daughter Dolly and . . .' He always hesitates and looks at my mother, stunned. I know she has just kicked him under the table. So he regroups and does it again. 'This is my daughter Dolly, and this is my daughter Jill.' He's been blowing his introductions like that for years."

"Yes," says Jill, "I guess you can say we have a gay family. We have close friends who are a part of our gay family. We've got our next-door neighbors and their kids. They're part of our family . . . and you know it every time one of the kids comes knocking on the door asking for cookies. 'Real family' is when you're comfortable enough to come ask for cookies and comfortable enough to say, 'Hey, I'm in trouble and I need some help.'"

"My parents are simple people," Dolly explains. "They take people at face value; they don't try to analyze you. My parents were scared when they found out I was gay because they thought I carried men's clothes in the trunk of my car and as soon as I left work I dressed up as a man. But we talked and I told them it was nothing like that. Then they met Jill, and over the years we've been together, it's been good."

"I couldn't have asked for a better family if I'd picked them myself," Jill continues. "They've made up for some of the things I missed with my own family. In some ways I think they treat me better than their other daughters-in-law."

"And how do you treat them?" I ask.

"I try to treat them pretty good," Jill says. "We know Dolly's mother likes shrimps, so if we're shopping and we've got some extra money, we buy them shrimps. When they're a little short at the end of the month, Dolly gives her father fifty dollars, knowing she doesn't have to ask me, because they're retired and we both know they need it. I don't have to treat them any special way. I just fit in with them like I've been there all my life."

• • •

The end of every telephone conversation with my own father is always the same. He says, "I love you . . . Give Valerie a kiss for me." And, of course, I "cash in" on the kisses my father sends to Valerie. When my father was seventy years old, my mother had a surprise dinner party in a local restaurant. She asked that Valerie and I get there early and put the place cards on the table.

"What do you want me to do with the dais?" I uncomfortably asked.

"Put Dad and me in the middle, your brother and his wife on one side, and you and Valerie on the other side," she answered. "I told them to set the dais for six."

"Mom," I asked her anxiously, "do you know what you're doing?"

"Yeah, I'm telling you how to arrange the table for your father's party. What do you mean, 'Do I know what I'm doing?' What's the matter?"

"Well, it's like you're making a public announcement to the whole family about Val and me. And I want to be sure you understand what you're doing."

"You know," she hissed at me, "I really don't give a damn anymore. Anyone has anything to say, let them look at their own kids."

"Okay, if you're sure you . . ."

"I told you," she interrupted, "you want me to tell you again? Your father and me in the middle, your brother and his wife on one side, you and Valerie on the other side."

I realized after talking with my mother that I was more afraid for *myself* than I was for her. Ironically, I drew the courage necessary to deal with the day from *her*. Her acceptance of Valerie and me as a couple enabled *me* to better accept us as a couple in potentially "unfriendly" terrain. I discussed it with Valerie and she was willing to sit at my side on the dais. We all survived the day—my father had a wonderful birthday party.

Not all parent-related gay stories have a happy ending. I spoke with a man whose parents had disowned him when they learned he was a homosexual. "That was nine years ago," he said. "I've tried to see them several times over the years, but they won't see me. What scares me is that they're getting older and they're going to die . . . and all these years will be such a terrible waste. I can't stand the pain of that, but it's a pain and a hurt I've got to absorb because I've got to move beyond it."

Another man sat in a restaurant with me and cried at the table. "I was raised in a very liberal family. My parents had *friends* who were gay. So when I realized *I* was gay I didn't see any problem in telling them. They want nothing to do with me. I don't understand why if they can have gay friends they can't have me as a gay son. My kid sister was getting married and she wanted me to come to her wedding. My father didn't want me there: he told her and he told me. She begged me to go to her wedding. She said it was important to her and she wanted me to be there. I *wanted* to be there. So I went. When my father saw me, he physically threw me out of the reception . . . in front of all those people. My sister was standing there in her white gown, crying . . . she just kept crying."

Every lesbian and homosexual had or has parents. There are many painful stories. However, there are also happy stories. I never wanted my parents to know I was a lesbian because I believed they would reject me. And yet their struggling to accept me has helped me in my own struggle to accept myself. We all have our different reasons for either telling or not telling our parents. And only each individual can determine whether or not his or her reasons are valid. One woman explained to me: "My parents are elderly. They live in another city. Tell me, what am I going to achieve by telling them? Why inflict confusion on them at their age? Why use them on my trip to establish my gay identity."

A man explained to me: "I'm out and active as a gay. I'm somewhat of a spokesman for gay rights in this city. I've been on television and I've been interviewed. But I still haven't actually told my parents, and they live here. And I'm not going to discuss it with them until I have a stable relationship . . . someone I can bring home for Sunday dinner. I guess what I want to be able to say to my parents is, 'This is my partner. We're homosexuals and we share a life together.' I want to say 'I'm gay,' but when I tell them I want it to be a happy thing. And until it's a happy thing, it's not worth what it may cost me to tell them. I do think they know, but they're waiting for me . . . and I'm waiting until I have a good and stable relationship."

Fred is a decorator friend who had been working on some picture frames for me. I thought it odd that when I had called him the previous Monday to say I would be there on Friday he said firmly, "Make *sure* you're here Friday night. I'll be waiting for you."

He nervously showed me the frames within seconds after I arrived. There were no social amenities—he quickly wrapped them and sat down at a worktable.

"Sit, please," he said, "I want to talk to you. I've been waiting all week to talk to you."

"What *is* the matter with you?" I asked. And then, jokingly: "By the expression on your face, I really don't know if I want to hear this."

"I really hate myself," he began. "Pat, my eighteen-year-old daughter, told me she's gay. My little girl is a lesbian. And I don't know what's the matter with me."

"What do you mean, you don't know what's the matter with you?"

"I've been an interior decorator for over thirty years. I worked and socialized with gay people all these years. I never had any problem. I never saw any difference. I feel like such a hypocrite. All these years I said I understood gay people, could see where they were coming from. But now it's my *daughter* and I can't figure out what's troubling me so."

"Fred, do you really expect yourself to jump up and down and say, 'Gay is great.' Do you think that's realistic for you as a father?"

"She told me she wanted to talk to me," he explained. "She was so cute and innocent sitting there. She just came right out with it. She said, 'Daddy, I want you to know I'm gay. I want to come out.' She also told me she thought she might be bisexual. But she's dating other girls. She's already had a relationship, and she wanted me to know she was going to continue seeing girls. She was so up front."

"How did you react, Fred? Is that what's bothering you?"

"How could I react? She's my little girl. After she finished talking, she asked me if I would hug her. And I hugged her probably harder than I've ever hugged her before in her life. It was like I didn't want to let her go. But I hate myself because I'm not ready to defend my own daughter. I'm not ready to take on the relatives and her grandparents. I don't want anyone to know my daughter is gay—me, the great liberal. She says she wants to be 'out.' I don't want her to be out—I want to protect her and I don't want her to get hurt. And I'm a rotten father because I don't want to have to defend her if she's out."

"Fred, the fact that she told you and your wife says something for the kind of parents you are. She must know you love her if she could tell you. She must trust you."

"My wife has been crying for a week. We've only spoken about it twice. Maybe it's the grandchild business. We're not going to be grandparents—this daughter is not going to produce a baby for us. And isn't that selfish of me? Did I love my daughter with a price tag attached—'I'll love you and I'll raise you and you produce grandchildren for me'? Is that the kind of father I've been?"

"Pat only told you last week. Will you give yourself a break. Give yourself time to absorb it and sort it out."

"But did I handle it right, Mary? She wanted to know if she could bring home girls she is dating. I said, 'No.' I told her I couldn't deal with it yet. I also told her I didn't want her getting involved with boys if she was just experimenting. I don't want to see her hurt any young guys while she's trying to prove she's not gay. I just don't know if I handled it right."

"You handled it the way you had to handle it," I said.

"What's that supposed to mean?"

"Fred, you were honest and sincere. She knows you love her and accept her. But you have to be who *you* are, too. And right now this thing is so new. Once it settles in, you might be able to deal with her bringing home a girl she's dating. Give yourself time, and give her time. You both have to sort out who you are and where you're coming from. If you want to tell her anything, tell her that you and your wife need time. Let her see that it's a process for you just as much as it's a process for her. Do you think she told you she's bisexual so it would be easier for you? Maybe she was padding it for you."

"Yeah," he answered, "I thought that. But what do I do now?"

"Nothing. Just keep talking to her. Just keep hugging her. Fred, life is difficult enough for a girl her age. Now she's got another whole identity thing to deal with. She needs you and your wife. But she doesn't need you to say, 'Gay is great.' She needs you to support her, accept her, and understand her. But be yourself, be real. If you're not, she'll see right through it. She'll know you're doing a number and she'll cut you off. Once that communication is gone, you're in a lot of trouble."

"I keep looking at her—all this week I looked at her. She hasn't changed—she looks the same. She's still the same daughter I had two weeks ago. I look at her and I think: 'What's so terrible, what's so different?' It's *me* that's got the problem."

"Okay, it's you that's got the problem. Tell her you're trying to work things out in your own head. She's still the same daughter, only now her emotional and sexual preferences are different than you thought they were."

"I was wrong telling her I didn't want her to bring home girls she's dating?"

"Would you want her to bring home boys she's dating?"

"Of course I would," he answers. "I'd want to see them. I'd want to know who she's going out with."

"You just answered your own question, baby. She's not your gay daughter or your straight daughter. She's your daughter. That's the issue—not her sexual identity."

•   •   •

I ask Em and Louise about the "extended gay family." "Of

course we have a gay family," Em answers. "I have seven sons and a daughter and they all know I'm gay. That makes a gay family. Even my ex-husband knows I'm gay. It doesn't bother him as much as it bothers his new wife. She keeps telling us how we're going to hell. And I keep telling her that God is love, and because we love and are good people, there's no way God is going to send us to hell."

"Okay, Em," I say, "you have a couple of sons left at home whom you're raising in a lesbian relationship. How do you think that will affect their growing up?"

"I don't worry about my sons because they're being raised by two lesbians and living in a lesbian family. Christopher is a handsome, red-haired fourteen-year-old. He's already got himself a little girl friend. I'm sure his little girl friend is aware of our lifestyle. We're not raising my sons to love either a man or a woman: we're just trying to teach them to love. Who they love is their own business . . . I just want them to be good, honest, and decent men."

"Em," I ask, "you accept your lesbianism, but how would you feel if one of your sons told you he is a homosexual?"

"One of my sons," she laughs, "has already told me he's a homosexual. You didn't expect me to answer that way, did you? But let me tell you something: he and I go out together and we have a great time. He understands my lifestyle and I most certainly understand his. Of all my sons, he's the one with whom I have the closest relationship."

• • •

We asked the gay community: "If your parents are aware of your gay marriage/relationship," how have they reacted? Their responses were as follows:

40%   their parents accept their relationship (e.g., invite them and their partners to family functions)

36%   their parents are not aware of their relationship

21%   their parents treat their relationships as simply two friends living together with no commitment

3%   their parents refuse to see them and their partners together under any circumstances.

GAYS and THEIR SIBLINGS

And because most people have at least one brother or one sister, "Speak Out" also asked: "If your brother(s) and/or sister(s) are aware of your marriage/relationship," how have they reacted? The respondents indicated as follows:

53%   their siblings accept it (e.g., invite them and their partners to family functions)
29%   their siblings are not aware
16%   their siblings treat their relationships as simply two friends living together with no commitment
1%   their siblings refuse to see them and their partners together under any circumstances.

FINANCIAL PARTNERSHIPS

As more and more women enter the job market, the greater the psychological imbalance of heterosexual marriages. Traditionally, the person earning the money is the person with the decision-making power, and that power has historically been claimed by men. Women are now not only contributing to the support of their families, but in some instances they are earning as much as, if not more than, their husbands. Perhaps this economic power struggle in heterosexual relationships is the basis of their role identification problems: "I man, you woman. I support family, make decisions. You clean house, make babies." Although men cannot make babies, women most certainly can make decisions—and *they can* make money. Perhaps these socioeconomic factors will soon enable heterosexual couples to enjoy the same equal rights and the same financial partnerships most gay couples enjoy.

"Speak Out" asked: "Do you and your partner have a financial partnership, planning your spending as a couple?" Seventy-one (71) percent of the respondents said Yes; 29 percent said No. Of the total number of men who answered this question, 70 percent said Yes; of the total number of women, 72 percent said Yes. Thirty (30) percent of the men answering said No; 28 percent of the women said No. In terms of the men and women who responded to "Speak Out," there does not seem to be much of a difference between the way lesbians and homosexuals handle their finances as couples. Perhaps financial "planning" is the pattern for gays. While for straights, it is financial "decisions," and those decisions are usually made by the person with the greater earning power.

It would be quite difficult for two people to earn exactly the same amount of money. We asked: "Do you and your partner pool all or part of your individual paychecks to cover essential living expenses?" The responses were:

41% pool part of their paychecks
29% pool their total paychecks
25% do not pool their paychecks on a regular basis
5% do not pool their paychecks because only one partner works.

GAY COUPLES:
OWNING and RENTING THEIR HOMES

We know that lesbian and homosexual couples are living everywhere. But how are they living? Based on the "Speak Out" responses, we found that:

50% they rent their house or apartment
24% they and their partners jointly own their residence
15% they own their residence
11% their partners own their residence.

I do not want to startle the real estate industry, but there does seem to be a large gay market. If you look at the last three figures, a lot of sales are obviously being made to gays. Although 50 percent of the men and women responding to "Speak Out" rent their residences, the other 50 percent are living in residences either jointly owned or owned by one or the other of the partners. Is gay *not an issue* when it comes to real estate sales and commissions? Or are we, as gays, so "normal" that realtors do not realize they are selling to us? Or do the realtors know and hope the other members of the community do not realize they have just let one of us into the neighborhood?

I am sure no gay would flaunt his or her gayness in a real estate office on a Saturday or Sunday afternoon, and never in a bank somewhere out there in mid-America where they are applying for a mortgage. However, I do find it difficult to believe that the realtor who just sold a house to two women actually believes the two women are always cousins. And the realtor who sold the house to those two men: Does he or she really believe the two men are always "just a couple of buddies" looking for a tax shelter? I am cynical enough to believe that when it comes to economics, it is okay to be gay—as long as you can pay. Gay dollars have no problem with acceptance. However, regarding equal rights for homosexuals and lesbians, it will be decades before we enjoy the first-class citizenship to which—based on our tax dollars—we are entitled.

Like heterosexual couples, not all gay couples can afford to own either a house or co-op or condominium. However, like heterosexual couples, they do jointly own other things. "Speak Out" provided a list of "things" a couple could own together and asked the gay community to check as many of those things they *jointly* *own* with their partners.

59%   household furnishings
26%   cars and motorcycles
8%   businesses
8%   land
7%   country homes
4%   savings accounts and other investments.

HEALTH INSURANCE / DISABILITY INSURANCE

With the rising costs of medical care, health is a major influence on any couple's financial stability. No one can guarantee anyone continuous good health. And I have often thought that the most serious illnesses seem to strike when you are walking around believing you are in the best of health.

Valerie and I never really had a "honeymoon." We officially began living together on May 1. On May 10, I found out I had a tumor; on May 16, I learned I had four tumors. There was no way I was going for a third opinion. It seemed to be costing me more and more money to find out I had more and more tumors. There is no way to describe the emotional and psychological pressure during the three weeks prior to surgery. It was during those weeks that I became most aware of the mental luxury of a solid program of medical insurance. All I had to worry about was my health. I did not have to concern myself with being financially ruined by doctor and hospital bills.

"Speak Out" surveyed gays about their health insurance. We found that 87 percent of the gay community has health insurance; 78 percent said their partners had health insurance. In a heterosexual marriage, both partners need not necessarily have health insurance. With most plans, the insured's spouse is included: a husband's medical plan will include his wife and his children. A working wife's coverage can often make up the difference for expenses not totally covered by her husband's plan.

However, the health insurance situation for lesbian and homosexual couples is one of the finest examples of inequality under the law. It is also among the most important issues regarding legal marriage for gay couples.

I have an exceptionally good health insurance program; Valerie's is less than adequate. Although *we* consider ourselves married, my medical plan does not include her. However, if she were to become seriously ill, we—our relationship—would absorb the costs of that illness. For a married man with the same exact plan as I have, several dollars more a month provides medical protection for his wife and all his dependent children. Even though I might be willing to pay much more than several dollars a month to include Valerie in my plan, no insurance company is ready to underwrite a health plan for our lesbian marriage. Regarding health insurance, heterosexual common-law couples are in the same precarious and dangerous situation.

My friends Carla and JoAnne have been together seven years. Carla has a nine-year-old daughter, Marie. Although JoAnne has an excellent health care plan, it does not cover Carla and Marie. Carla does not have health insurance, nor can she afford to purchase it as an individual. Marie, like other children, gets sick. Carla and JoAnne must pay the total costs of those medical bills. They are a gay family with none of the same insurance protection enjoyed by straight families. Because they are not legally married, JoAnne's health insurance cannot include Carla or her daughter, Marie.

However, even if lesbian and homosexual couples were permitted to legally marry, that is no guarantee insurance companies would recognize the marriage and "insure" it. Most insurance companies still persist in only insuring the traditional family unit: legally married husband and wife and their children.

Unlike legally married heterosexual couples, gay couples cannot depend upon the conventional structures to ensure their financial solvency. They must depend upon themselves. For all gays, but particularly for gays who either own property together or whose standard of living is based upon both their incomes, health insurance and disability insurance are imperative. Yes, it is a very unjust situation. And yes, it costs more money to insure a gay marriage than it does to insure a straight marriage. However, whether or not it is unfair is not the issue. The issue is making certain our relationships are financially protected. We simply do not have the support systems enjoyed by heterosexual couples. No one is going to take care of us but ourselves.

PLANNING for OLD AGE:
LIFE INSURANCE and WILLS

Of the total number of men and women who responded to "Speak Out," 95 percent said they believe and hope they and their partners will grow into old age together. Like heterosexual couples, lesbian and homosexual couples also plan for old age.

•   •   •

Paul and Michael believe planning for old age includes both planning to retire together and planning for the security of the surviving partner when one or the other of them dies. "We don't see any financial problems with old age," says Paul. "Financially," Michael explains, "we've made provisions for each other. We've had wills made out leaving each other all of our assets. We both have life insurance naming the other as beneficiary. We've tried to do all that is legally feasible to provide for the remaining partner."

"We haven't done nearly as much about planning for old age as we should," says Charlotte. "We'd like to have life insurance," Nancy explains, "but basically we live on my income and the state disability Charlotte receives. We can't afford it. We've got a savings account which we call our 'dream account.' We'd like to get enough money together for a down payment on a house. That's what we think about when we talk about our 'old agehood' together."

"Bob and I decided early in our relationship," Robert says, "that it would be better to buy a house than to keep renting. That's what we did, because eventually the house will be paid off. So financially we're set for old age. When we furnished the house, we bought expensive furniture that will last us for our lifetime. We plan to live until we're eighty, and it will be nice to grow old comfortably and gracefully." Robert talks about retirement: "I want to be able to sit back, retire, and be happy—that's what I want out of life. Right now, I'm heavy on financial security. But when we retire I don't mind becoming a hermit as long as we're together and happy."

"Louise and I have life insurance on each other's life," Em explains. "That should help both of us if either one of us dies. We also own this house and we see it as a way of investing our money. We expect to be able to sell it when we're old, and then we'd like to travel."

Debra and Beverly jointly own a condominium and country home. Both women have wills bequeathing to each other all their assets. They have life insurance and mortgage insurance. "Financially," explains Debra, "we'll be fine. We have pensions from our years of teaching. And we'll both be receiving Social Security benefits. We've also saved money and bought some stocks. We're planning to retire here and rent our condominium as income-producing property." "Financially," Beverly says, laughing, "we're in very good shape for our retirement. The problem is we're only in our early forties and we're ready to retire right now."

For Troy and Ed, old age is part of their *immediate* future. They both have life insurance naming each other as beneficiaries, and they both have wills, each bequeathing their properties to the other. "The older we get," Troy says, sighing, "the more of our friends die, and we have to watch it happen. That's the part of getting older that we don't like. As for retiring, I don't have a pension plan, which means all I will have coming in are my Social Security benefits. I don't have any money saved. Basically, I have nothing. But hope does spring eternal in the human breast. Ed and I are writing a book, which a publisher has already signed for. If that's a success, I'll kiss my work goodbye, play my harpsichord, go back to painting, learn another language, look out the window, visit with my boyfriends: basically, enjoy life.

"But exclusive of the book, Ed does have a good pension. Plus he'll get Social Security. So we can add my Social Security to that. We have a friend who's already retired. The three of us are thinking of pooling whatever retirement income we have and living together. As older gays, I think we're in a position to build a mature family: friends who love each other by choice, who take care of each other by choice."

• • •

Responding to "Speak Out," 73 percent of the people said either they or their partners had retirement plans. Twenty-seven (27) percent said that neither they nor their partners had retirement plans. Fifty-six (56) percent of the men and women responding said either they or their partners own life insurance naming the other as beneficiary. Forty-four (44) percent said that neither they nor their partners had life insurance.

"I see old age," says Ann, "as absolutely delightful. I see myself in a rocking chair with a book. Kate is sitting next to me. Or it's a Sunday morning and we're reading the newspapers—we read each other parts that we think are exciting. I feel lucky knowing I'll have Kate to grow old with. I don't want to rush into old age, but I'm looking forward to it. Even if Kate were to die before me—it would be difficult, but, if she weren't there, I'd have the memory of her and the memories of the life we had together. As long as you have your health, I don't think old age affects you so much. Old age is an adjustment: it's not being able to do the things you'd like to do. But at least, hopefully, we'll have the mental faculties to share different kinds of activities. Even now we share memories. It's not old age but it's what I see old age as being. We have some hilarious memories, some heartwarming memories, and some traumatic memories. All of those experiences are a part of our present relationship . . . and they'll be a part of our future relationship, which will be our old age together."

Kate and Ann both have life insurance naming each other as beneficiaries. They jointly own a house, land, and stocks. "We plan to have wills drawn up," says Kate. "Wills are the only way we can protect each other from society and from our respective families. My parents, for instance, think I own things which actually both Ann and I own. It's not only because of what we own—a will is important to make certain that our parents don't interfere in our wishes for the role each of us would play in the event of the other's death."

• • •

"Speak Out" asked: "Do either you or your partner have a will bequeathing to the other either all or part of monies, properties, etc.?" Of the total number of men and women responding, 45 percent said Yes; 54 percent said No. Of the total number of men responding, 44 percent said Yes; 55 percent said No. Of the total number of women responding, 46 percent said Yes; 54 percent said No.

Why life insurance and wills? Tom and Bill are fictional characters created for the purposes of an explanation of what can and does happen to a gay couple.

Tom and Bill met and lived together in an apartment for two years. They decided to buy a house, and together scraped up every penny they could find for the down payment. They knew both their salaries were necessary to make the monthly mortgage payments.

Having purchased the house together, it was jointly owned and the mortgage was in both their names. As anyone who has bought a home knows, the first few years in a house are financially the worst. It took every penny Tom and Bill had to pay their mortgage and run the house. Therefore, they had no extra money to either save or to purchase life insurance.

Tom died suddenly of a heart attack. Tom's family approached Bill and demanded 50 percent of the value of the house because Tom and Bill owned the house as "tenants in common" not as "joint tenants." Therefore, Tom's portion of the house became part of his estate. Had the house been owned in "joint tenancy," Tom's portion of the house would have gone directly to Bill. Bill, of course, was defenseless. There was *no will.* And although the house was jointly owned by both of them, Tom and Bill had not known enough to specify a "right to survivorship" or "joint tenancy" clause when they purchased the house. For a legally married heterosexual couple who jointly own a home, the "right to survivorship" is automatically included. Of course, for a gay couple, no such right is automatically included. And because Tom and Bill had not been able to afford life insurance, Bill did not have the money to pay Tom's family 50 percent of the assessed value of the house. Bill, therefore, had to sell the house and give Tom's family 50 percent of the amount for which the house was sold.

Even if Tom and Bill had known enough to specifically ask for a "right to survivorship" or a "joint tenancy" clause in their deed, Bill would *still* have lost the house. No, he would not have lost it to Tom's family. They would have had no automatic claim to 50 percent of the house. Bill would have lost the house for financial reasons. Remember, their ability to make their monthly mortgage payments was based on *both* their incomes. After Tom's death, alone, Bill could no longer afford the house based on only *his* salary. Had they had life insurance, a policy on Tom's life naming Bill as beneficiary, Bill would have had the proceeds of that insurance policy to make up the difference for the loss of Tom's salary. A life insurance policy would have eliminated the force-sale situation with which Bill was confronted: alone, he did not have the income necessary to support the house. Therefore, he was forced to sell it. And Bill walked away a broken man—he had lost his lover and he had lost the home they had struggled to build together.

Philip Perl was a real person: he died in 1978. Stanley Saul was his lover. The two men had lived together for ten years in a Manhattan co-op owned by Philip. Philip had purchased the cooperative apartment five years before he had met Stanley. Less than one year after Philip's death, Stanley was in court trying to save what had been their home.

"Two homosexuals who live together," reported the *New York Times,* "no matter how long or close their relationship, do not constitute an 'immediate family,' according to a ruling by a judge in New York City Housing Court. . . . Stanley contended that he and Philip had for all intents and purposes lived together as a family unit: he and Philip had shared the same household and its expenses, ate at the same table and slept in the same bedroom, wore each other's clothes, enjoyed the same friends, attended the same social functions, took vacations together—and operated for all purposes as a family. Stanley contended in court papers that the term 'family' was not restricted to 'relatives by blood or marriage.'

"After research on the issue," the *Times* continued, "the court has been unable to find any authority that holds [that] homosexuals living together constitute a family."* Basically, Stanley had no legal claim on the four-room cooperative apartment he and Philip had lived in together for ten years. The property, or the money from the sale of the property, would go to Philip's estate—to his immediate family.

The last paragraph in the *Times* story is most interesting: "Marvin S. Lerman, Mr. Saul's lawyer, reportedly plans to appeal the decision. But Irving Perl, a Manhattan lawyer who has represented his *late* brother's estate during the litigation, said, 'In my view there is no law that would uphold Mr. Saul's position" (italics mine).†

And into his (Mr. Irving Perl's) pocket will go either all or part of the monies realized from the sale of that Manhattan cooperative— in which his dead brother, Philip, had lived with his lover, Stanley, for ten years. What the *Times* did not say: although Philip had lived in the apartment for five years before he began living with Stanley, he, Philip, had never during their ten years together transferred ownership to both his and Stanley's name. Was it something Philip always meant to do but never got around to doing? Did Philip and Stanley "always mean to" have wills drawn up? Had Philip and Stanley been legally married, Philip's property would have automatically been inherited by Stanley, his surviving spouse. Because

---

* "Two Homosexuals Living Together Not a Legal Family, Judge Rules," *New York Times,* May 6, 1979.
† Ibid.

they were not legally married, and because there was no will, Philip's immediate family inherited his property.

The law does not protect us. However, we can use wills and life insurance as vehicles by which we can protect ourselves and each other. And even though a will can be contested, a family might be less likely to take a surviving lover into court if there is a slight possibility they may lose. If the sanctity of our unions as gay couples is not respected while we are alive, we are naive if we believe our unions will be respected when we are dead. And even though a family has *accepted* the gay marriage of one of its members, should that member of the family die, dollars can then become the issue.

6

KNOCK-KNOCK.
Who's There?

Welcome to Main Street, State of Confusion, U.S.A. Knock at any door and there is no way you will ever be able to predict who will answer. Nothing is as it seems—except the aluminum siding and the manicured lawns. Let's take a walk around the neighborhood to check out lifestyles and values. . . .

- The white house there on the corner: Mrs. Smith and Mr. Jones live there. Both are retired; both widowed. They decided to "live together" instead of marrying so they both could continue to collect their Social Security checks. Mrs. Smith and Mr. Jones giggle a lot about being "too old for sex." But they do so enjoy the touching, the cuddling, and the companionship. Both of them have grown children, none of whom approve of the relationship their respective parents are having.

- In the next house, the one with the green shutters: Bob and Clara. They were married to each other for seven years, and they have been divorced from each other for five years. They married in college and divorced—for tax purposes—in their early thirties. Neither of them want children, and both of them practice Transcendental Meditation.

- The house with the toys on the lawn: Margaret and her two children. It is what sociologists call a single-parent family headed by a woman: she and her husband divorced three years ago. Margaret believes in the new celibacy: rechanneling her sexual energies into self-improvement programs.

- And the condominium complex, there, as you turn left at the corner: Alice and Frank have the ground-floor apartment. Alice is white; Frank, black. They have been living together for six years. They have chosen not to legally marry because they do not plan to have children. They both feel society is barely ready to accept them and not at all ready to accept any mulatto children they might produce.

• In the apartment directly above Alice and Frank: Joe and Jerry, a homosexual couple who have been together eight years. They would like to legally marry, but, of course, they cannot. However, they have had a religious ceremony in a gay church commemorating their commitment to each other. Joe is interested in spiritualism. Jerry is sometimes interested in spiritualism, but mostly he jogs.

• In the apartment directly adjacent to Joe and Jerry is Victor. In his late twenties, Victor is now a full-time student again. He divorced his wife two years ago and is now living on his alimony payments. He is involved with another woman, however, he does not want to remarry because he will lose his alimony. And if he lost his alimony, he would have to go to work. And if he had to go to work, he could not be a full-time student anymore.

• Downstairs, in the apartment adjacent to Alice and Frank, are Liz and Fred. Although they have been living together for almost seven years, Fred has not yet divorced his wife. Therefore, he cannot marry Liz. Liz supports Fred, who supports his wife and three children. All the neighbors think that Fred and Liz are married. And Fred and Liz let all the neighbors think they are married.

• Peter and Ann live in a little studio apartment in the condominium complex. Peter's father bought it for him when he graduated college. They are in their mid-twenties, and they both believe in living together for several years before legally marrying. They see marriage as a viable institution, but only after an intense live-in period of engagement.

• Across the street from the condominium is that lovely Tudor. Bill and Sarah live there; they have three teenage children. After being married for fifteen years, they decided it would be much better for their relationship if they divorced. However, for the sake of the children and for financial reasons, they have continued to live together. Both of them are trying to find themselves. And although they feel they may remarry each other later in life, for now they choose to remain single.

- Carla and Esther are the lesbian couple who live in the blue house across the street from the lovely Tudor. They have been together eleven years. Esther was married to a man for three years prior to meeting Carla. For Carla, Esther was her first relationship of any kind. Both of them are health food "freaks," although when Esther is teaching evening yoga classes, Carla cheats and eats pizza for supper. She puts the pizza boxes in the condominium complex garbage cans.

- Down the street, the brick house: George and Arlene. They have been married for nine years. Although none of the neighbors know it, George and Arlene are a swinging couple. They belong to a swingers group of switching couples on the other side of town. Initially, swinging was George's idea. However, since Arlene has realized her bisexuality within the context of swinging, George no longer wants to continue with the group.

Scattered throughout the rest of the neighborhood are an assortment of first-time marrieds, remarrieds, and divorced people. What do the straight people in the neighborhood have in common with the gay people in the neighborhood? Do their values differ? And if they do differ, what are those differences, and on what are they based? Are there not more similarities than there are differences? Are the differences only a thin veneer of acceptability enjoyed by the heterosexual majority? An interracial heterosexual couple might be frowned upon, but at least they are *normal.* Society tends to frown upon men and women who deviate from conventional behavior. Society ostracizes homosexuals and lesbians. Are we ostracized because of the main difference—our emotional and sexual preference? Or are we ostracized because there are too many similarities, which a heterosexual society either does not realize or cannot comfortably acknowledge?

SIMILARITIES and DIFFERENCES

"The important similarity," says Bob, "is love. That's the universal. I love Rob, he's my partner. And that's the major similarity between us and any straight couple. There's differences between all kinds of marriages. I have a woman friend I grew up with. She and her husband have decided not to have children. As a couple, they're different from my sister and her husband, who've chosen to have three children. I don't know how you pinpoint the differences between gay marriages and straight marriages. They're all marriages but they're all different because of the different choices made by the different types of partners in the marriages. Society is more geared toward straight marriages. Therefore, the people in those marriages can feel more comfortable about being 'obviously' married. Society services straight marriages. Society doesn't support Rob and me, but that doesn't make us any less married."

"It's harder to have a gay relationship," argues Kate. "All of society works toward the perfect relationship—a heterosexual, legally married man and woman with children. Other than that, no matter what sex or age the people are, they have a lot in common in terms of establishing a relationship. We all have to build love and trust and commitment with our partners.

"Society plays a tremendous role in destroying gay relationships. Ann and I walk down the street: she wants to hold my hand, and I won't do it. I'm so constrained by these thousands of amorphous people who may see me and judge me a horrible creature. Society constantly pressures people to move toward what is best for the preservation of society—legally married units with children. And anyone who goes against that is made to feel there's something wrong with them. You think it's easy for straight couples who decide they don't want to have children?

"Gay couples certainly become pariahs. There are just so few places you can be free to be a couple. You dare not exhibit the love and affection you have for a woman in a heterosexual society. Social pressures cause a lot of miserable traits in gay people. You have to compensate for the oppression so you go to the other extreme. Gays develop an arrogant or defensive attitude because they know they're seen as freaks. You either thumb your nose at society . . . or you die."

"Love and understanding," says Bob, "are the priorities in our relationship. It's the same for straights. The other day Robert and I were looking at brochures on these little remote islands—out of this world and out of this rat race. Everyone, gays and straights, looks at it the same way—let's go back a couple of hundred years to the islands, let's get lost together for awhile. The world would be happier if we all slowed down. None of us, gays or straights, have enough time to think. We're always rushing around and we don't make the time to stand back and look at what our marriages are about. Look at the pace of gay and straight couples who are trying to raise children. Why are there so many divorces? We're not taking the time to sit back and ask ourselves what it's all about. As gay and straight couples, we have to take the time to resolve the little problems in our relationships—the plateaus. Get the plateaus out of the way and you're safe. I don't think there are any differences between gay and straight couples. As couples, we have to stick to the basics of marriage. That's the only way you can hold it together."

Both Beverly and Debra believe there are differences between gay and straight couples. "If you have two men or two women living together," explains Beverly, "you think you should do more things together because you're the same sex—that can create problems. It's accepted that a husband and wife will do different things."

"I see compatibility as a major difference," says Debra. "Because Beverly and I are the same sex, there are certain things we don't have to discuss. We're both women and we think the same way about certain things. I think two gay men can enjoy this same type of understanding and closeness."

Regarding similarities, Beverly says, "Gays and straights enjoy the same things: your sexual life, your free time together. We have the same problems as straight couples: external pressures, in-law problems, how you handle finances. We don't see our relationship any differently than we see straight relationships. Basically, we're as middle class as any straight couple in terms of our lifestyle and our values.

"My married sister," continues Beverly, "once told me my life with Debra is much the same as her life with her husband. My sister thinks Deb is very much like her husband, Bob. I think she's right. It doesn't have anything to do with being gay or straight. It's the way my sister and I were raised that makes us much the way we both are."

"Bob and I have talked about it," says Debra. "We've discussed 'the sisters' and how similar they are. He and I know opposites attract. Bob is a greater risk taker than Bev's sister. He's a manipulator and he maneuvers: he makes things turn out right. He and I will spend money. Bev and her sister are less willing to spend money, less willing to risk."

"I see differences," says Troy, "and I see similarities between gay and straight couples. A big difference is that gays are less frequently obliged 'to stay together.' Ed and I don't have the kids,

the high cost of divorce, the in-laws, and the financial entangle-
ments to keep us together. We also don't have all the support
systems that straights enjoy. I think gays have more career conflicts
than do straights. For every negative difference, there's a positive
difference. Gay in-laws can't and don't make the same claims and
demands which straight in-laws consider their prerogatives.

"As to similarities," Troy continues, "the making of the relationship is the same. Meshing lifestyles, friendships, tastes, goals: it's
two people coming together. Learning each other is the same—
when to yield the right-of-way to your partner; who shall 'parent'
whom and when and how and under what circumstances. We all,
gay or straight, deal with the same things: in-laws, loyalties,
commitments, liaisons—and, always, the division of labor within
the household."

"The most important difference to me," says Lisa, "is the
pressure gay couples suffer because we're not accepted by society.
We don't receive the same supports straight couples have. In many
cases, you have to live 'closeted,' and that's a terrible pressure on a
relationship. As far as similarities, Marje and I are no different
from any straight couple. We've got a lot of problems to work out.
And the problems aren't any different from the problems straights
have: financial, sexual, in-laws. It's the same for us as it is for any
straight couple. However, what's different is we don't have a lot of
the structures straights have to help them solve their problems. We
have to do it on our own and so it's harder for a gay couple to stay
together and make their relationship work."

"The big difference," argues Nancy, "is that heterosexual
relationships have validity built right into them. The support a
straight couple receives from society gives their relationship validity. No one gives gays anything. As a committed gay couple,
Charlotte and I have to establish our own validity, and it's hard
work. I'd like to see gay relationships recognized and acknowledged for what they are—two people working damn hard to make
their relationship work. Charlotte and I have a gay relationship and
we work at that, we don't work at emulating any heterosexual
model of what a relationship should be."

"The big similarity between a gay couple and a straight couple,"
explains Timothy, "is that we're all wishing for the same things. We
all want our relationships to last. We all want a home and a decent
life with the person we love. I think everyone, gay or straight, has

the same wishes and the same needs. Together, Angel and I are the same as anyone else."

"But straight couples," adds Angel, "are more worried about marriage licenses and divorces than we are. First, they worry about getting the license—that's the big thing. But then, if they split, they worry about who's getting what. For a gay couple, if they want to come together, they make the decision. If they want to split, they make the decision. I also think straight couples worry too much about roles—who's going to be the bigger breadwinner, who's going to stay home and take care of the kids, who's going to be the domineering person in the home. Now the man has got to be the bigger breadwinner, which means he's going to be the domineering person in the home. The woman has to stay home and take care of the kids. They've got all this stuff to worry about, and we don't have to worry about any of it."

Em smiles. "The most important similarity between gays and straights: staying in love with each other. Louise and I have that, but we've got to work at it. We've got our ups and downs but we know we've got to stay in love with each other because, if we do, we'll come out on top together no matter how rough the road gets.

"The other thing that's really important," Em continues, "is a hug. You're smiling at me, but hugging *is* important. Louise and I hug each other a lot, and we hug the boys. 'Cause, if you hug someone, they feel wanted and they feel loved."

"I knew I wanted love," Louise explains. "I knew I wanted to be hugged and wanted. Like I told you, I didn't have it when I was married to a man. I didn't know how to get it or find it until I fell in love with Em. That's the difference between a gay woman and a straight woman. It wasn't possible for me to have hugging and love with a man—it had to be with a woman. If a person is gay, like I am, you can't make them happy in a heterosexual relationship. Once I realized I was a lesbian, I followed that course. I'm not sorry for what I did, and I will never go back to being what I was. I belong loving a woman, this woman. I belong loving Em and loving her boys. I never really knew love until I entered into a lesbian relationship. That's the only difference—loving another woman."

• • •

When I queried Bishop Robert, he answered, *"People* love." And two people who love each other want and need a public acclamation and a public declaration of that love. The institutional churches enable straight couples to publicly acknowledge their love and their relationship. Gay people have the same need and the same desire to publicly declare their love and their relationship: the Holy Union Ceremony enables gay people to do just that. Gay people have just as much right as straight people to publicly acknowledge their love before God. If the couple is of God and of love, then they belong together. It's important to the church because we must acknowledge and bless all of God's love. The church is the means by which people can make a pledge to each other and publicly acknowledge their love of each other and their love of God. Jesus said, 'Feed my sheep.' And this is what we are doing here at Beloved Disciple through our Holy Union Ceremony. The Holy Union Ceremony can spiritually strengthen and feed the souls of two committed gay people who are floundering in this hideous mess of disapproval and prejudice."

Of the lesbians and homosexuals who responded to "Speak Out," 41 percent said commitment is the major similarity between gay and straight couples. Nineteen (19) percent feel companionship is the same for straight couples as it is for gay couples. Eighteen (18) percent wrote they believe the interpersonal relationship between two men or two women is the same as it is between a man and a woman. Among the other similarities cited by those completing the questionnaire: love; permanence; a shared emotional life; communication, mutual dependence.

Forty-seven (47) percent of the men and women who responded to "Speak Out" believe societal approval is the major *difference* between gay couples and straight couples. Sixteen (16) percent of the men and women responding believe the economic relationship between two men or two women is different from the economic relationship that exists between a man and a woman. Fourteen (14) percent of the men and women believe the interpersonal relationship that exists between two members of the same sex is different from the interpersonal relationship that exists between two members of the opposite sex. Regarding parenthood: 10 percent of the men and women see this as a difference between gay and straight couples. Other areas of difference cited were the inability to legally marry; lack of support systems for gay couples; the inability of a gay couple to have a child together; nonacceptance as a gay couple; the inability to show affection in public.

TURNING IT AROUND

Several years ago, an aunt and uncle celebrated their fiftieth wedding anniversary. They marked the occasion with a beautiful dinner for over 200 people. Of course, all their nieces and nephews and their respective husbands and wives were invited. Ranging in age from twenty-five to forty-five, we filled two adjacent tables. All my cousins were, of course, in couples. I was alone.

That night was probably one of the most important nights in my life. It was the first time in years I had been with my entire family at the same time. It was also the first time I had seen any of my relatives since my lesbianism had become "public" knowledge. I was scared. I did not know who knew or who did not know, who had heard or who had not heard.

These were my cousins I was sitting with, the other kids in the family with whom I had grown up. These were the people to whom I had never measured up. They all had married in the fifties and in the sixties, moved from Brooklyn apartments to Long Island and New Jersey suburban homes, increased and multiplied and filled the family with grandchildren. My own life had not evolved in the same way. I was always—even as a child—somehow different. They were "boy crazy" or "girl crazy"; I read a lot. They dreamed of big weddings; I wanted to go to college. They become engaged; I joined the army so I could become a writer. They married and settled down; I became a nun. When, at twenty-six, I realized my lesbianism, not only was I then just different than they were, but they were now *better* than I. I courted my inferiority and self-hate for seven years.

What I realized the night of the anniversary party was that while I was into my lesbian self-flagellation trip, my cousins had also suffered. Prior to that night, I had *known* about their problems because I had heard about what was happening to them. But seeing them all together that night, I saw them as they really are—not as the people I had idealized. Some arrived at the dinner with their second husbands or their second wives. I saw in some of their faces the unhappiness I had only heard whispered about. I knew of some of their marital problems and of their temporary separations. Some of them looked older than their years. Talking with several of them, I found they sounded tired and bitter. They laughed too loudly; they smiled too much. Throughout the evening, we talked about the past. Was it easier for us to talk about our collective past as we remembered it than to discuss the present as we each knew it?

Perhaps, I thought, sitting with them, *I'm not the only one in the family who can't talk about my present life.*

I sat facing a wall of mirrors with my back to the dance floor. I watched them, couple by couple, as they danced with their respective husbands and wives. I could see myself in the mirrors, but I could also see *them* as I had never been able to see them before. Looking at them in the mirrors, I could ask myself: *Why am I so different from them? Why are they better than I?* I realized my own life had not been as tumultuous as some of theirs. I realized my secrets and sins, if they were sins, were no worse than theirs. They had failed as I had failed. They mourned their broken dreams as I mourned my own. They had had problems and struggles as I had had problems and struggles.

Looking at my own reflection in the mirrors, I asked myself a question only I could answer. *Why have you tortured yourself for years? Because you're a lesbian?* I found myself laughing in my own face. *You stupid fool. Look at them: they're no different than you are. We're all only the illusions and images of what we're "supposed to be." Look at yourself when you look at them, you haven't done too badly. You're a good person, as they are good people. You're not better than they are, but goddamn, you're just as good. Your life has as much dignity and integrity—as much confusion—as any of theirs.*

"Goodbye, angst," I laughed, as I left the restaurant, walking into the midnight air. I was drunk with self-acceptance and self-actualization. It was a clear, cold January night. It was the beginning of a new year and a new life for me—I was free. I had left the anniversary party behind me. I had also left behind me all the mirages of people to whom I have never measured up. I had used society's yardstick to measure myself. And while society evaluates heterosexuals on the basis of their lifestyles, their values, and their achievements, it evaluates me, as a lesbian, only in terms of my sexual preference.

Now I would evaluate myself. I would measure myself based upon my life and my values. *Goddamn,* I thought, *they're as good as anybody else's. And I'm as good as anybody else. Society can continue to measure me as society chooses to continue measuring me. But they can take their yardstick and shove it because they haven't been using the same yardstick to measure me as they've been using to measure my cousins. And what's worse, I let them hand me their yardstick by which I then measured myself—then beat myself to death with it because I never measured up.*

Self-acceptance is like a delicate and fragile bud: if it is strengthened during a good spring, it will flower. I had a good spring that year. I became ill and I was afraid I was going to die— organ by organ. The possibility of one's own death has a tremendous way of putting life into perspective. If I was going to die, the only thing I was going to be sorry for was my ill-timed and premature death—*nothing else.* I would not be sorry for being a lesbian. I would not be sorry for the years of struggling to win my own self-acceptance and self-respect. I would not be sorry for never measuring up to society's standards, because society had clay feet just like me. Of all the things I would be happy about, the most important: I had loved and I had been loved. Well, I did not die. And as soon as I knew I was not going to die, I knew I would never again apologize to anyone for being who I am. Never again would I bend a knee to either religious or social values that are no better— nor any worse—than my own.

My self-acceptance gave birth to self-pride. I was no more proud of my lesbianism than someone else is proud of their heterosexuality. However, I was proud of myself as a decent and productive human being. I became proud of my life of which my lesbianism is a part. I had bought the ticket I was preconditioned to buy; by negatively focusing on my lesbianism, I had overlooked the merits and the quality of what was my total life. I had overlooked my goodness as a person because I was preoccupied with the secret of my badness: my lesbianism. Once I had accepted my lesbianism as an aspect of my personhood, I was free to look at what was the total picture of my life.

More and more, I began to feel I would take on any heterosexual who wanted to take me on—lifestyle for lifestyle, relationship for relationship, value for value. I became less and less afraid and less and less ashamed to measure my life against anyone else's. I had established me and everyone else on equal footing and at the same starting line. My lesbianism is not a "flaw" in my personality just as heterosexuality is not a "flaw" in someone else's personality. There are no handicaps, and no one gets or loses any extra points for anything.

I have continued to be proud of who I am. However, I have had a great deal of help along the way. Perhaps the greatest impetus to my growth has been this book. I am proud to be associated with the men and women interviewed within these pages. Their human dignity, their positive self-images, and their self-respect have helped to strengthen my own convictions and my own self-image.

GAYS and THEIR SELF-IMAGE

Because my lesbianism had made me feel less of a human being, I asked those I interviewed if they feel—or have ever felt—less of a man or a woman because they are gay.

• • •

"I've been a homosexual since I was twelve years old," says Paul. "I've never known a heterosexual relationship nor have I ever had a desire to. But I've never felt less of a man. God had His own reasons for having made me as I am. I feel I'm a better person because I've done the best I could with the life God has given me. I'm one of five children in my family, and I can honestly say of the five of us, I think I'm the happiest."

"At the beginning of my relationship with Paul," says Michael, "I did think of myself as less of a man. It's apparent to me now that I fought my homosexuality throughout my marriage to my wife. But I've come to grips with myself and who I am. Now I don't believe that sexual preference makes you less of a man or less of a woman. I no longer feel I'm less of a man because I'm a homosexual."

"The older I get the more I feel like a woman," says Kate. "And I've never felt less of a woman because I'm a lesbian or because I love Ann."

"I don't know how you define a woman," says Ann, "because it's been defined in heterosexual terms for so long. For myself, I'm a more complete person because of my relationship with Kate, and I don't know if I would feel this way with a man. But I definitely don't feel less of a woman because I'm a lesbian. I feel very complete."

"I don't feel less of a man because I'm a homosexual," Robert explains. "My generation was raised to believe that men don't do certain things: cooking, cleaning, etc. These are things I enjoy doing, and if that detracts from my manhood—well, that's one way of looking at it. But I don't look at it that way. I don't feel any less of a man. I like to cook but I also love stock car racing. I would love to have been a stock car racer. Does that make me manly? But then, I like to clean. I watch 'Wide World of Sports' every Sunday. Does that make me more of a man? I most often watch it with my sister. Does that make her more of a man? If it does, it's ridiculous because I know she's very heterosexual. Masculinity, manhood, womanhood—what's it all about anyway?"

"I certainly don't feel less of a man because I'm a homosexual," adds Bob. "I would have to agree with Robert: a lot of this manhood and womanhood nonsense is simply stereotyping people. If you behave a certain way, you're stuck in a certain role. My role is to act like myself, be myself: there's no way that could make me less than the man I am."

"My parents didn't raise me to be a woman, a man, a lesbian, a homosexual," says Debra. "When I was growing up at home, I was taught to believe I could go out and accomplish whatever I wanted to accomplish. Being a woman never interfered with what my parents taught me I could do as a person. That's how I was raised and that's why I have a hard time taking a subservient role to anyone because of anything. I've never felt less of a woman because I'm a lesbian. I am who I am."

"I've never felt less of a woman because I'm a lesbian," explains Beverly. "I don't see myself as being any different than I would've been had I been married to a man instead of being committed to Debra. I am the way I was raised to be. Yes, I've changed, but I haven't changed as a woman—I've changed as a person. Those changes I experienced as a result of the women's movement are the same changes that would have occurred had I been with a man."

"Less of a man?" Bob asks. "I feel much more of a man—not because I'm a homosexual but because I've come to grips with my sexuality. I am more of a person, therefore I am more of a man. Straight people have conceived of the stereotyped gay person. And I don't see myself as the straight world sees me. I just feel damn good about myself as a person."

"Look"—Rob shakes both of his hands at me—"neither of us have limp wrists. I'm a dancer but even *I* don't wear dresses. I've known I was a homosexual since I was twelve years old. I didn't feel less of a boy then because I was screwing every girl in the neighborhood. And I don't feel less of a man now. Bob and I love each other as two men."

"I don't even know how to answer that question," says Nancy, smirking. "I am a lesbian. How would I know what it feels like to be a nonwomanly lesbian? At one point, I thought of myself as less of a person because I was a lesbian, but never less of a woman. It was back in the early sixties. I went to a psychiatrist for three years. He was one of the few people back then who realized the validity of accepting yourself as yourself and not trying to change. Through him I began to appreciate myself as a person without changing my sexuality."

"As two women," adds Charlotte, "Nancy and I have a loving partnership. We have a shared faith life and a shared prayer life. We share our values as Christians. I don't feel less of anything because I am a lesbian."

"Definitely not," says Timothy. "I've never felt less of a man because I'm a homosexual. I don't feel any less masculine because I'm gay. I never even thought about it in those terms. Sometimes I even feel more masculine than some of my straight friends. This macho image is just a put-on, it's just an act. Angel has helped me see, especially because of his Cuban background, that macho is something you have to concentrate on being: it's not real, it's not natural."

"I was guilty about being gay," adds Angel, "and I did see myself as less of a man. In my culture, if you're a man you have sex with women. What does going to bed with a woman have to do with being a man? I now consider myself as much of a man as any men I know, whether they're heterosexual or homosexual. The words *man* and *woman* have to do with what sex a person is. They don't have anything to do with how a person loves. I love: I love Timothy. We have a sexual relationship. I love my friend Anna very much. She's gay and she helped me to accept and understand myself. But there is nothing sexual between us. Does that mean I don't love her? Does that mean I'm not a man because I don't have sex with this woman I love very much? My brother-in-law told me this love I have for Anna could turn into something sexual if I let it. Then I would go to bed with her and I would be a man. It all doesn't make sense to me. Feelings are the same for men and women—we love. But we love persons, not sexes, and we love different people differently."

"I don't feel less of a man," says Richard. "I love a person: Charles. That person happens to be a man, but I don't believe my loving him and the commitment we have makes me less of a man."

"No," adds Charles, "I don't feel any less of a man because I'm a homosexual. I never have. My homosexuality, my commitment to Richard, our trust and compatibility: it's all very natural to me. I don't see myself as less of a man. I think of myself as a useful and productive human being . . . a good citizen, a good person."

I LOVE—THEREFORE I FEAR

Fear, like love, does not distinguish between gay or straight. Happiness, like pain, does not know black or white. The texture of our emotional life is such that, when we do love and we are happy, we are afraid. The richer our lives become, the more we are threatened: we become more and more vulnerable to both real and unreal fears.

It was a school night; therefore, it was after nine when I came home. I noticed Valerie was wearing the same clothes she had worn that morning for work. When I kissed her hello, she held me too long and too tightly for a casual, "Hi, I'm home. How was your day?" I noticed, too, that she was not looking at me. The doorbell rang. It was Kathy and Steve, the couple next door. Rather than letting them into the apartment, Valerie stood in the hallway talking to them in a whisper. I was sitting on the couch when she came back into the apartment. It was then that I saw her scraped legs, her torn hose.

"Did you fall?" I asked. "What happened to your legs?"

"I was pushed," she answered, still not looking at me.

"What's wrong?" I asked, cupping her face in my hands so she could no longer avoid my eyes. "Tell me," I said. "What happened?"

Sitting next to me on the couch, she explained she had been mugged and robbed in front of the apartment by eight teenage girls. She was very calm as she spoke. I could feel my hands turn ice cold; my stomach was in knots. I held her as she finished her story.

"I didn't want to give them my pocketbook, my personal things, so I gave them my money and then they grabbed me and pushed me down the steps. By the time I could get myself up, they were running away. The woman on the first floor came home and helped me clean up the lobby. We don't have milk for coffee in the morning."

I found myself holding her and rocking back and forth as we sat on the couch. I was clinging to her for life—for dear life. I lay next to her in bed that night watching her sleep. I touched her face, her hair. I ran my fingers along the shadows on her cheeks. On and off throughout the entire night, I would doze off and wake up, sometimes cold, sometimes sweating. *Dear God,* I thought, *in a minute a bunch of anonymous punks could have taken her life, taken her away from me, taken me away from her. They never would have even known or cared who she was.*

I realized during that long night that all the previous phantoms of my mind had become a reality in the form of eight teenage girls. During the time we had been together, the happier I became with Valerie, the more afraid I became of losing her. And even within my fear of losing her, the blind hope: I will never lose her. People are attacked and killed every day on the streets of our cities. And yet it was inconceivable to me that anyone would dare touch her or hit her. It seemed incomprehensible, absurd. But how could I possibly think we were untouchable, that it could not happen to us?

Loving does not protect us from loss. And it is loving that makes loss an ever-present threat. I asked the men and women I interviewed, "What is your greatest fear?"

• • •

"In the past," answers Michael, "my biggest fear was that homosexual relationships weren't taken seriously. I wanted the same serious relationship as I'd had with my wife while we were married. My life with Paul has helped me to believe that a homosexual marriage can have the same depth, fidelity, and permanence as a heterosexual marriage. Now my biggest fear is our health. I don't have a good track record regarding health. Paul is a borderline diabetic—that's why I was so afraid of his drinking. My biggest fear now is losing Paul through illness."

"My biggest fear," Paul says, sighing, "is to be without Michael. I constantly worry. He's on the road a lot and I'm afraid of an automobile accident. I'm constantly pressuring him to drive safely, to make certain the car is in good operating order. What would I do if he died? What would I do if he just didn't come home from work someday? I can't even think about it, it's devastating to me. At this point, I feel I would commit suicide. I would not want to live without him."

"My greatest fear," explains Debra, "is being out of control of what's happening to me, being in situations where I can't take care of myself. I try to plan things so I'm always in control. I expect to outlive Beverly."

"I'm not afraid of losing Debra," says Beverly, "because she's right: she's going to outlive me. My biggest fear is my own death because I haven't come to grips with dying yet: I want to live forever."

"We're aware that death is one of those things that *is* going to happen," continues Debra. "Beverly is always dying of something: the other day it was lockjaw. There's nothing between lockjaw and cancer. I think our relationship is going to go on forever. Beverly will die before me, but not much before—and I'm going to live until I'm eighty-five. Then I plan to terminate my own life so I can be in control of my own death."

"My greatest fear," explains Robert, "is being left alone without Bob. We're still young now. But what if I were to lose him, my spouse, when I'm fifty? How would I go through the rest of my life, even if it were only twenty years, without him? My biggest fear used to be my own dying. Now my biggest fear is Bob's dying."

"That's it," agrees Bob, "losing the person you love and the person you share your life with. The person you make all those plans with. That's my biggest fear: losing Robert . . . spending the rest of my life without him."

"When Ann is away," Kate says, "I think, what if she died, if I lost her? That's my greatest fear in terms of our relationship. Sometimes I think: what if I died, if she lost me? Then I feel terrible. I feel so sad because she would be hurt and because she would be alone."

"I'm afraid of Kate dying," says Ann. "I don't know how I would adjust to her death because she's so much a part of my life. What would I do? It would be a double loss because so much of me would die with her. I'm a survivor and I know I'd survive, but it would be awfully hard."

"If Troy were to die," explains Ed, "it would be a tremendous adjustment. I would go through many of the same problems as a heterosexual man who loses his wife. We've been together twenty-five years: there's no way to explain the emotional impact of that loss. I think when a husband or wife dies, a lot of the unfulfilled hopes or the unresolved problems create pain. I think that's what mourning is: an attempt to come to terms with all that is now and can never be fulfilled or resolved. Add to that, of course, the fear of being old and being alone."

"I used to think," says Troy, "that the possibility of my dying was outrageous, that the great 'me' would cease to exist was absurd. Now my survival doesn't seem that important to me. Now it's losing Ed, losing my friends. I want me and everyone else to die in our sleep. I don't like the idea of pain and suffering, and I like it less in terms of my loved ones and my friends. I don't want to watch people I love wither away and die in pain. My fear is that it seems to be happening more and more."

"That Charlotte and I might die," explains Nancy, "without having known our full potential as human beings: that's my greatest fear for both of us. That we might die too soon, never having realized or satisfied our individuality or our personhood: that's what I'm afraid of."

"Loneliness," says Lisa, sighing, "is my biggest fear. That threat: maybe things won't work out for Marje and me, and I will be alone." Marje adds: "That's it for me too. My greatest fear is loneliness: the loneliness that comes with having failed in a relationship."

7

EXIT 8: *Gay Divorce*

Ι t was a Sunday morning. Nothing had happened that weekend that had not happened before, that would not happen again: the conflicts, the struggling, the tearing each other apart. I knew it was over: I knew I would leave Paula. There was only pain and a terrible sense of failure. I loved her that Sunday morning as I am sure I will always love her. But even though I loved her, I knew I could not—would not—continue to live with her. You can love someone and yet intuitively know you cannot go on living with that person: love is simply not enough. Our relationship, I believed, had become destructive to both of us.

I could hear Paula dressing upstairs. We had not slept together the night before, as we had not slept together on many other nights. *She's no longer who and what I need, I thought. And I'm no longer who and what she needs. We are as we have become, and neither of us is going to change. And is it worth it for either of us to become something we're not just to keep the marriage together? Paula is Paula, I can accept and understand her, but I don't want to spend the rest of my life with her. I don't want to go on living as we've been living. I'd rather be alone than go through this.*

Sunlight streamed through the living room windows. The forsythia bushes were just beginning to bud. The ground was thawing. I sat on the couch looking at our home: I would leave it, and I would leave Paula for the last time. It was a silent decision: a decision I would never waiver in during the months that followed— a decision I would never regret. I believed I was doing the right thing for both of us. I stared at the dining room set we had picked out together when we had bought the house. I looked at the drapes, the new rocking chair pillows. Everything I looked at hurt. Everywhere I looked I saw pain. These were *our* things. They would now become *her* things and *my* things.

When your marriage ends, it is not the tangible house you sell; it is not the furniture you divide between the two of you. It is the broken dreams, the lost hopes, the plans that will never become a reality. The house represents something you tried to build together. And yet you know, no matter what it costs, for the sake of your own survival you must walk away.

Sitting there in the living room, I remembered many things and I wondered about many things. Paula and I had known each other for over two years before we became lovers. It was a first relationship for both of us: we had "come out" together. During our first years as lovers there had been no commitment. I dated other people, both men and women. But no matter whom I was seeing or sleeping with, there was always Paula. I might have been involved or infatuated with other people, but I loved Paula.

When finally we made a commitment to each other, it was a marriage for both of us. And now I sat on the couch wondering where our marriage had "gone wrong." How had we grown so far apart? What had happened to the love both of us had believed would last a lifetime? Had we both changed so much during the nine years we had known each other that we had become strangers? Had I changed so much that she could no longer be the person with whom I would share my life? No one was to blame: our divorce was not her fault, nor was it my fault. A marriage is not ended because of a divorce. A marriage is ended by a slow process of deterioration to which both partners contribute. Then one or both partners lose hope, therefore divorce.

The house was sold and I returned to Manhattan. It was weeks after I moved into my apartment before I began to unpack. I would come home in the evening, stare at the cartons awhile, and decide not to begin unpacking. I was afraid to see what was inside of the cartons: gifts she had given me, things we had bought for the house, something of hers I might have packed by mistake. About two months after I had returned to Manhattan, I had a business trip. Without thinking, I rented a car and began the long drive to the meeting site. Suddenly, before I realized it, I was at Exit 7 on the parkway. I panicked. The next exit was Exit 8: this was where Paula and I had lived together, this was the turnoff to our house, this was where I had failed, where I had lost. As I drove past Exit 8, I began to cry. I turned off the parkway at Exit 9, stopped the car, and sat there crying. I did not know who I was anymore. I did not know what I wanted or what I needed. I did not know what to do with my pain. I could not believe our home still existed right off Exit 8. I could not believe someone else was actually living in our house. How could other people possibly be living in our home? You mourn a lost marriage as you would mourn a lover who has died. And perhaps it is during this period of mourning that people begin to redefine their lives, their needs, and their direction. Perhaps it was passing so close to the gravesite that forced me to acknowledge and absorb the fact that my marriage was truly over. Only then could I begin to rebuild my life.

Now, almost four years later, I still find myself sighing whenever I pass Exit 8 on the parkway—where Paula and I used to live. I do not cry anymore, but I still feel a sense of sadness and a sense of loss. When you have spent any number of years of your life loving a person—building, growing, and sharing—that person remains a part of you even though you live apart.

"OUR INCOMPATIBILITY: HIS WAS A MARRIAGE OF NEED; MINE, A MARRIAGE OF WANT. I WANTED HIM, BUT HE NEEDED ME."

Bernie, in his early thirties, is a Ph.D. research scientist. He and his ex-lover, Tom, met in a hospital where Bernie was a patient.

"I'd had a back injury," Bernie explains. "Tom was an orderly in the hospital, and we became friends. It was after I got out of the hospital that we became lovers. We lived together for seven years."

"What is your definition of a marriage, Bernie?"

"To me, a marriage is a total commitment whereby every facet of my life is committed to the other person. It's a relationship wherein I would do most anything for the other person without any reservations whatsoever. If I had any reservations, it wouldn't be a marriage, because I wouldn't be totally committed. It could be a comfortable ongoing relationship, but not a marriage based on my own definition."

"Did you consider your relationship with Tom a marriage?"

"In all outward appearances, it was a marriage. Other people looking at us would've considered it a marriage. But because of the way I felt inside, it wasn't a marriage: at no time did I think it would last forever. I always knew that unless we could overcome the problems the two of us had, it wasn't going to last. I always worked toward resolving the problems, but never did I believe they would be resolved to a point whereby I would be satisfied with the relationship."

"What were the problems?"

"Sex was a problem. We most often had no sex life together. Yet he was constantly having sex with friends and strangers. He was into bathrooms and roadside rests. I don't think his tricking around affected the love he had for me. Nor did it affect the love I had for him. His having sex with other men interfered with our having a one-to-one relationship. His need for a variety of sexual partners was in itself not the problem. Had we had a good sexual life together, I probably could have become comfortable with some of the other problems. When I entered the relationship with Tom, I made a commitment to him, and I strongly believed in that commitment. He was honest—he told me he couldn't make the same type of commitment to me I had made to him. He wasn't monogamous. Although I wanted a monogamous relationship, I didn't practice monogamy during my years with him. I thought if I were having outside sex, it would somehow balance out the relationship so that we could better deal with his outside sexual activities. I was prepared to have either a monogamous or a nonmonogamous relationship. However, I knew the roots of the problems were much deeper than the sexual dimension of our relationship."

"What were the roots of the problem?"

"I think the roots of the problem were his constant need to trick. It was more than just satisfying sexual needs. There was something he needed which wasn't being supplied at home. I asked him about it, but I don't think even he understood it. I told him if there was something out there that would make him happier, he should leave me and go out and try to find it. But he never would."

"Bernie, if this went on for seven years, why did you stay with him?"

"Well, that brings me to another problem. Tom was a functional illiterate: he could not read nor write very well. His illiteracy created a lot of problems for him in his own mind. I kept making excuses for those problems. I believed if I was patient with him, if I tried to help him and understand him, we'd get to the roots of his personal problems. And then, knowing what they were, we'd be able to deal with them. But we never got to the roots of things. He agreed to be evaluated at a psychological evaluating center. The center determined that his problem was related to his fine motor controls. His gross motor controls were good, and the center believed they could work on his fine motor control and raise his literacy skills to a point where he would be able to function rather normally in society: read a newspaper, complete a job application."

"Bernie, wait—stop. Let's look at this: you have your doctoral degree, you function in a very sophisticated world, you're upper-income level. What were you doing? What needs of yours were being satisfied by such an unequal relationship?"

"I believed that when you made a commitment to someone, it was forever. I can't go into a relationship and then, when things go wrong, just get out. I believe you work at it and try to make it work out."

"For seven years? You took traditional standards on marriage and divorce and applied it to your relationship with Tom?"

"That was part of it. My other need or belief was that when you are with somebody you can experience their side of life no matter how different or similar it is to your own. It didn't matter to me that Tom was not my intellectual equal, that we could not discuss philosophy or whatever together. Through him I was able to experience, appreciate, and understand a dimension of life I'd never been exposed to. I loved him, and, as I experienced his life, I wanted him to experience the side of life I could show him."

"How did you and Tom function socially as a couple?"

"My friends were constantly telling me he wasn't right for me. They thought I could do better. But whether or not I could do better wasn't the point. I didn't believe in ending the relationship because we were incompatible. I think it's very difficult to find someone you're totally compatible with. I think you need patience, understanding, and communication in any relationship. I felt I had a lot I could offer. I guess I was hoping I could supply the added attributes that would hold the relationship together—and I did for seven years."

"What finally ended the relationship? Was it a mutual decision? What happened?"

"Sex. I come from a sexually oriented family. Although sex is a very minor part of life, when it isn't given freely from one partner to another, it can cause severe problems. It took two years for the relationship to finally end. We hardly had any sex life together. I believed that I loved him and that the physical attraction I had for him was caused by the love I felt for him. I desired him but he didn't desire me. I don't want to feel I'm forcing sex or anything else on someone. I tried to talk to him. I told him, 'If you don't get turned on by me, or if I turn you off in some respect, tell me what it is and we can try to work it out. Let's end it or let's work it out.' We argued about it, he would promise to change. The promise would be good for a while and then we'd be back to where we were. We'd fight, he'd promise me things would be different. They'd be different for a while, and then we'd be back to where we were again.

"Finally, I decided it was over. He was working part time as a janitor and going to school at the psychological testing center. I was supporting him. I told him I would continue to support him if he'd pay for fees—no more than forty dollars a week at the center. We tried to continue living together as a divorced couple but it didn't work. Then he dropped out of school, and that was it. I told him I wanted him to leave, but he wouldn't. He wanted a thousand-dollar settlement from me, which I wouldn't give him. So he sold over fifteen hundred dollars worth of furniture in the house. One night he came in with three or four friends—they were drunk. They literally wrecked the house. I called the police the next day, and when he realized I was serious, that was finally the end of it."

"Okay, you had a seven-year relationship with Tom. Within that time you had certain irreconcilable problems. Were they exclusively gay problems or were they human problems?"

"I think the basic problems were human problems. In terms of the exclusively gay dimension, I'd have to say that the availability of outside sexual partners is uniquely gay. If we'd been a straight couple—say, Tom was the husband—he simply wouldn't have had the freedom to be tricking with twenty different women. A husband who tries that would never get away with that type of behavior. He'd suffer the consequences of it. His wife would probably never tolerate it, he'd be under pressure from his family and his in-laws. I think Tom's behavior is much more tolerated in gay society than it would be tolerated by straight society were he a heterosexual married man."

"Are you saying that the availability of free sex is exclusively enjoyed by gay men? Or is it men in general? If we could eliminate screaming wives and irate in-laws, do you think a straight man having marital problems would behave as Tom behaved?"

"I'm a man, and I think men in general, gay and straight, are more susceptible to tricking—whether they're tricking with other men or with women. I think the degree to which a man tricks is based upon the availability of sex and upon the threat of censure. There may be more pressure on straight men in terms of restricting this kind of behavior, but then, I think straight men go underground—it's restricted to business trips. There's a lot more freedom for gay men, and a lot more availability. A gay man doesn't have a wife waiting at home with dinner on the stove. So if he wants to trick on his way home from work, there's the freedom of time and the freedom from censure. I think straight men would act much in the same way."

"You're talking about the lifestyle of gay men. Have you ever felt less of a man because you're a homosexual?"

"Never, not at all. And that's probably because of my aversion to roles of any kind. I don't think it's good to be all masculine or all feminine. I don't even like having to use the words *masculine* and *feminine*. What we've done is label traits as either masculine or feminine. I think it's important to have a well-balanced personality which encompasses many traits—and not assign a gender to those traits. My masculinity, personality, self-image, or whatever has never been threatened by my homosexuality or what role I might play in bed."

"Do you believe a third party breaks up a relationship between two people?"

"Absolutely not. No third party can break up a relationship between two people. The two people cause whatever problems they have, and that's what allows a third party to work his way into the relationship. I never felt any animosity toward any of the people Tom slept with. It wasn't their fault: these were problems which existed between Tom and me. If two people love each other, if they have a good relationship: no way can a third party break up that relationship. If there is something wrong in a relationship between two people, a third party comes between them only because of the defects in their relationship."

"After seven years in a relationship that ended in divorce, what did you learn, Bernie?"

"A lot of things: some negative, some positive. I'll be less likely to be so giving in a future relationship. I learned it's important to withdraw a little bit so I won't be hurt this way again. You know, Mary, I was only twenty-one when I became involved with Tom. As for positive aspects: you live and you share with someone for seven years. I'm a scientist. I don't judge experiences as bad or good—just as experiences to learn from and appreciate. I think you can grow and learn a lot about life even from bad experiences. I don't regret my years with Tom. I don't feel I made a mistake by staying in the relationship with him as long as I did. Nor do I feel I made a mistake when I finally ended it. I did what I had to do at that time. However, I know enough to know I will never repeat a one-way relationship again. I think in the future I would try to better protect myself emotionally by not becoming too involved too soon. I'd probably be more demanding in a relationship—I'd have certain expectations. I would be more selective about a partner. I'd want someone who could cope with life situations and also someone who liked himself. I don't think Tom ever liked himself. I think now I'd be able to more quickly detect a person who didn't like himself and who didn't love himself. And I'd get out sooner."

"Do you still believe you can have a permanent ongoing relationship with someone?"

"Do you mean have I become so jaded as a result of my relationship with Tom that I wouldn't be able to have the type of relationship I wanted when I committed myself to Tom? I do believe I can have the type of relationship I want—absolutely. I'm looking for a primary relationship. I'm looking for a person I can share and spend the rest of my life with."

"And you believe such a relationship is possible for you as a homosexual?"

"Very definitely. I believe such a relationship is possible for me as a gay man. I think it's something very precious and it doesn't happen to many people in their lifetime. I think I'll be able to recognize it when it happens to me, and I'll hold on to it for dear life. Getting to know someone goes on for a lifetime, and that's the fun of a relationship. It's also important that you never really get to know that person totally. It's learning from him and with him for the rest of your life. Such a relationship is possible for me, and I don't think it has anything to do with being gay or straight."

"IT GOT TO A POINT WHERE I HAD TO GET AWAY FROM HER."

Bonnie and Linda had been together for almost ten years. After dating each other for four months, Bonnie and Linda moved into an apartment. A year later, they bought a suburban home.

"It was a beautiful relationship," says Linda, sighing. "We were two people who loved each other very much. We were friends—we shared a lot. We loved our home and taking care of it. We had a good and healthy sexual life together. Never during our ten years together was I ever with anyone else. She trusted me completely because she knew how much I loved her. And I trusted her completely. I can only hope now that she was as faithful to me as I was to her. I loved her, but when I realized that love was turning to hate, I left."

"What happened, Linda?"

"I became ill, and in the beginning I didn't even know it. I was always tired, always sleeping. It got to be a joke: we'd go to someone's house for dinner and I'd fall asleep. My tiredness began to affect my personality. Bonnie kept insisting I go to a doctor. Our friends were constantly pressuring me to go to a doctor. But I wouldn't go: I resented the idea that I could be sick. Finally, I yielded and went to a general practitioner. He couldn't find anything wrong with me. I was still exhausted all the time. He advised me to see a specialist, and, of course, I wasn't going to rush into that. I simply wouldn't accept the fact that there was something seriously wrong with me."

"Linda, what are we talking about in terms of time? How long was it between your becoming ill and the point at which your medical problem was diagnosed and treated?"

"About nine months. Bonnie would want to do something and I was simply too tired. I didn't have the strength. When I went to bed, I would kiss her good night and that was it. She would try to stimulate me sexually, but nothing would arouse me. I didn't have any energy at all. I wish she'd been a little more tolerant: she recognized that I was ill even if I wouldn't accept it. But I don't blame her for it—I blame myself."

"And after your illness was diagnosed and you were improving, did you try to work things out?"

"It was too late. Bonnie had met a younger woman. Bonnie and I are both in our early forties. Bonnie is an attractive and intelligent woman, so she had no difficulty finding the personal and sexual satisfaction she needed somewhere else. However, it would've been easier if she were just sexually involved with this younger woman; but she was also emotionally involved. It was difficult for her to separate herself from this woman when I started to get better."

"What broke up the relationship: your illness, the younger woman?"

"Neither. My pride destroyed the relationship. As far as breaking up, it was the last thing in the world I wanted. But when I found out she'd been seeing someone else, it was the most crushing blow I've received in my life. I just couldn't believe or tolerate it. Even though I'd become physically capable of having sex again, I didn't want anything to do with her. I was so hurt that she'd do this to me, knowing that I was sick. We continued living in the house together, but I'd sleep on the couch. Then I started drinking a lot so I could sleep, so I wouldn't have to hear her coming in at all hours of the night."

"Linda, what kind of pride do you have? You and Bonnie had had a good life together for ten years."
"It was more than my pride, Mary. I was so hurt. It took everything I had for me to realize my love for her was so much more important than my pride. I realized that by not going to the proper doctors, I had contributed to this thing. I was as much to blame as she was. I knew I wanted her back badly enough to give it another try. She promised me on a Sunday night that she'd give up the other woman. But then, she didn't come home at all Monday night. She didn't want to lose me, but either she wasn't ready or she wasn't strong enough to give up the love she had with this other person. It was a different type of love than she had for me, but, whatever it was, she wasn't giving it up."

"What happened after that?"
"She again promised me she'd give up this other woman. But I didn't believe her and I was right. She continued seeing her. Things started to get pretty vicious. I was afraid I was becoming an alcoholic. She was constantly on my mind and I was going nuts. I knew I had to straighten myself out and I knew I had to get away from her. I was afraid something bad was going to happen. It was after she broke her second promise that she asked me to go to a marriage counselor with her. But I was beyond that point.

"In order for me to survive, I had to get away from her and give up the house and everything I loved. When I say 'the house'— Bonnie was the house to me: it represented everything we had built together. In leaving her I left all those things I most treasured in my life. But I had to do it because nothing was worth the hatred I was feeling toward her."

"Emotionally, what did you experience after you moved out of the house?"
"Relief. I was relieved to get away from her. Getting away from her was the most important thing to me."

"Why was it so important?"

"The situation had become so intense. I felt sick when I left, but I knew what I was doing. I didn't know then that it would probably become, for me, the sorriest day in my life. I probably should've stayed in our home. If I'd stayed, either of two things would have happened: we would have killed each other, or we would've worked it out. I did what I thought was the most logical thing: I left. I was afraid of some sort of violence, and I wanted to leave before that happened."

"When you left, did you feel like a failure?"

"I didn't feel like a failure and I still don't. But at the time, rather than watch everything be destroyed, it was much easier for me to move out."

"Between the time you realized Bonnie was involved with someone else and the point you actually moved out, what are we talking about in terms of time?"

"About a year, and it was hell. I stayed in the house and withdrew into a shell. I guess I was hoping that we could still get back together again. Oddly enough, I did meet a woman that summer. I was honest with her—she knew I didn't want to get emotionally involved. I spent weekends with this woman. She kept me from going completely crazy. My relationship with this woman was going to be a fun thing, and that's exactly what it was. My heart still belonged to Bonnie—I loved her so much."

"And when you finally moved out, what did you then feel for Bonnie?"

"It was terrible, but I hated her. I hated her for doing what she'd done to me. I'd planned so much—I'd built my whole future around her. She was my life: I actually lived for her. I did everything I could to make her happy. And it hadn't been one-sided, either. I knew she loved me. But all my love turned to hate. Later that hate turned to resentment.

"Eventually, she started coming around. We went out for dinner several times. I realized I didn't hate her—I could never hate her. Even the resentment vanished. I knew I'd been to blame for what had happened. I should've listened, gotten proper medical care sooner. Maybe our breakup could have been prevented. For a while we saw each other occasionally: shopping, antique hunting. We'd always been good friends throughout our years together. Our friendship was rekindled, salvaged. But we never became lovers again. Eventually, the younger woman she was involved with moved into the house. But they've since broken up—Bonnie is living alone."

"Linda, in terms of what happened to you and Bonnie, do you believe your divorce was because of exclusively gay problems?"

"What happened to us could've happened to anyone: two men, two women, a man and a woman. Our relationship didn't end because we were gay. It ended because of some very unfortunate incidents that seemed to get out of control."

"It's two years since you left the home you and Bonnie had shared for almost ten years. Where are you now? Would you consider a reconciliation with Bonnie? Remarrying, so to speak?"

"I'm selfish to the extent that I don't want her to be happy unless it's with me. I've thought about going back to her, but I don't know. I still love her. Perhaps I'd go back with her, but I don't know under what terms. I think we could be friends, but I don't know if the love of lovers could be rekindled again. At this point in my life I would have to say that Bonnie and I might never be able to be lovers again."

"What did you learn from the experience, Linda? What would you do differently?"

"I sure learned my pride is a little bit much—too much. I learned I should be more human. I won't allow myself to ever again be as vulnerable to anyone as I was to Bonnie. I was hurt too much and I'll never put myself in a position where it can happen again. I also learned that you can only trust yourself. I don't want any commitment, and I'm not looking for any permanent relationship. I'm damned frightened of relationships like I had with Bonnie. I put everything I had into it. It was too many years to be with someone, to feel you had everything, to feel you knew the person— and then to find out you really didn't know her and she really didn't know you."

"THE MAJOR CONFLICT BETWEEN US WAS MONOGAMY."

Charles, in his late twenties, is a registered nurse. When he first met Phil, a minister, Phil was married and living with his wife and children.

"We were lovers for five years. During our first three years," Charles explains, "Phil lived with his wife, I had my own apartment, and we shared a third residence: an apartment in another nearby city. He'd live a week with his wife and a week with me. When I first met him he made it very clear he wouldn't divorce his wife. But then she asked him for a divorce and he agreed. He left the ministry after his divorce, and during the two years we lived together, he practiced law. He's since returned to the ministry."

"Would you define your relationship with Phil as a marriage, Charles?"

"Not during our first three years together when he was still living with his wife. After his divorce, during the two years we lived together, I considered myself married to him. To me, marriage is a commitment between two people. I think it should be a closed relationship. I believe in monogamy—two people building a relationship with no third parties involved."

"Why do you think your marriage with Phil failed?"

"The main issue was monogamy. I found out that he had another lover, a man, in another city. He was being sexually unfaithful."

"Sexual infidelity can be a sign of other problems in a relationship. Do you think there were other problems?"

"The underlying problem was probably the lack of communication between us. He had to have a separate business phone in the apartment, and I wasn't supposed to answer it. I lived there and I felt I should be able to answer both phones. But it wasn't the phone—it was what my not being allowed to answer the phone did to my self-esteem and self-image. But you know, Mary, as much as that phone bothered me, we never discussed it. Then, when I found out he was involved with someone else, we never discussed that either. It all just built up over a period of time—all the big and little problems we never discussed. Once I knew he had another lover: it was all downhill from there. Communications broke down on an important issue—his other lover. And then we stopped discussing anything and everything else."

"What did Phil's having another lover represent to you, Charles?"

"I lost trust in him and I never could get it back. Trust is a big issue with me, and I wanted to be able to trust him. If he was away on business, I was always suspicious after I found out about this other man. Sexual fidelity is important to me because it was a big part of our love."

"Why is sexual fidelity so important to you, Charles?"

"Sexual fidelity involves a very deep level of intimacy between two lovers. It's not so much the act of sex I resent sharing: it's the intimacy. I felt that because he had another lover, the personal intimacy we'd had together was lost. I think sexual intimacy is a personal thing between two people and I don't think it should be shared."

"How did Phil respond to your attitudes on sexual fidelity? Did he share your feelings?"

"When we first came together, he wanted the same type of relationship that I did. But he had a broader range—he could deal with both. He felt he could give me love and everything else I needed and also have outside relationships. I think having more than one person was a big part of his self-image. He'd always had two people. He had his wife and he had me. He had me and he had another man. He still maintains a very unusual relationship with his wife even though she's remarried."

"Are we talking about a difference in values on the question of sexual fidelity?"

"I think that was the basic conflict between us. Toward the end we argued about everything, but sexual fidelity was the basic issue. He had his point of view and I had mine. I couldn't live with his system of values. To me, it was pointless to go on. He wanted us to continue in the relationship, but I just couldn't. I couldn't even have sex with him anymore."

"What was that about? Why couldn't you have sex with him?"

"Well, when I knew he had another lover, I started seeing other men. I couldn't have sex with my lover and go out with other men. I felt guilty about not maintaining the monogamous relationship to which I'd committed myself. I get that from my very religious background. I believe in monogamy. Once that was gone, I began seeing other men. I couldn't have sex with Phil."

"Did you and Phil try to do anything to reconcile your differences regarding sexual fidelity?"

"We maintained our relationship for about a year after I found out about this other man. I tried doing what he wanted, living it his way. But we didn't have sex together during that period. That's when I started seeing other people. The final decision to end the relationship was mine. Our commitment had failed. We'd committed ourselves to a monogamous relationship. Neither one of us was any longer monogamous. I couldn't see continuing."

"Charles, do you think a third party breaks up a relationship? For instance, when you found out about the first man Phil was involved with, did that first man break up the relationship?"

"No, I don't think so. I don't think a third party breaks up a relationship. I'd felt his indifference and his insensitivity toward me for a long time before I found out about the other man. There seemed to be other things that were more important to him than our maintaining a stable relationship."

"Did you believe, after Phil left his wife, that your relationship with him was a permanent relationship?"

"I considered it a marriage, but I never considered it permanent. He didn't really want to divorce his wife because he wanted to stay with his children. Somehow I was never secure within the relationship. I never felt it would last a lifetime. And, of course, when I found out he was involved with another man, I was very threatened."

"How did you feel after you left Phil?"

"A lot of mixed feelings. I was disappointed that it didn't work. I felt I'd probably never have a permanent relationship with anyone. For a while I thought it would be better to have a variety of sexual partners. I was afraid of another relationship because my relationship with Phil had been so disappointing. I was hurt. It was also damaging to my own self-esteem because I'd made a commitment and it hadn't worked."

"Did you feel like a failure because your relationship with Phil didn't work?"

"I felt it was a failure on both our parts. If we'd communicated with each other, we might have been able to solve our problems. If we had sat down and talked to each other, reasoned with each other, maybe I could've given in some, he could've given in some. I think if we had just talked, we would've been able to work things out and we'd still be together. It was a failure on my part not to initiate this type of communication between us."

"Why didn't you initiate these conversations?"

"Probably because I was afraid of the truth. It was fear of his actually telling me he'd been with other men. I was afraid of having to cope with that. And also, I didn't want him to see this other side of me. I didn't want him to know I had these deep feelings about fidelity and intimacy. It was too personal to even share with him. I felt they would scare him away and then I'd have to deal with that.

I'm passive and I'm too flexible and I was afraid for him to see that."

"You said before you were turned off to permanent relationships after you left Phil. But you're involved now in trying to build another permanent relationship. What made you believe again?"

"I really don't know what made me believe again. I wasn't looking for another permanent relationship—it just happened. Somehow I let it develop. I gave having a permanent relationship another try; and at the same time, I'm trying to be more open, to communicate better."

"After your relationship with Phil, what did you learn for the future in terms of how you now define what you want and what you need?"

"I've learned I've got to be more open with myself and more openly express my feelings to my partner. I've learned that it's hard for two people to live together and adjust to each other—you have to establish what are your habits and you have to get used to your partner's habits and his lifestyle. You have to give and take. You have to accept your partner for who he is and he has to accept you for who you are. Then you grow together from there. You grow as two individuals and you grow in terms of maintaining your relationship. You both learn from each other and you both come out better people."

"How does a healthy relationship enable someone to become a better person?"

"For me, if I'm in a happy and healthy relationship, I can feel more secure. I'm not afraid of losing my lover. I'm not afraid of the different points of view we may each have. If I'm secure with my lover and, say, I have a certain prejudice, I'll be free to express that prejudice. And then maybe my lover can show me a better perspective."

"Even a better perspective on sexual fidelity? Do you think homosexuals are more open to discussing sexual fidelity than say a heterosexual male married to a woman?"

"Yes, I think male homosexuals are more open to discussing sexual fidelity. And if both men agree on an open relationship, that's fine. It's a decision made between two consenting adult men who can both deal with an open marriage. I think straight couples should have the same type of openness regarding their sexual lives—whether or not a man or a woman wants a sexually exclusive

or a sexually open relationship. For me, I want monogamy. I want
a one-to-one relationship with my partner. It has to do with what I
believe about love, what I believe about the kind of intimate
relationship I want. In terms of my security as a person, it's what I
need."

"Have you ever felt less of a man because you're a homosexual?"
"I've never felt less of a man because I'm a homosexual. I was
born a man and I don't feel any less of a man because I love men. I
also love women, but in a different way than I love men. That
doesn't make me less of a man. I love men sexually, but I don't love
women sexually."

*"Are you saying that the love that leads to sexual intimacy is what
you experience with men and not with women?"*
"Yes. My emotional preference is toward men and it has been
since I was a child. I knew I was gay when I was six years old. There
was no specific incident that made me realize that—it was just
something I knew. I felt differently about men than I did about
women. It wasn't in terms of sex—I knew nothing about sex when I
was six. I felt that I wanted to be close to men all the time—I
wanted to be with them. I didn't feel that way about women. I
knew I was different from other little boys when I was six. Most
boys knew they were going to have relationships with girls, but I
never felt that way. I knew I was going to have relationships with
boys. I don't know how I knew that, but I knew it. When I was
thirteen, I knew what was happening. I went with girls as a
teenager, but I was never happy. I never felt fulfilled."

"And now, Charles, as a man—how do you feel?"
"I'm fulfilled. I feel good about myself. I have a good relationship with God and I don't think it matters to God that I'm a
homosexual. I think everything is fine between us—God and me."

"COMPROMISE DOESN'T WORK WHEN
WHAT YOU'RE COMPROMISING IS YOURSELF."

Eileen, a social worker, is in her late twenties. She and her ex-
lover, Sandy, met while they were college students. They knew
each other as lovers for approximately two years before they began
to live together. And they lived together for three years. "I used to
have a definition of marriage or a permanent relationship," says

Eileen. "Right now I don't have any definition—I'm looking for a new one."

"Was there any gradual decline in your relationship with Sandy, Eileen?"

"Not one that I'd admit to. I'd gone to spend the holidays with my family without Sandy. When I came home, I knew I couldn't handle the relationship anymore. At least, not the way it was. It wasn't a good thing for me. I was ready to chuck the whole thing, but we did attempt to change things. For a couple of months I kidded myself into thinking it was going to work. Then I got involved with someone else, and that made me realize my relationship with Sandy wasn't going to work. It was the way I felt when I was with this other woman—I felt good about myself. I started liking myself again. My relationship with this other woman was a supportive relationship. I wasn't taking care of her and she wasn't taking care of me."

"What were the problems in your relationship with Sandy?"

"Monogamy was a problem. When we first began living together, we decided on a monogamous relationship. It was an experiment for me because I'd never been monogamous before in any of my lesbian relationships. I didn't like being monogamous—I simply didn't function well. Whether or not I'm acting out my preference for a nonmonogamous relationship is irrelevant. I need to have the option. It wasn't the sexual exclusivity of monogamy that I couldn't deal with. I couldn't deal with the emotional monogamy that was demanded of me. Sandy wanted to make sure my emotional energies weren't going anyplace else. She was jealous of my friends; she was jealous of my involvement with the gay community. Wherever I went, she had to go with me. If I was going to a meeting and I didn't want her escorting me, she'd say, 'If you were a good lover, you wouldn't mind having me there.' It was so clinging. But I allowed it to continue—that was my compromise. By allowing her to cling to me, I was proving to myself that I could be monogamous, that I wouldn't fool around. All of this so our relationship would endure. If I went out and she stayed home, I'd feel guilty. Then I'd come home to a scene. I just became fed up and angry."

"Were there other problems, Eileen?"

"We ended up emphasizing each other's negative points. Sandy was normally a dependent person—she became even more dependent. I have a need 'to take care of.' I ended up running her life for her."

"Specifically?"

"She was trying to get her career together. I was working as a vocational counselor at the time. I made the big mistake of doing social work at home. I helped her get her résumé together. I pushed her and I goaded her. She needed pushing, but she needed to push herself. She wanted me to run her life for her, but she didn't want me to run her life for her. We ended up losing respect for each other. I only want a relationship with someone I can respect and someone who respects me. To me, respecting someone means they maintain their personhood, their individuality. We lost respect for each other."

"You say you helped her with her résumé, Eileen. What's the line between helping someone and running their life? What about mutual growth?"

"Perhaps neither of us had enough self-respect to even approach the relationship as one of mutual growth. We were clinging to each other desperately. We'd just finished college. We weren't students anymore and the world was very different for us. We were both scared and hiding from the world. We weren't growing; we were simply matching neuroses. We weren't meeting each other as equals and supporting each other's goals. We were helping or doing just to get the thing completed. It's the difference between giving someone a loaf of bread or teaching them how to make it. I should've been offering her suggestions about her career when she asked for them. I assumed she had to automatically report to me on what was happening in her career and I was making the benchmarks as to whether or not she was successful. If I'd been assisting her, she would've run with a piece of information I'd given her. Instead, I got her the information and did the running for her."

"Where do you feel you were wrong?"

"First, I was wrong to myself. I made compromises that I shouldn't have made. By being false to myself, I was false to Sandy and to the relationship. I was wrong in that I did for her, lived her life for her. In terms of my own personality, I became a lot of destructive things. I lost my gentleness and my caring. I became pushy, and Sandy is a very sensitive person. We were both suffering through it so we'd stay together. We were just banging each other around emotionally. I don't see it as a function of one of us being wrong. We have different ways to arrive at our goals in life, and those ways are just not compatible. I was tired and fed up with trying to make the relationship work. Tired of not feeling good about myself. The relationship endured based on the fact that we were still together. The relationship existed, but it wasn't doing me any good. I'd heard all the promises, but I didn't have any hope anymore that the relationship would swing around and become a good relationship. I didn't have any energy left to put anything else into it. I lost hope when I no longer believed it would work. She said she believed we could work it out. But I don't know if she really believed that or wanted to believe it for the sake of her own security."

"So, then, the decision to separate was not a mutual decision?"

"No, it wasn't completely mutual in the beginning: I wanted to break up and Sandy did not. We were in couples counseling. It was what I needed to end the relationship. At first, we worked as a couple with the therapist. But it wasn't helping, so then the therapist started seeing us as individuals. Our breaking up was much easier because we worked toward it—we planned for divorce. We were getting our emotional support from a third party. By letting go of each other, we were giving each other emotional support—we weren't strangling each other. I didn't have to feel guilty. Couples counseling and our individual therapy enabled me to end the relationship in a safe place without having Sandy bouncing off the walls."

"When do you think compromise becomes a negative instead of a positive?"

"Compromise doesn't work when what you're compromising is yourself—when the changes you make are opposed to both your personality and to your goals for yourself. I have a tendency to compromise rather than argue, to compromise rather than deal with something I'm really against. Making certain the relationship endured was the goal. It was a mistake. What we should've been looking at was whether or not both of us were growing in the relationship, whether or not both of us were being nurtured by the relationship."

"What you're saying is the relationship as an enduring entity becomes more important than the people in it?"

"We put such expectations on a relationship. And there's such disapproval when a relationship ends. Why don't we just let them end when they're over? People come together for love, for needs, for mutual support, for whatever. They spend time together. They learn and they grow—or they don't. And if they don't, they separate and live apart. We've got all these expectations of what 'should be' rather than working with 'what is.' It's got to last 'forever and ever.' Your friends mourn for you when your relationship breaks up. And if you're into double-digit numbers in a gay relationship—well, that makes it even more dramatic. What's the difference if it's one year or ten years? Instead of friends carrying on because your relationship has ended, why don't they say, 'It's over. Do you need any assistance? Your life is going to change—let me be a friend and help you go on from here.' We get into a habit of security and we don't want to let the relationship end. Why don't we let it end when it's over instead of trying to hold on to a relationship that's over or should be over?"

"How did you feel when the relationship finally ended?"
"Relieved. I'm not angry. But sometimes I'm sad—sad that all the good and wonderful feelings which existed between Sandy and me don't exist anymore. I don't feel like a failure because I didn't set myself up to be a failure. I didn't enter the relationship believing it would 'have to' last into old age. A successful relationship, for me, isn't measured in time. It's measured in terms of what I've learned from the relationship, the good feelings I experienced, the good times I enjoyed. If I've grown as an individual as a result of a relationship, then it was a successful relationship. I don't measure the success of a relationship by the amount of time it lasted."

"What did you learn in your relationship with Sandy?"
"I've learned a whole lot more of what I need and want out of a relationship. And I've learned what I'm willing to invest in a relationship. What I want out of a relationship is caring and a certain amount of commitment. I've learned I need a lot of emotional space to allow other people in my life whether they're friends or lovers. I need a lot of honesty. I've really made myself responsible, as Sandy has made herself responsible, for making the breakup work. Call it planned divorce. I'm cautious about other relationships, but I wouldn't be afraid of going into another committed relationship. Right now I have different space requirements than I may need or desire in a couple of years."

"If you were to make another commitment, what type of person would you be looking for?"
"We'd have to have shared values. I'd want the other person to have goals. She'd have to have something else in her life that

mattered to her other than me. I don't want to be the thing that matters more than anything else. What happens then is your marriage becomes your career, and that's fine if other people want it that way—but I don't."

"In terms of your problems with Sandy, were they gay problems or human problems?"

"I don't think there's any difference between gays and straights as far as a divorce. I don't think Sandy and I broke up because we're gay. I haven't found any difference between gays and straights as far as the problems. I say this as a professional and as a gay person who has been through a divorce. It's the same type of things, the same type of hurt, the same type games. However, the one difference is that gay people can't talk about their breakup every place; a straight can talk about it anyplace."

"How do you feel about monogamous relationships now?"

"There's no universal truth as to whether or not monogamy is going to work for everyone. It was positive for me in terms of my relationship with Sandy because I had to learn to stick something out and deal with it until it was time to go because it couldn't be worked out. I used to seek out other people so as not to deal with the problems in a relationship I was running away from. Monogamy can be a safeguard: I am monogamous, therefore I have to work on the relationship. Learning that I didn't function well monogamously had a positive effect on me. If you're not going to be monogamous, you have to be really honest with yourself about why you're in whatever relationship you happen to be in. What motivated you to get involved with someone else? Was it to run away from something or to add something? An outside relationship can bring something to a primary relationship in the sense that it brings something to the individual engaged in it—it has a ripple effect."

"Eileen, have you ever felt less of a woman because you're a lesbian?"

"Yes, at one point I did. I felt people didn't accept me as a woman because I was with another woman instead of a man. You get points for being with a man. When I was married to my husband, my parents treated me like an adult. When I divorced my husband and when they found out I was gay, they reverted to treating me like a child. To them, I was only an adult if I was attached to a man. Being attached to a woman was only second best—it didn't count."

"How did your parents find out you were gay?"

"While I was going through my divorce, the only settlement I wanted was that I wanted my things. My ex-husband wanted me to walk away without any claim on anything. He blackmailed me, threatening to tell my parents I was gay if I insisted on taking anything with me. And he told them."

"Eileen, what do you want now?"

"I've been married to a man and I've been married to a woman—now I'm looking for something that works. Of course, I no longer feel less of a woman because I'm a lesbian. I'm free to search for androgyny. I can be whatever I want to be."

DIVORCE: ANOTHER PERSPECTIVE

After my own divorce, my continued affection and caring for Paula frightened me. Did I unconsciously want to be reunited with her? Was I still in love with her? Had I done the wrong thing? Even after Valerie and I came together, occasional "Paula thoughts" would scare me. I discussed it once with a friend. "Mary," Pat said, "you spent nine years of your life with this woman. You have good memories and you have bad memories. Do you think all those years and all those memories are just going to disappear because the relationship ended? Do you think the hurt of breaking up with Paula destroyed the years of affection and tenderness you shared?" Pat did manage to minimize my fears. However, it was only one year ago that I truly resolved the emotional conflicts and confusion I experienced regarding Paula. It happened at the Church of the Beloved Disciple, where I was doing an interview for this book.

"Love is love," said Father John, "once and for always. Love is love. You have it today and you have it forever. It may be that in time you have changed and it's no longer necessary or desirable for you to live together. The desire and the drive to stay together may die, but the love never dies. You will carry that love with you from one person to another. You carry it forever. People don't think of love that way. We're blinded by narrow and provincial heterosexual values. Gays don't have to accept heterosexual values—we can find our own values.

"Love is out of time, and love is sacred. You will carry the love of a relationship with you, even if it ends, to your grave. You have been touched and changed by that love; therefore it is a love which will always remain with you. You'll never be the same person again. I believe this concept of love, as I'm trying to explain it, is part of the gay heritage. Gays can be much more realistic than straights about relationships. Our minds are more flexible than heterosexual minds. I believe gay people are more fortunate than straights, because if their relationship ends, they can acknowledge that 'end' and still begin anew."

"The important thing is the love," Father Philip elaborated. "It doesn't matter how many people you love—one love is the extension of the love that went before it. You may love another person later, and that love may be completely different. But the love itself is the same. Love is love. As we grow, we may grow apart, but that doesn't negate the loving. With love, there's no such thing as the death of love. The death of love is only in our minds. Our psyches kill our love—we destroy the beauty of what was really there. We try to bury it, throw it in the closet. We don't want to acknowledge it anymore—it's something of our past we want to forget.

"Love is not like that," Father Philip continued. "We choose to make it like that. We're wrong in that once something goes wrong with a relationship we're in, we try to cut that relationship out of ourselves. In doing so we forget the good parts of that relationship—we forget the value that relationship once had in our lives. Instead of salvaging the good parts when a relationship ends, we throw out the good with the bad. As gays, we're too caught up in the values of the heterosexual world and straight marriages. I believe it's as Father John said: the love you have had for one person will follow you to the grave. In ending a relationship with a person, why destroy all the good and all the love which existed between you? Acknowledge that the *relationship* is over—not the love."

8

PROFESSIONALLY SPEAKING

Since I believe the essence of a relationship is the same between members of the same sex as it is between members of the opposite sex, I also believe the problems are much the same. And just as there are common problems, there are also problems that are unique to gay couples and problems that are unique to straight couples.

Those things one personally believes are fine for subjective fireside chats with friends. However, in terms of a book, those beliefs must be documented and substantiated. In order to lend credibility to what are my personal beliefs, I decided to explore the issues with professionals who would either support or invalidate my thinking. My criteria: the psychiatrists with whom I would talk would have to have both gay and straight couples and individuals as patients.

DR. KENNETH BERC

Dr. Kenneth Berc, a board certified psychiatrist, is a graduate of Harvard Medical School. He received his training at Columbia University and St. Luke's Hospital in New York City. He has practiced psychiatry in both New York City and Long Island for over ten years. In addition to his private practice, Dr. Berc is presently a faculty member of both the College of Physicians and Surgeons of Columbia University and Brookdale Center on Aging of Hunter College's School of Social Work.

"Dr. Berc, do you, in a therapeutic setting, treat a gay couple any differently than you would treat a straight couple?"

"My only training in couples therapy was in terms of working

160

with straight couples. So, when I began working with gay couples, I used the identical techniques and they worked well. Later I added modifications for particular problems a gay couple might be facing *because* they are gay."

"Are there major differences between the problems experienced by gay couples and the problems experienced by straight couples?"

"Basically, there are more similarities than there are differences."

"Can you review some of the more common problems experienced by both gay and straight couples?"

"People generally come to discuss their relationships because they are dissatisfied, fighting too much for what they expected, or are not experiencing as much pleasure as they expected, either physically or emotionally or both. They may simply be experiencing 'staleness,' which is usually due to poor communications. One or both partners thinks he or she knows what the other will say, do, or feel, so that person stops listening to the other. The doors for growth, change, and continued excitation are closed. Often those doors were closed long ago. Then one must backtrack to a time when the relationship was fulfilling in order to rediscover its positive roots.

"Sometimes there are more specific complaints: disagreements, the discovery of sexual relationships outside of the primary relationship. The causes for the problem are often the same for straight and gay couples: one partner is bored with the other, or one partner feels his or her esteem has been lowered in the other partner's eyes. Or sometimes there's some type of anger between the partners, communication breaks down—the anger may be expressed through outside sexual activity.

"Financial difficulties are a problem for both gay and straight couples. However, we're seeing more of it now with straight couples because women are no longer willing to accept second-class financial status. Financial imbalance is a problem because, culturally, we associate money with power.

"Job reassignments are more a problem for gay couples than for straights. An employer, not knowing a single employee is gay, might transfer this person to another city. No provisions are made for the gay person's partner. As far as the company knows, the person is single. Whereas with a married heterosexual, the company is less likely to transfer the person and his or her partner. And if they do transfer a married heterosexual, provisions are made for the person's husband or wife. Of course, there is the case where one partner does not wish to move, which causes power issue problems.

"The presence of a particular mental problem in one's spouse creates the same situation for gay couples as it does for straight couples. One partner's mental problem is affecting the relationship, and then both partners, as a couple, sometimes go into joint therapy. They work on the problem together, often as a symptom in their relationship as well as working on it as a symptom one partner has exclusive of the relationship.

"Family interference is another common problem, although it's more subtle—it's not the complaint presented by either gay or straight couples. The couple is having problems because of pressure from in-laws; there's a third party trying to sabotage the relationship. However, in-law pressure is often overlooked as the underlying problem by the therapist working with a gay couple. It's just recently that we're beginning to think of gay people as even having families."

"What are some of the problems that are unique to gay couples, Dr. Berc?"

"In terms of social position, gays are a minority. Minority group status makes any particular situation different. Gays are different from the average white middle-class couples. Although they're not that different from a poor black or Hispanic couple in terms of destructive social expectations.

"What I mean is there's a large amount of incorporated self-hatred in the gay population. There's the idea among gays themselves that gay relationships don't work. And it's that idea that's reinforced by so-called gay friends, who can disrupt the relationship with this type of thinking rather than, as a friend, try to help to improve it. For straight couples, there's more positive reinforcement in terms of making the relationship work. Part of the problem is that there's no word for a gay couple's relationship. A culture which has no word for something usually arrived at that point because there was no value for that concept.

"It's harder for gay couples to get support for their relationships from their families because so many gay couples haven't shared their relationships with their families. However, my experience has been that when a gay couple *has* shared their relationship with their families, the healthier families are often much more supportive than ever I would've thought they'd be. Often members of the family will share their heterosexual experiences with the gay couple. It's a very positive thing for the gay couple when this does happen because it short-circuits a lot of therapy."

"What is your greatest difficulty in terms of dealing with a gay couple as opposed to dealing with a straight couple?"

"As a psychiatrist, I guess the most continuous thing I see is the internalized self-hatred of gays. The more I practice, the more I see how pervasive it is. I see it in terms of the gay person's lowered self-esteem, their inability to believe that they have it within themselves to solve their problems. In short, I see the effects of prejudice. I've seen the same thing in some older black people who fight against the belief that maybe white people really are better."

"Where does the self-hatred and the lack of self-esteem come from?"

"It comes from identifying with a culture that says that gay people aren't as good as other people, that gay relationships aren't as good as straight relationships. That's why therapeutic gay groups are so important. When I was training, one of my professors explained that we should *never* put gay people together in a group because they reinforce each other and it doesn't help them at all. However, that very type of reinforcement we were told was a negative is one of the fastest methods for getting through the tremendous internalized self-hate—the social sense gays have that there's something basically wrong with them. This type of positive reinforcement—gays supporting gays—can help gay people see that there's nothing basically wrong with them, that their problems can be solved. Sometimes, when this self-hatred is the only problem and is resolved by the person, the other problems can easily be solved and no further therapy is necessary."

"What are gay couples better at than straight couples, Dr. Berc?"

"Gay couples are better at openly communicating with each other than are straight couples. Gay people are a minority. They've had to learn to survive, to be more soul-searching. And they've had to learn to put up with certain amounts of pain in order to survive. I don't mean to say that heterosexuals don't have pain—only that on the average gays have more pain to deal with. When gay couples feel that there's hope for them and their relationships, they actually seem more able than straight couples to draw from past painful experience, apply it, and grow. It is a much different viewpoint than some writers, who believe gay people are less able to deal with pain, frustration, and disappointment, and, therefore, are more 'narcissistic' than average.

"Also, for gay couples, making a go of it has the added advantage of special pride, since their success will fly in the face of prejudice."

"What do the straight couples have going for them that the gay couples do not?"

"First, straight couples have a lot more positive reinforcements in terms of society and in terms of their peers, as I have said. They're able to at least feel secure in that they're on the side of trying to reproduce the species. There is the special case of couples who decide not to have children. Several such couples have reported peer pressure as destructive as the pressure imposed upon gays. If, as it happens for some straight couples, the pair only wants to do 'what's right'—have children, make money, support one's family and participate in the community, those people obviously will have less work to do to bring their relationships into concord with their expectations. Gay people just don't have that luxury of saying, 'But we have the house, the car, our children are well—what more do you want?' And so they silence deeper questions. I'd also like to comment on a view held by some that straight couples have the advantage of difference, in the 'opposites attract' sense. This is true on the surface. But gay couples need only to begin to realize their differences from each other and validate those differences as complementary to achieve the same state.

"One major advantage, until recently, has been the willingness of heterosexual women to end power struggles by yielding to their husbands. This yielding has been culturally validated and often the sense of the 'marriage working' offsets the woman's ensuing depression. In homosexual relationships, the power struggle solutions are more complicated. However, as cultural expectations are changing for heterosexuals, these power issues are also getting as complex as they are for gays. I include here issues of who earns more, whose home the couple moves into, etc."

"Throughout my interviews, I've had people explain the merits of having a partner of the same sex. What are some of the benefits of having a partner of a different sex?"

"You have a straight marriage, one man and one woman living together. If things go wrong between them, it's culturally acceptable for the man to say, 'All women are crazy,' or for the woman to say, 'All men are crazy'—that kind of thing. When you have two people of the same sex, if they attack their partner's gender they are attacking themselves and putting down their own gender. By attacking their partner's gender, they themselves suffer the blow—it leads to more despair and more lack of fulfillment. That's one of the advantages to a male/female marriage—one can attribute disagreements to the partner's gender crazies. It's a crazy approach, but it does help in straight marriages, because it helps create some distance when necessary and helps negotiate disappointment.

"Lesbian and homosexual couples often expect their partners to be the same as they are, to enjoy the same things. Gay couples have to learn to appreciate the differences in their partners as persons. Gays don't have the luxury of blaming these differences on gender; it'd be absurd—they're the same gender."

"Is instability inherent in gay relationships? Do gay people enter relationships expecting them to be unstable? Are gay relationships predestined to fail?"

"I'll challenge you on your use of the word 'inherent' because it's a tricky word. Yes, gay people do go into a relationship thinking it will be unstable. And yes, in a sense, gay relationships may be predestined to fail. However, their failure is not inherent in the psychology of humans who happen to be gay. That's what a lot of antigay and homophobic psychiatrists would have gays believe—that as gays, well, it's the nature of the beast that's defective, and therefore, doomed to failure. And, of course, two defective beasts having a relationship together have got to produce a defective relationship. Certain psychiatrists would have us believe that gays, like schizophrenics, are sick, so what can you expect but failure? If you have very sick people, you don't ask too much of them anyway. If they want to be queer, crazy faggots, and dikes—why not?

"Look, there's a large group of psychiatrists who say that gay relationships are inherently doomed to failure. This type of psychiatrist can be very destructive to gay couples. Through the politics of psychotherapy, the psychiatrist can subtly get the two people involved to end their relationship by alluding to the fact that this *gay* relationship can hurt you. The therapist wouldn't even explore the positive aspects of the relationship with the couple because it's a gay couple.

"Let me give you an example of two women, a lesbian couple, I recently treated. They'd been together for fifteen years. They'd come to me because, among other things, they were having trouble with their relationship. In their own minds, even though they had been together so long, their problems were proof that such relationships couldn't work. Remember what I said before about the importance of families to gays? Well, both mothers had advised their daughters at the outset and often during the years that doom was sooner or later inevitable. They had to do extra work separating their own judgments from those of their mothers. Gradually, they were able to pin down enough positive judgments of their own to believe that what they were doing was right for them despite what others said. I would add that they are beautiful people and the story has a happy ending. They overcame their own homophobia."

"Do I hear you correctly? You're talking about gay homophobia."

"Yes. I see homophobia in gays as their internalization of cultural value. Anyone exposed to society internalizes or makes a part of themself the values of the society. People behave in certain ways that are consistent with society. People dress appropriately according to societal standards. Their thinking becomes appropriate to society. Gay people, some as young as three or four years old when they realize they're gay, grow up knowing they're gay. These gay children struggle to fit into what is appropriate to society. In that process of trying to fit in, they begin the process of identifying with the aggressor, the aggressor being a heterosexual society which is down on lesbians and homosexuals. As that person or child begins to identify with the aggressor, they begin 'aggressing' against themselves. While they are trying to fit in, they begin picking up the values of the people who are trying to suppress them. They—the gays—then begin to suppress themselves. They suppress themselves in the way they behave, dress, talk, walk.

"Sometimes this self-suppression is conscious. Those are the gay people who are 'dysphoric,' to quote the new psychiatric term. They'd rather be dead than gay. They disgust themselves. But more often, it is unconscious. Because, the way the mind works, complex linkages occur so that one idea which is anathema can link into many other ideas which otherwise might be uncontaminated. The most simple way I can demonstrate this is to ask you if there's a different feeling to the statements 'a black lawyer' versus 'a lawyer who is black,' a 'woman doctor' versus a 'doctor who is a woman,' 'a gay author' versus 'an author who is gay.' I think that these expressions all feel different from each other. I also feel that the differences occur because of complex unconscious expectations that occur and are rekindled by many circumstances—in this circumstance by simple use of adjectives. All people's minds work more or less the same, thus gay people are subject to homophobic ideas."

"What is your definition of homophobia, Dr. Berc?"

"I'd describe homophobia as a general fear or uneasiness about homosexuality. People are often unaware of this fear or uneasiness, but it does, nevertheless, influence their lives."

"As gays, historically, we're predestined to failure. As we grow up, we're preconditioned to our impending failure by society. But do we become so preoccupied with this legacy of failure that we ourselves make it a self-fulfilling prophecy?"

"What you're describing, Mary, is the person who's generating his or her own internal anxiety. Too much anxiety can prevent a person from functioning. Therapy then should address that very problem: Why is the person generating his or her own anxiety and actualizing this self-fulfilling prophecy? The therapist must help the person explore why they are convinced of failure. In both cases, that in which the person begins to believe in the possibility of success or that in which the person realizes that the relationship is not right for them, the realization will help decrease anxiety. When anxiety drops, coping skills will return and they function better. Usually, if there are no other problems involved, the person can then resolve the problems he or she is having with little further help. The therapist doesn't have to tell them how to fix things."

"Are you saying, Dr. Berc, that once you can get a gay person to trust in their gayness and the wholeness of that gayness, a lot of the other problems are simple problems?"

"For the average gay person, yes. That's why all these un-qualified, so-called 'therapists' are so successful. They offer the gay person peer identification, peer safety. This peer support helps gays to lower their anxiety levels by getting rid of the fear, the internalized self-hatred. Once that's done, the person gets better or solves their other problems on their own. If there were more serious problems involved, it would take a lot more than peer support and unqualified therapists to resolve them."

"What I hear you saying is that gays have to rid themselves of their preoccupation with failing and get preoccupied with succeeding. But how do you get gay people to believe in their own right to hap-piness?"

"I challenge the roots of their unhappiness. I make them prove to me they're failures. I compare and contrast it to other successful areas of their lives—jobs, successful interpersonal relationships.

Then you get to the area of their gayness—suddenly, they're failures. The question then becomes: How can you be successful in all these other areas, but be a failure in anything pertaining to your gayness? You have to help the person see the inconsistency of their thinking. Sooner or later, they begin to question why they see themselves as failures because they're gay, and yet see themselves as successful in other areas of their life. If people begin to compare and contrast who they are as people and put their values as gays in line with their values as people, there's a tremendous shift in their pessimism, antigay and antiself thinking. Everything else in their lives is working just fine. Why shouldn't their gayness work just fine, too? Sometimes, gay people also have to change their behavior to conform to what they are proud of."

"Change their behavior in terms of what?"
"Some behavior may come from internalized self-hatred—the seedier gay behavior, certain types of promiscuity, abusive behavior. Society has shortchanged them, so they shortchange themselves. Sometimes they have to stop this type of behavior so they can feel proud about themselves again. But again, the root of the problem is often self-hate—they hate themselves because they're gay and because being gay is an antisocial act. When they can bring the rest of their behavior into responsible social terms and try to focus on their total personality, they realize there's nothing more or less bad about being gay, as there's nothing more or less bad about other dimensions of their personalities."

"If a gay is unaware of his or her own antigay feelings, can those very feelings be causing the other problems in their lives?"
"Yes. I have a couple of patients who are alcoholics and whose drinking comes out of a sense of gay despair. They think they're alcoholics simply because they're alcoholics. But their inability to control their drinking is a manifestation of their self-hate. If they could stop hating themselves, they might be better able to fight their drinking patterns. I had worked for months with a patient whom I tried to get to stop drinking. Three weeks after he confirmed that he had developed a playful attitude about his sexuality, he announced that he was having too much fun to keep poisoning himself with alcohol. He had changed how he related to his own sexuality, had overcome, if you will, his homophobia, and with it his sense of inferiority and despair."

"Are there other areas where a gay's antigay feelings cause other problems?"

"Finances. Let me give you an example of a man I was working with. Salarywise, he believed he was doing the best he possibly could . . . for a gay person. The fact that he'd failed in a relationship many years before affected how he looked at himself in business. As he began to look at his personal life and how he felt about himself, he also began to look at his professional life. His low self-esteem and his poor self-image, because of his gayness, made him totally unaware of the fact that he was capable of earning more. As his self-image as a person improved, so did his professional image. He realized he was worth more as a person and more professionally. He went out and got another job, doubling his income."

"What you're saying is that gay homophobia and gay despair are a result of gays internalizing the antigay attitudes of a heterosexual society?"

"Yes, but I do want to qualify some of this. Being gay has a lot of real hardships attached to it: real pain, real suffering, real rejection. Add to the real pain the feeling of worthlessness that has been imposed upon gays by a heterosexual society, and you have gay despair. The real hardships of being gay, plus the internalized self-hate, can create a situation of chronic depression. Another qualification on gay homophobia and gay despair: these conditions do not exist in all gays, and, where they exist, they exist in varying degrees. Look, the fact that a person is gay doesn't cause all of this. It's a gay person's coming to terms with the status of gays in society. There are many heterosexual women who have to come to terms with the status of women in society. I worked with a heterosexual woman lawyer who'd been told that unless she gave up her aspiration to be a brilliant woman lawyer and raise a family instead, she'd never be happy. Just as there are many women who've come to terms with the status of women, so there are many gays who've come to terms with the status of gays and have gotten beyond it."

"Beyond it to what?"

"Beyond it to self-fulfillment. To being people who realize their own natural human potentials for whatever level they strive to achieve. Beyond it to being able to compete with what are their very real abilities. Beyond it to living the fullest lives they possibly can."

"Gay people accept the instability of their relationships as part of their life until they get to a point where they unlearn all of that. Let's look at straights. Does the high divorce rate cause straights to go into marriages believing their marriages aren't going to work?"

"Absolutely. I have a patient—a heterosexual woman—who has given the symptom you've just described as one of her reasons for being in therapy: her fear that her marriage will fail. She's not about to give up her heterosexuality. But she's adopted the attitudes of the affluent subculture in which she lives toward marriage, and she's internalized them as fearful—marriages tend to work only for a while but then can be 'traded up' for another, perhaps better one. She wants *her* marriage to work the first time around.

"As psychiatrists begin to see societal pressures as a human problem, they'll be more open to gays and the effect societal pressures have on them. It's the social pressures associated with a particular lifestyle that cause many of the problems. There's nothing wrong with a woman who wants to be a brilliant lawyer. What's wrong is the pressure imposed on her because she doesn't want to be a traditional housewife. Those pressures of deviating from society's standards cause the problems."

"Why is it that, after a short-term affair has ended, gay people act as if a fifteen-year marriage has ended? When gay people say they've been married five times, are they really talking about marriage or are they talking about five affairs? What is this seemingly emotional immaturity among gays?"

"I think you've hit upon something important with that one, Mary. The average heterosexual adolescent—sixteen, seventeen, eighteen—begins to form relationships which are generated by sexual interest. Even if there's no actual sex between the two youngsters, the basis of the relationship is a desire to be together plus a sexual interest in each other. Such relationships are classically marked by massive dependency on each other: they're on the phone for hours, they're both despondent if they have a fight, they're jealous. And it's all quite normal for youngsters that age.

"The gay adolescent at that same age is already hiding, therefore not learning from peers or anyone else how to handle relationships. With a straight teenage girl who has a fight or breaks up with her boyfriend—well, she gets all the support and advice she needs from her parents and her girl friends. The gay youngster is more than likely already ashamed of his or her sexual feelings, and even if they are having a relationship, they're not about to discuss it with anyone. And that's where the emotional immaturity you're asking about comes in. It's not because gay adults are emotionally immature; it's because they haven't had the opportunity to have the same learning experiences or the same adult guidance a heterosexual youngster enjoys. So you can have a gay person getting into a relationship at twenty who's doing what they should've actually been doing at sixteen.

"Part of the problem is that gay people don't realize that a first relationship might be a practice relationship—just the way a heterosexual teenager has practice relationships with different boyfriends or girl friends. Between the first dependency or practice relationship and the real one, there may be other relationships that backfire because the person is not yet skilled in choosing a partner."

"Acquiring skills in choosing a partner is an aspect of development for the heterosexual adolescent between the ages of sixteen and twenty?"

"Yes. And in choosing—I mean in terms of one's values—the lifestyle one would prefer. It's appropriate to choose a spouse who shares enough of your values—it helps the relationship work. It's a whole process because we learn to choose on even deeper levels. One professor of mine once said that it's important to choose a person that has the right kind of neurosis—one that doesn't bother you that much, one you can live with. Learning to choose involves the subtle understanding of the particular person's problems."

"Are you saying that because of society's oppression of gays, gays become slow learners in terms of their emotional development?"

"I'd even be more up front about it. Gays are robbed of a certain phase of development which they have to go back and get later on in their lives."

"Does the process of accepting one's gayness slow the person down in terms of dealing with their human needs and wants in a relationship?"

"Yes. That happens more times than it doesn't. I would say about twenty percent of the gays escape this, but that eighty percent, to one degree or another, get torn apart by the struggle for self-acceptance as gays. Accepting one's gayness is the first level a gay person must achieve. Then they can begin to see themselves as people and get beyond that to determining their needs."

"Is my sexual preference part of my emotional preference? Which comes first? When I love someone is that love then expressed sexually?"

"Probably the basic roots of emotional preference happens first and sexual preference happens later. Sexual preference without emotional preference in the gay or straight adolescent can make sex an overwhelming drive. Clara Thompson, writing some years ago, made one of the first breakthroughs against some of the antigay psychiatric literature. She said that it is the emotional preference which is paramount in a healthy sexual relationship. And she felt if a person could get in touch with the emotional person they needed to relate to and could then express that sexually, they'd be the most healthy. She was talking about the union of emotional preference and sexual preference in one person. This applies to both gays and straights. It is putting one's emotional needs with a person who is of the sex that is most attractive. There is 'something' that the person definitely gravitates to as a primary drive, and I don't mean just sexual. I'm not comfortable saying it's affectionate, emotional, or sexual. I think it's a whole lot of things that come together in the right person. And the 'right person' will include gender, include a kind of personality of gender. That gender person will have the kind of lifestyle the person needs."

"In my relationships with men, I felt 'in love,' infatuated. But there was always something missing. I always felt as if I was watching something—almost an observer in my own life. Throughout these relationships with men, there was a relationship with a particular woman—simultaneously. I knew I loved her—she was number one. She was the first woman I was ever involved with. Having a relationship with a woman troubled me, but not enough to make me end the relationship."

"It is very difficult for me to discuss something so personal and individual without asking many more questions. At the risk of being simplistic, I might understand you to mean that there's something about women and your feelings for women that permits you to be really close and expressive. However, there is something about men and your feelings about men that causes you to keep some distance. Since your reason for being with a man was out of social responsibility, your whole heart wasn't in it. On the other hand, without being told to do so, you found your way to loving a woman. I'd have to say that that drive was very strong. Even though that drive was not biologically reproductive, I have no reason to doubt that it wasn't as much built into you at the factory, so to speak, as is heterosexual primacy built in for others. At twenty-six, you accepted this and you moved into your gayness. For some people, it would be a frightening experience. As I said earlier, there are some who would rather be dead than deal with what they've learned about themselves. Here we get into the social stigma again. You obviously didn't feel any danger for yourself in experiencing fulfillment with this woman and you went forward from there.

"You say in the beginning, when you first came out, there was some degree of a problem. If you were my patient then, I would have suggested that you try to set aside your fears and explore exactly what that problem was—what you were afraid of. In your personal case, you had already demonstrated that you were neither exclusively heterosexual nor exclusively homosexual. This is certainly not unusual. What you had were two complex sets of feelings, both of which could tell you much about who you were as a person and what your needs were so that, should you choose to do so, you could follow your own lead to your own life.

"The thing is not to be frightened by whatever feelings you have. And to the extent that people can remain unafraid, that makes them healthier people. Even if you were afraid of 'becoming a lesbian,' I would have advised you that it would be worth exploring the feelings you had for the woman as well as for the men. If you'd decided you wanted to be heterosexual, it would have enhanced your heterosexuality. And if you decided to be a lesbian, you would also have more to work with."

"Dr. Berc, you're using words like 'decide' and 'choice.' Are you saying there's a choice involved in being a homosexual or a lesbian?"

"Yes, for some people I think there is. The terms *homosexual* and *heterosexual* evolve out of Western culture. These terms are probably superficial: they attempt to label people in two categories. Human beings never fall into categories—they fall into broad bands and spectrums. There is a percentage of people who are absolutely homosexual or absolutely heterosexual. There are other people who feel relatively more comfortable with one sex than they do with the other. Between the people who are absolutely one way or another, there are a lot of other people who can exercise some degree of choice. I've known some people who are the so-called bisexuals—who some people say don't exist. But they do exist and to these people the actual gender of another person isn't so important. Bisexuals can and do choose which side they're going to be on and when."

"Is switching more of a problem for gay couples than it is for straight couples?"

"I would have to guess that there are far more self-labeled heterosexuals than there are homosexuals who have decided to give up their homosexual drives or leanings than the reverse. I do not refer to those heterosexuals with *occasional* homosexual thoughts or actions, but to those who clearly prefer homosexuality and who can engage in heterosexual behavior some of the time. So there are more people who would rather be homosexual living as heterosexual. But I cannot believe that the pain would be less for either group—homosexual or heterosexual—if the person had to behave and relate in a way that was less satisfactory than another one open to him or her."

"We've talked about gay homophobia and internalized self-hate. As a population, are gays sicker than straights?"

"I would have to confess that I don't see homophobia by itself as sick. I know we throw terms like *sickness* and *health* around in our society, even calling society itself sick. But by sick, I can only relate to the medical model, which in psychiatric areas defines such things as 'psychoses,' 'anxiety reactions,' 'phobias,' etc., as sick. Within those strict categories, homosexuals and heterosexuals share equally the burdens of sickness and health. The importance to the understanding of the specialness of gays has nothing to do with their being more or less sick. But when they do get sick, a therapist with a clear understanding of the special problems they face will have a better chance of helping. What I hope your book will accomplish, among other things, is to enhance preventative mental health."

"What about a mixed world, Dr. Berc—gay couples interacting and sharing with straight couples as couples?"

"I think we're getting a little closer to that ideal. With more awareness and sophistication, healthy heterosexual couples are becoming less afraid of their gay neighbors. Some of them never were afraid and are now glad their gay neighbors are becoming less afraid of them. Communication always helps ameliorate fear. I would like to see heterosexuals who haven't already done so try to find out more about gay people by meeting gay people. And I would like to see gay people less ashamed to accept the overtures of friendship when they are offered. Most people seem more than happy to help their neighbors raise their barns without asking too many questions as to why it burned down. I say this to those who fear the moralists.

"Lastly, I should like to relate an anecdote. An elderly woman asked her neighbor how long he knew his male roommate. When he responded with the exact date, thirty-four years before, she shared the fact that she, too, knew her husband thirty-four years. He did not respond. So on the date he'd given her, she baked a cake inscribed 'Happy Thirty-fifth' and the names of both the men. Her neighbors looked at the cake and blushed, but refused to eat it. They feigned total bewilderment. Hopefully, the next generation won't miss that boat."

DR. JEAN MUNZER

Dr. Jean Munzer is both an analytically trained psychiatrist and a social psychologist. She received her medical degree from New York University, and she earned her Ph.D. in social psychology at Columbia University. Her psychiatric residency was completed at Bellevue Hospital in New York City. Dr. Munzer, who has been in private practice since 1952, is presently on the faculties of both the Fielding Institute and Adelphi University.

"Dr. Munzer, I'm interested in similarities and differences between gay and straight couples in terms of problem solving."

"As with most questions asked about human beings, there are both similarities and differences. In my experience with both gay and straight couples, the similarities greatly outweigh the differences. The problems of gay couples, by and large, closely correspond to the problems of straight couples."

"What are some specific similar problems?"

"I've counseled both gay and straight couples for many years, and their problems are the problems of two human beings living together: compromise, conflicts regarding dominance and submission, financial problems, sexual problems, infidelity."

"A lot has been written recently about power struggles in straight couples in terms of women now earning more money. What do you see as power struggles in gay couples?"

"Power struggles in gay couples are frequently similar to the power struggles in straight couples. There is no statistical data to support my opinion, but my overall impression is that there aren't as many power struggle problems for gay couples as there are for straight couples. However, whether it's two men or two women living together, if one partner earns a great deal more than the other or has a more prestigious job than the other, there can be a good deal of unhappiness and rivalry.

"Our sexist society has contributed to a great many of the problems experienced by heterosexual couples. A sexist society programs both the man and the woman for role behavior which may not suit their individual preferences or abilities. These role problems aren't reflected that much in gay couples. Comparing gay and straight couples, each has strengths, strains, and support systems the other may not have. My overall impression, contrary to popular stereotypes: I've found a more optimistic outlook in gay couples, particularly women, in terms of staying together. And often they stay together at the expense of social approval and frequently with the loss of support from their original families.

"Gay couples, in many ways, have a compatibility that many straight couples don't. I'm not in a position to say how much of this is biologically determined or how much of it is influenced by the fact that our sexist society raises boys and girls without ever teaching them to like each other. In gay couples, there's a basis for liking and understanding each other which can strengthen the union when the normal stresses of living are causing divisive things to occur."

"Do you find this same type of compatibility among both gay men and gay women?"

"Although I have a relatively large practice, I am not able to speak in any terms from which one can make reliable generalizations. A large practice still only represents a very small segment of the population. With that as a qualification, I would say the lesbian couples I've counseled have presented fewer power struggles and more of a willingness to compromise. I think this might be due to the fact that lesbians are brought up in the same sexist society as are straight women. And generally, women are trained to be more cooperative and less competitive than men. Competitiveness is more of a problem among gay men than it is among gay women, although less of a problem for gay men than it is for straight men."

"Is instability inherent in gay relationships?"

"I believe a certain amount of instability is inherent in human relationships. I have no evidence to support the belief that instability is generally more frequent in male homosexual or lesbian relationships than in heterosexual relationships."

"Do gays accept impermanence in their relationships as part of their gay pathology?"

"There, I believe I agree with that. Remember, now, the gay couples who come to me are couples who want to stay together in at least a semipermanent relationship. And I don't find they show more instability than the straight couples who come to me. However, I do believe that a number of our young gay people have come to accept a lot of the negative stereotypes about gays. Many of them feel they have to, so to speak, 'put up with' a lack of monogamy or lack of fidelity. A great many young straight people don't feel they have to 'put up with' these things."

"Dr. Munzer, let's talk about this 'put up with' concept in terms of how you deal with it with your patients."

"This is, of course, not true of all my patients. One thing I want to emphasize is that there's about as much variation among gay couples as among straight couples. But I do find that a distressing proportion of the gay couples I work with—particularly the men— has accepted some of the really negative stereotypes about gays. So that a young man deeply involved with his partner may still feel he somehow doesn't have the right to say, 'Look, I want you to be faithful to me.' One of the ways I try to help the couple is to make them see that they don't have to 'put up with' behavior which is not doing their relationship any good whatsoever. I will say, 'What is it that makes you feel you have fewer rights and privileges in this gay relationship than you would have if you were in a conventional straight relationship?"

"And what is it that makes them feel they have fewer rights and privileges?"

"I think that comes from the same sad roots that make blacks accept stereotypes about their race, that make Jews accept negative stereotypes about their specific ethnic group. Minorities who've been persecuted or discriminated against throughout history have, unfortunately, tended to accept some, if not all, of the negative stereotypes held against them by the majority."

"Sometimes, I think, as gay couples, myself included, we tend to adopt the most negative aspects of heterosexual marriage."

"I think, Mary, as a population, gays are greatly discriminated against, and they are therefore very defensive. I go back a long time in terms of working with discriminated-against minorities. I'm a feminist; I was active in the civil rights movement. When human beings are defending themselves against bad treatment, misunderstanding, and discrimination, they're faced with hard choices. Sometimes the way in which they defend themselves is by almost caricaturing the behavior of the more fortunate majority. Others defend themselves by rebelling and leading more or less outrageous lives.

"My fairly extensive experience with minorities has convinced me that if there could be greater acceptance of all people by all people, much of the behavior which is criticized as offensive and antisocial would disappear. Gay couples who've found acceptance in their communities live very quiet, law-abiding, and often attractive lives. The so-called misbehavior that is sometimes observed is almost invariably a defensive response to the lack of acceptance. Personally, Mary, I hope to devote the rest of my professional life to doing what I can to speak for the acceptance of all people by all people."

"Do you think the divorce rate has the same negative impact upon straight couples as the impact of instability has upon gay couples?"

"I suppose every generation has felt it's living in particularly difficult times. But, in spite of acknowledging this as background, I believe young people today are facing more rapid change and more instability than perhaps has ever been faced by any generation throughout the history of mankind. Gay couples and straight couples alike are supported by far less in the way of structure. Religion, social sanction, the extended family that stays together, stable neighborhoods—we've lost so much of all that. Couples coming together are very much threatened by all of this. For straight couples—they're threatened by the increasingly high divorce rate. For gay couples—the knowledge that so many of their friends who have formed what they'd hoped to be lasting unions have broken up after any number of years. It's an unstable time when values are changing, when new lifestyles are being considered and practiced, and when the whole of society is in a state of flux. Many people need help to try to live constructive and happy lives in spite of the unstable society where a lot of threatening forces are impacting upon them."

"Dr. Munzer, is my sexual preference part of my emotional life? First, I love all different people in different ways, and then I choose a

partner as part of my ability to love. And when I choose a partner, it includes a sexual dimension."

"There's no question in my mind that optimally one's emotional investment and one's sexual attraction and fulfillment are found in the same person. In ninety percent of our population, it happens with a person of the opposite sex; in ten percent of the population, with someone of the same sex. People do vary all over the place. There are some people who make their emotional investment with one sex and find sexual pleasure with the other sex. But my feeling about committed relationships—whether they be gay or straight—is that the emotional investment in the other person is the primary and most important part of the relationship. And then, obviously, one turns to one's friend and intimate partner for sexual satisfaction as well."

"I've never had sexual intimacy with men, although I've had sex with men. I've had that intimacy with women. How would you, as a professional, explain this?"

"To the best of my knowledge, Mary, no one has been able to explain love, and I'm not going to try to do it here. I will say your experience is by no means a unique one. Not all, but most of the gay people with whom I've worked have had at least some relationships with members of the opposite sex. The majority of them have reported very much of what you've said: they had sexual satisfaction but there was something very important that was missing."

"What's that important something that was missing?"

"You don't give up, do you? Maybe I can best explain it by sharing a personal experience with you. I'll explain it in terms of what I feel should be there. Actually, the experience was one of the most impressive I've ever had with a patient.

"Like most analytically trained psychiatrists, I do not socialize with my patients. However, for many years I have felt that I could attend important ceremonies, such as weddings. A gay couple whom I'd counseled at one time decided to celebrate their union and their relationship. As a married woman myself, I'd attended many heterosexual weddings. But I had really mixed feelings about going to this same-sex celebration: a 'Holy Union Ceremony' was the way the invitation was worded. It was in the Metropolitan Church, and I went. I don't think I've ever been more impressed with the dignity and solemnity of a religious service. It raised my own consciousness a lot."

"I'd like to explore the area of intimacy, Dr. Munzer. What is 'intimacy' in terms of a healthy committed relationship?"

"Intimacy is hard to define; I suspect it can mean quite different things to different people. To me, perhaps the single most important component of an intimate relationship is mutual trust. One must trust the other sufficiently to allow oneself to show one's true vulnerability in the presence of that other. Within an intimate relationship, one could expect to feel safe, trusting, and trusted, loved, cared for, supported."

"What is the basis of a person's fear of intimacy with someone else?"

"I believe that most of our fears are learned. I think someone who greatly fears intimacy with another human being is someone who has had bad experiences probably beginning in infancy, certainly in early childhood, where the intimate relationships have not been safe ones."

"Safe as opposed to threatening, and threatening in terms of what?"

"The threatening aspects could vary greatly. Probably all of us develop our basic trust or distrust largely due to our early experiences with being mothered. The mother who really cares for her child unambivalently or relatively unambivalently, the mother who is capable of what we call 'good enough mothering' is a mother who can help her infant, and later her toddler and her preschool child, develop what we call basic trust. The mother who is rejecting, hostile, depressed, or very anxious may not be capable of 'good enough mothering,' and her infant and young child grows up lacking the kind of ability for trust which is so basic to the ability to form good relationships throughout the rest of life."

"Why is intimacy different from 'merging' with another human being?"

"Intimacy, true intimacy, is totally different from merging. Intimacy is a valued attribute and quality which occurs when people have been able to grow up with relatively good mental and emotional health. Merging is not a good quality. It is one which develops when the growth process has been distorted. The healthy mother helps her small child separate from her. This happens usually around the toddler period, when the mother helps her child go out into the world and meet it. When mothering has failed, the small child is unable to differentiate himself or herself as a separate little being: that is what we call 'merging.' The child has a symbiotic relationship with the mother, a relationship where the child is not a separate little being. It is from healthy little children that autonomous self-confident adults develop."

"Does intimacy have to mean dependency, Dr. Munzer?"

"Most definitely not. Dependency, again like the merging we've just been discussing, is something which we do not associate with mental health. Dependency is fine in small children. But part of the process of growing up is to become increasingly independent and increasingly clear about who you are and what you stand for. The person who has attained a reasonable degree of mental and emotional health is not a dependent person, and certainly not someone who is going to be prone to merging. The healthy person will be capable of a truly intimate relationship in which he or she, as an independent human being, can relate in a warm, trusting, and intimate way with another adult who has also attained a certain degree of autonomy and independence."

"Is intimacy more of a problem for gay couples than it is for straights?"

"I see no reason to believe so. As I think I've mentioned before, no one has yet found any correlation between any human attribute, good or bad, and either straightness or gayness. I have treated both gay and straight people who have problems with dependency or with a lack of clear ego boundaries. But as I said, there is no correlation between these undesirable developmental deficits and sexual orientation. As a footnote to this, I think to the extent that there is any difference at all, my hunch would be that intimacy might be a little bit easier with gay couples, simply because of the fact that, by definition, both partners in the gay relationship have had similar experiences in the socialization process. Both partners have been brought up as little girls or little boys. They've shared many experiences and many of the same cultural pressures. They've conformed in many of the same ways. So in a theoretical sense, at least, intimacy might be easier for them."

"Dr. Munzer, would you comment on the sexual act as opposed to sexual intimacy?"

"It is, unfortunately, true that the sexual act is possible without any true intimacy at all. We see this in casual one-night stands or in those people who think of their sexual behavior as promiscuity. In its most extreme form, of course, it occurs in rape. The sexual act—

as I say, unfortunately—does not have to include intimacy. In my mind, there is no question that the sexual act is at its most desirable when it is associated with true and total intimacy between the participants."

"Do gay couples have more serious problems than straight couples?"

"I do individual and group therapy as well as couples therapy. I work with male homosexuals, lesbians, and heterosexuals. I've frequently told my gay patients that homosexuality or lesbianism is no protection against various forms of psychopathology. Unfortunately, ours is a troubled world. There are a number of poor relationships—gay and straight—where one or both partners are seriously disturbed. But I cannot say that I've found more problems among gay couples than I've found among straight couples.

"They sometimes have different problems. Gays are frequently estranged from their families, which is a difficult situation. There are frequently children involved in rather complicated relationships between their parents—a lesbian mother, for instance, who has joint custody with the children's heterosexual father. Maybe that heterosexual father has remarried. Children and stepchildren present more complicated problems for gay couples than for straight couples.

"However, I have not seen any more disturbance in the children where one of the parents is gay as compared with children where both parents are straight. I think it's very nice if children can grow up with their biological parents, who love each other—this is the ideal family situation. However, I haven't seen any difference in the amount of disturbance shown by children from broken marriages where one parent is either a homosexual or a lesbian."

"I have a heterosexual woman friend who divorced and remarried. She raised her two children with her second husband. However, when her children go to visit their natural father, he'll ask them, 'How's your mother, the whore?' I interviewed two lesbians who are raising two children. When these children visit their natural father, he asks them about their mother, the 'lessie,' or their mother, the 'dike.' As adults, do we victimize our own children by laying our crazies on them?"

"Those are two stories of equally appalling proportions. But they do illustrate the point I've been trying to make: there are troubled people in any ethnic group and of any sexual orientation. I believe there are also evil people—people who deliberately hurt other people. There are also good and compassionate and understanding people in any group, whether they be gay or straight. If people care deeply for their children, they will try to make certain they're not victimized or used as pawns. If one is a really troubled person, then one can and may do damage to one's own children. Whether one stays in a marriage or ends it, whether one is gay or straight, there is no correlation between the basic goodness of people and their color, creed, or sexual orientation."

"I'd like to look at remarriage, Dr. Munzer. In terms of establishing a second relationship, do straight couples experience the same fears and reservations as gay couples?"

"That's one of your questions where I'd have to say I've not found any difference between gays and straights. The remarriage situation is very much the same for gays and straights."

"What is the situation and what are the similar problems?"

"If something was not good about their first marriage, people are afraid they'll make the same mistake again. Unfortunately, many people do. One of the most typical and unfortunate repetitions is teaming up for the second or third time with an alcoholic. And that happens with the same frequency among gays and straights. And it happens to gay and straight people for the same reasons. Those reasons need treatment; some people choose partners time and again where there will be misery for both. Again, this seems to happen in the gay population with the same frequency as it happens in the straight population.

"On the other hand, if there has been a good relationship which has been terminated by the death of one of the partners, the surviving partner is apt to again find a partner with whom he or she can have a good relationship, whether it's a gay relationship or a straight relationship."

"Are you saying that successful remarriage depends upon the mental health of the person, where they're at?"

"I truly believe that in most cases happiness does indeed depend upon the emotional and mental health of the person. In the great majority of cases, it's what each of us brings to life that determines whether or not that life is going to be happy. Generally speaking, external circumstances are far less important than we believe."

"Does being gay become an excuse for gay people who don't want to deal with what might be their real problems—problems that have nothing to do with their gayness?"

"It certainly can. Parenthetically, I find looking for a cop-out very human, even if it's perhaps not very admirable. People who are looking for a cop-out will seize upon anything they can. If one happens to be gay and failing in a job, failing with human relationships, or generally having difficulties, it's easier to say, 'It's because I'm gay.' Easier than perhaps to admit, 'This is because I failed to assert enough energy, because I'm hostile, because I'm overcompetitive or not competitive enough.' In a sense, this leads into what therapy is all about: to help people face the real issues with honesty and courage—not to blame their failures on gayness, blackness, Jewishness, the poverty of their parents, hard luck."

"Dr. Munzer, do you believe there's such a thing as gay homophobia?"

"No question about it. In the course of my professional life I've worked with anti-Semitic Jews, antiblack racist blacks, and antigay homophobic gays. A child who grows up as a member of a despised or rejected minority almost invariably internalizes some of the negative things he or she hears said about the minority group of which he or she is a member. The gay child growing up learns very early to believe that being gay is wrong, bad, sick. These are terrible and difficult things for a vulnerable child to assimilate. Some children have enough strength within them not to grow up homophobic. Others are exposed to people who are helping them, and they may not grow up homophobic. Unfortunately, a great many gay children don't have anyone who will understand them and help them. They grow up hating themselves."

"How is homophobia manifested in gay people?"

"Unfortunately, self-hate is not limited to any group. It's more widespread than it should be. I have a strong conviction that people are generally decent, and I wish people would like themselves. But the homophobic gay, like the anti-Semitic Jew, grows up hating himself and hating what he is. He can't change what he is, and he or she, in fact, feels inferior, sick, or sinful. This child then has low self-esteem; doesn't believe in his basic worth as a human being, and frequently manages to see to it that he fails in life. It's what we call a self-fulfilling prophecy. If you're convinced there's something awfully wrong with you, it's not that hard to somehow manage your life so that you never amount to anything. This is a phenomenon we see in all groups of people, but certainly more frequently in those people who've grown up in especially discriminated against minority groups."

"What's the answer for this type of person? How do you break out?"

"That's a big question and there's no easy answer. All mental health professionals have been struggling for years to help people overcome their lack of belief in their own self-worth. A good therapeutic experience, whether it be individual or group therapy, can help. Happily, there are a number of groups now which are trying to help all types of children. This entails better education for teachers, clergy, parents—not just for gay children, but for all children growing up in this country who are not part of the favored majority. All of them need help. The sources of help can be in many places and provided by people of good will who want to reduce the unnecessary suffering of people everywhere."

"What about a good emotional adult relationship for the gay child?"

"There is one especially sad thing about the gay child: in the majority of cases, a gay child is the only minority group person who grows up without a sharing kind of understanding from his or her own family. This is, of course, also true of the handicapped child. However, of the larger identifiable minorities, the gay child is the only one who is a stranger even in his or her own family. A black child may be a member of the only black family in the community, but he or she has the support of family who share in the child's blackness. Compare this with the gay child, who, in the great majority of cases, is the only gay child in the family group and frequently the only gay child in the community."

"What does this type of gay child need?"

"Supportive emotional relationships are absolutely essential for people anywhere. Since you're oriented to the particular problems of gays, I'll say that the sooner the gay child can be recognized and receive support, the likelier it is that the child will grow up a fulfilled and happy human being.

"We've only scratched the surface in the entire area of lesbianism and homosexuality as regards the problems that may or may not be present. One thing I do want to say: the age at which the child may realize his or her differences, of course, varies tremendously, depending upon the child and a variety of circumstances. But as soon as the potentially gay man or woman can be identified by self or others—this is the time when true understanding and informed emotional and educational support should be available."

"Dr. Munzer, why is it that some gays need to hang on to an 'I am different' attitude or idea?"

"My first response is because they are different. But the way you phrase the question—'Why do they have to hang on to the idea'—I think you're asking me to address myself to the defensive quality: 'I'm different, you can't tell me I'm not.' This is present in the gay population as it is with many other minority groups. The most usual social-psychological explanation: when any group has been subject to prejudicial discrimination, the group becomes highly defensive. In part, they accept the negative stereotyping. Then they defend themselves against it by saying, 'Yes, I'm different—what are you going to do about it?' It becomes a rebellious stand."

"Does what you just said tie into the self-hate of gay homophobia?"

"It certainly does. It's the other side of the same coin. There could be the gay person who'd say, 'You're right. I'm inferior, I'm sick, I'm bad, I need help.' That's similar to the old-fashioned black attitude, which is happily far less prevalent today: 'Yes, you're right. As a black, I can't compete; there's something about me that's genetically inferior.' It's a tragic acceptance of the negative things that this person—gay or black—has heard about himself or herself. The other side of the coin, the turnaround, is the man or woman who responds to this kind of negative stereotyping by becoming rebellious and defiant and saying, 'You say I'm different. Okay, I'm different. But gay is good, black is beautiful.' And all of us Americans have a historical precedence: *Yankee* was once used as a tremendous put-down word by the British for the colonials. But the proud colonials sang 'Yankee Doodle Dandy' and used *Yankee* as a word of pride."

"When can this turnaround be a healthy thing for the gay person?"

"Until discrimination has ended in an ideal future we haven't yet attained, this kind of turnaround is almost always a milestone on the growth toward health. It's far better to become defiant about what is negatively said about oneself as a minority person than to passively accept the negatives. So the defiance is a good place to be for a while. In growing toward total maturity, the minority person gets through his defiant period and comes to understand what all the miserable discrimination has been about. He or she forgives the oppressor, develops confidence in his or her own identity, and no longer has to be defiant."

"What has to happen to us as gays for us to see ourselves as the complete people we are?"

"I think the women's movement can help the gay movement. I'm a strong advocate of consciousness-raising, or C-R, groups. The C-R groups which were introduced to this country through the women's movement can also be tremendously helpful for gays. When a group of gay men and gay women can get together and talk freely and honestly about who they are, where they are, and how they got there—that kind of mutual support can help people get in touch with individual as well as collective strength. It can help people get in touch with their own human dignity. Then gays will be better able to confront and refute the negative stereotypes that don't fit them."

"Let's go in another direction now. By constantly being defined and defining ourselves in terms of sexual preference, don't we as gays contribute to the definition of being totally sexual creatures?"

"No question about that. I'm not sure what kind of constructive comment I can make. Until the heterosexual majority can be persuaded to stop characterizing the gay minority in terms of their sexual preference, gays are pretty much stuck with that characterization. It's similar to blacks being stuck with being identified by skin color rather than by their human attributes, which are considerably more important to them."

"Do straights look at gay love relationships as different and therefore inferior to their own heterosexual experiences with love relationships? And do we as gays contribute to their attitudes toward us by maintaining the 'I am different' platform?"

"I believe there is truth to both parts of that question. It would be a mistake to speak for all straights as it would be a mistake to speak for all gays. But certainly I think a great number of heterosexuals see homosexual relationships as basically different, therefore inferior. So far as the second part of the question, I think there's no doubt that gays support this attitude themselves by assuming the defiant 'Yes, we're different' posture. I think gays should work patiently and intelligently toward persuading the heterosexual majority of the basic similarity of themselves as human beings and of their relationships as human relationships."

"Personally, Dr. Munzer, I believe in universal emotional experiences that are shared by all people, whether they be gay or straight. I

think what most hurts and enrages me is that my love is not seen as valid or that it's seen as an inferior love because I am gay—and when my marriage is seen as less important or less worthy of respect because I am married and committed to a woman whom I consider my spouse."

"Mary, I can only respond to what you're saying within the context of a young woman with whom I am now working professionally. She has just lost, by death, her female lover with whom she had been living in a marriage-equivalent relationship for nearly four years. When her lover died, her gay friends all recognized the magnitude of her grief. They recognized that she had been widowed, bereaved. And they rallied to her support. In marked contrast, her family was totally unable to identify with her and extend to her the kind of compassionate understanding which they had extended to a sister of hers who'd lost her husband. It was a startling demonstration of how difficult it is for even quite decent and loving people—in this case her parents—to be able to understand how totally identical her feelings were even though her choice of sex object had not been the one that they would have chosen for her."

"As a lesbian, what can I personally do to help change the negative images of gay people?"

"As in so many other human problems, the best answer is the hard answer. Until and unless more healthy, effective, and socially productive gay human beings come out publicly as gays, it will be extraordinarily difficult for all gay people to emerge from their unfavorable position in our society. Men and women of distinction and accomplishment—doctors, lawyers, merchants and chiefs, supreme court justices, clergymen. When these people are recognized by the entire population as the fine people they are with a sexual preference that is different from the majority's, then and only then will all gay people have more opportunity to be seen for the complete people they are rather than being defined by only one attribute of their total being."

"Dr. Munzer, do you see a point—somewhere in the future— where gay couples and straight couples will be integrated—a point in time when they will be able to share the experiences of each other's lives?"

"I'm not sure whether you're asking me what I think will happen or what I'd like to have happen. Considering the present state of the world, I confess to being more pessimistic than optimistic about the overcoming of all kinds of prejudice. My hope is certainly that all prejudices will break down. I see the prejudice between gays and straights as very similar to ethnic prejudice, racial prejudice, sex prejudice, class prejudice, age prejudice. I believe that all of these make artificial barriers between people. I do have hope, and I will continue to work with the little bit I can do as an individual to try to overcome all kinds of divisiveness in the human family."

CHRIS ALMVIG *on* GAY SENIOR CITIZENS

Chris Almvig, in her early thirties, received her masters degree in gerontological administration from the New School for Social Research in New York City. Ms. Almvig is president of SAGE: Senior Action in a Gay Environment, Inc.

"I've always had an affinity for older people," Ms. Almvig explains. "When I discovered my own gayness many years ago, it seemed like a natural: I'd put my gayness together with my love for older people and create a career for myself in the field of gerontology."

"Ms. Almvig, what is SAGE?"

"Basically, it's a coalition of professionals in social service and gerontology. Plus we're mobilizing the available resources of the local homosexual and lesbian community. One definition of a community is that it cares for its more vulnerable members, so we're gays taking care of the special needs of our own gay elderly."

"What are those needs?"

"We're attempting to meet the needs of older gays which aren't being met by the traditional social and voluntary agencies. They're the needs of the aged: reducing their loneliness and isolation; helping them with shopping and maybe escorting them to a doctor; telephone contact; friendly visiting. We're training our volunteers to provide services to the homebound, the institutionalized, or frail gay. By doing this type of work, we enable these people to build new relationships and reestablish connections with the gay community."

"Are the needs of older gays different from the needs of older straights?"

"Most of the needs are similar. However, the situation of gays—let's say sixty and over—is unique in that they've lived hidden lives, some for fifty or sixty years. They've hidden and denied the most basic part of their persons—their sexual identity. SAGE wants to tell these men and women that they don't have to hide anymore— we understand where they're coming from and we're here to help them. It's gay adults reaching out to the older gay community."

"Help them how?"

"Many of these people have been involved in really long-term relationships. They've lost a lover with whom they shared their life for twenty or thirty years. They don't have anyone to talk to. They need to share their bereavement with someone, but who can they share it with if they've lived a hidden life? We have trained psychiatrists and social workers working with us. And maybe it isn't a professional—maybe it's just someone to talk to. Peer support is vitally important to all gays, but particularly to our elderly, who are cut off and isolated. These people simply don't have the support systems available to straights."

"A widows' and widowers' counseling service for gays?"

"That's only one aspect. Say you have two elderly lesbians in their seventies. They want to make a will, but they don't know where to go or how to do it because of the unique aspect of their relationship. Whether or not they want anyone to know it, they're a gay couple. We can connect them with a lawyer, where they can freely specify what they want in their will. Our volunteers will never discuss the individual's gayness unless the person wants to discuss it. But the fact that they're aware that you know they're gay can help them discuss private and personal things if they choose to."

"What are some of the common problems of widowhood for gays and for straights?"

"As a society, I think, we're very private and self-involved. Particularly in an urban situation, we're not sharing that much with our neighbors. Friendship networks are often confined to special interests. People become estranged and isolated in widowhood.

"Widowhood decreases a person's options. I think this is more of a problem for women—both heterosexual women and lesbians. Perhaps a bit less of a problem for the lesbian than it is for the straight woman. Women simply haven't been trained to ask. This is generally less of a problem for lesbians. A straight woman isn't going to ask a man to have dinner.

"For lesbians who've spent a lifetime passing for straight and living with their lovers in suburbia, it is a whole other set of problems. They may have thought they passed for straight in suburbia, but they never really became part of the neighborhood. A woman's lover dies and she's out there in suburbia, disconnected and isolated from her straight neighbors. Generally speaking, however, gay or straight, your friendship network diminishes as you get older.

"The financial problems are similar for gays and straights: if you lose your partner, you lose their Social Security income. And if you've been living on two sets of retirement incomes, you then have to make the adjustment to one. That's a burden for gays and straights. However, where a straight woman's retirement might be supplemented by her children, gay elderly people have no such financial resource."

"Let's look at the death of a partner. What's similar to gays and straights?"

"Mourning and bereavement are mourning and bereavement—sexual orientation doesn't have anything to do with it. People lose someone they've loved, depended upon, shared with. They've lost the person who's always been there for them—they've lost their significant other. It doesn't matter whether you're gay or straight—you can't replace that person.

"After a while the surviving partner wants to go out, wants to meet other people. But there's such fear of venturing out alone. When you've been with someone twenty or thirty years, you don't have to think about your self-worth: you've already been accepted. When that person who accepted you as you are for so many years is gone, your identity and self-worth come into question again.

"Straight women, no matter how old they are, are seen as sex objects. And it's difficult. You're sixty or sixty-five—how do you get it together so you'll be attractive? Older straight men are looking for companionship in another woman after their wives have died, but they also want someone who's acceptable and attractive-looking. Perhaps this appearance is less of an issue for lesbians. Looking good is important to lesbians, but not as important as the relationship they may be able to develop with another older lesbian.

"For older homosexuals, even though there may not be the possibility of another long-term relationship, there's always the possibility of sex. For the older straight man sex isn't that available."

"I'd like to look a little more deeply at the identity crisis a person might experience when a long-term partner or spouse dies?"

"All of a sudden you've got to look at yourself as a single unit. And that's very difficult when you've spent thirty years thinking in terms of two. You have to learn how to shop for one. Vacations—do you go away alone or do you go on a tour? How will you feel alone on a tour? And what do you do with your time?"

"What are the advantages of gay widowhood as opposed to straight widowhood?"

"There are some very pragmatic advantages. Gays are in a better position than straights because they haven't been into roles. Even if older gays were into roles socially because, for their time, it was expected, they didn't necessarily practice those roles in the privacy of their homes. Straight men have never been taught basic housekeeping. Straight women have always had a live-in mainte-nance man in the form of their husbands. Straight men have to learn how to cook for themselves, shop, maintain their house or apartment. Many of them have a hard time with everyday function-ing after they've lost their wives. A straight woman has to learn how to handle a checkbook, take care of insurance, worry about the car. These don't seem like big things, but learning is hard when you're older—it's all confusing and frightening.

"For gays, even those who've been into roles, there's been the opportunity to share some of the responsibilities of the respective roles. Gays are generally more autonomous. Lesbians didn't have a man to depend on to take care of their homes, budgeting, the car. And gay older men know how to cook, clean, and take care of themselves. Gay or straight, the sharing of roles makes the loss of a partner much easier."

"What about the emotional turmoil involved with the loss of a lifelong partner?"

"It's different for every couple, whether they be gay or straight. If the couple has been totally dependent upon each other, the loss to the surviving partner can be quite severe—you don't know who you are anymore. However, if the two people in the relationship have been two separate people, it can be a lot easier. Were they two personalities separate and distinct from each other? Did they have activities separate and exclusive of each other? Did they each have their own network of friends plus the mutual friends they shared as a couple? If they lived their life together as two separate individuals, bereavement is easier. The surviving partner can more easily pick up the pieces. I don't think that's got anything to do with being gay or straight—these are human questions.

"Creativity is important because it helps people to build new lives for themselves when they've lost their significant other. When I use the word 'creativity,' I'm talking about the ability to express yourself, the ability to create outlets for yourself. And perhaps this is one of those areas where gays are in a better position than straights. Straight people put all their energy into their children. As gays, most of us don't have children. We learn early on to put our energies into ourselves and into our relationships with our partners. For instance, many of us express ourselves through educational pursuits and careers. Now this is within the context of our relationships—as we grow with our partners, hopefully we're growing as individuals. For most straights, their whole life is their husband or wife and their children. What is then important to the straight person who's lost their partner? Gays are somewhat ahead because straights don't begin looking at second careers or whatever until their children are grown. Gays have been dealing with these things throughout their lives. Because young gays tend to look at their future less in terms of marriage than do straights, they know they have to depend upon themselves. I knew I wanted a career before a woman wanting a career was an 'in' thing. I knew I wouldn't marry and have a man to take care of me. So I began to think about taking care of myself at a very early age. Even now, within the context of my relationship, I'm established as an independent person with my own career and my own dreams."

"What can people do during middle age to help them prepare for the loss of a partner in their old age?"

"What you're talking about is better preparation for loss, because the loss of a loved one is an inevitable reality for everyone. I think in middle age we have to open ourselves up. We have to see ourselves as self and not necessarily in terms of the significant other in our life. Where can we go? How can we grow? We have to learn new things about ourselves and about our partners. We have to develop new friendships outside of our primary relationships. And if there's jealousy and possessiveness in our relationships, we have to get rid of them because they inhibit our individual life experience."

"Do you find in working with the gay elderly that they are less financially prepared for old age than straight people?"

"Quite the contrary. On the whole, gays are more financially stable than elderly straight people because they haven't had to spend all their money on children. They've been able to save. And they've been able to invest in their own careers. For instance, lesbians seem to have higher incomes and therefore more savings than straight women. Lesbians always knew they'd have to support themselves in old age, and they planned for it. Homosexuals and lesbians never counted on family support in their old age. They planned for themselves because there was no one else to depend on.

"However, there's another group of gays who bought society's telling them they weren't worth much. Therefore, they used whatever money they had to establish their worth. This type of gay never saved or planned for old age."

"What problems are unique for gay widows and widowers?"

"Who can you talk to? Who can you tell? Do you have a family member who understands? Do your neighbors know you lost your spouse and your lifelong partner—not your roommate? And where does an elderly gay person go to meet people? What if you're a widowed lesbian living in the suburbs—do you go to a city bar? There simply aren't any places for older gays to go where they can be comfortable. Their future options become very narrow. The most severe problem for the gay widowed: there's no one to confide in.

"We have to look at the history of many of our older gays who've lived in seclusion and in hiding with their partners. And their partner was maybe the only other person in the world who knew their secret. And now their partner is dead. What happens to these older gays is that they then become 'straight' to have contact with other people. All these older gays in these senior citizen community centers are living as someone they're not. But they don't have any choice. Isolation might have been all right when their partners were alive—they had someone to share it with. Now it's total isolation or playing straight with a straight seniors group. They compromise their identity for social contact. Think about it. They're forced to revert back fifty years, maybe to their teens, before they'd acknowledged their gayness. It's tragic to think that in the last years of their lives they've got to become someone they're not. And even at best, they're still on the periphery of a straight seniors group. These elderly straights are talking about their grandchildren. Or they're talking about their dead husbands or wives. They're sharing memories. The elderly gay can't share his or her memories. So they sit there quietly listening and never participating."

"What's the possibility of their meeting other older hidden gays in these straight seniors groups?"

"That can make it worse. My full-time job is, of course, in a straight seniors community center. I know of six gay men who attend this center. I couldn't understand why these six old men weren't friends. After all—and I was assuming—don't they have a common background and a common history? Then it dawned on me—individually, they're all in the closet. Put three of them on a bench sitting in the sun—they're afraid people will know they're gay. They isolate themselves from each other. They're paranoid about people seeing them together and thinking they're gay."

"Are you saying some older gay people would rather deal with their loneliness and isolation than deal with being exposed as a gay person?"

"They've lived a whole life of this hiding. They can't make major changes in their behavior and in their lives at sixty-five. Just because they're retired doesn't mean they can come out of the closet. They're afraid of being blackmailed. I know an older gay man who lives alone in a residential hotel. A couple of people who work in the hotel picked up on the idea that he is gay. They started to blackmail him: they told him they wanted him to give them money or they were going to tell the other people in the hotel he was gay. This old man was terrified—and he's eighty-two years old."

"What if I personally meet an elderly person I think is gay?"

"You may spot an older gay person. But this person thinks no one knows his or her secret. First of all, you can terrify an old man by hitting him with your gayness. And you could devastate an old woman by even alluding to the idea that you think she might be a lesbian. You first have to establish a human relationship. Reaching out has to be done with them reaching out to you—they have to come out to you. The issue of coming out is a big thing to older gays because they've probably turned off that part of their life many years ago. It's a delicate issue and it's very frightening to them."

"What do you do to reach these people?"

"SAGE would like to provide a nonthreatening and supportive atmosphere for these people, a place where they can come and participate in activities: a gay senior citizens center. We're not espousing separatism. We'd like to see a day when everyone can be out. We'd like to see social workers who are sensitive to the particular needs of older gay people. If that were the way things were, you wouldn't need an organization like SAGE. However, we know all of that is a long way off."

"That's SAGE. And right now there's only one SAGE, and that's in Manhattan. What do you see as the role of the adult gay community?"

"We must reach out to our elderly. The gay community should be connected to its older constituents. We don't have grandparents to tell us what it was like to be gay when they were younger. We don't have role models. These older gays have something to offer us. Younger gays should create or become involved with groups and organizations which are trying to reach out to the older gay. We can grow in one-on-one giving. Some of these elderly gay people have been totally alone for ten or fifteen years. Not only have they turned off their gayness in their loneliness, they've turned off themselves. Reaching out to them can enable them to renew a relationship with themselves within a community of gays. For an elderly gay, this can mean a whole new life of new friends, shared experiences, and shared memories."

9
TILL DEATH DO US PART
Gay Widowhood

MARY *and* SARAH

The trees on this street are old. Their branches cover the wood-framed houses like huge umbrellas. This is not the suburbia of the sixties and seventies—ranches and "splanches" extending themselves over manicured lawns. This is early suburbia—the post-World War II movement away from the cities. The sidewalks sag a bit and they are cracked. The leaves in the untrimmed and rather tiny front yards have not been raked away.

A small woman in her mid-sixties ushers me into the kitchen. "You want coffee? Cheese, crackers? Sit there," she says, pointing to a chair near the small kitchen table. "Put your tape recorder on top of the toaster. I really don't like those things, but I suppose I'll go along with you. I'm not holding that microphone—balance it on top of the cracker box. I'm not using any real names. We'll be Mary and Sarah. I'll be Mary; Sarah died in 1961."

"You want to know our background." Mary laughs. "Our background goes back to before you were born, kid. You got enough tape? I met Sarah in '33. I was eighteen; she was twenty-four. I was in college, living at home. I think my parents were aware I was a lesbian, but it wasn't brought out in the open. I think my father was relieved when I left home.

"At the time I met Sarah, she was pregnant, living in the city with her husband, George. When I moved into the city, the three of us got to be good friends. I ended up moving in with them. Those were hard times. The child was born in '34. Sarah and I became lovers while the three of us were living together. That was '36.

"I never anticipated Sarah and I being together—not for life. I didn't like the arrangement, but I was terribly attached to her and the child. She and George were having problems: no one had any money, he wasn't working, and he drank. We didn't have enough

197

food. Scraped up all we could to feed the child. Bad times. I was going to college, making twenty-five cents an hour typing. I graduated college in '36, got a WPA teaching job for twenty-two dollars a week—good money in those days.

"Summer of '37, George left. My whole life became Sarah and the baby. Their breaking up had something to do with me, but not entirely. I think my relationship with Sarah was a symptom of their marriage going sour.

"Sarah and I and the baby moved to another apartment in another part of the city. We moved in as two sisters—all our neighbors knew we were sisters. They accepted it. In those days, people didn't even think about it. Sometimes I might've dressed manishly, but no one wondered about it. We decided the child wouldn't be raised in a lesbian home. We were very careful, very inhibited. We lived like that for years.

"After we moved, we made straight friends in the new neighborhood. Sometimes we'd see other lesbians we'd known, but not that often. We didn't have the time or the money to go out. Our lesbian friends petered out. Sarah's husband had been giving her seven dollars a week for support, then he stopped. She went to court and the judge tried to reconcile them. It didn't work, but for a while he continued giving her money. Then he disappeared. I was holding down two jobs, supporting the three of us. Sarah, of course, was home raising the child. We were together, trying to survive."

"Mary," I ask, "did you consider it a marriage?"

She looks at me somewhat confused. "I didn't give it that name, but it certainly was a marriage. Neither of us would've walked away from it. I remember we'd been together for about eight years. I wanted to chuck the whole thing. I was always scrounging for money trying to stay alive. We were poor, but then everybody was poor."

"Why didn't you chuck the whole thing, Mary?"

"Because I loved her, and I loved the child," she answers. "That's why I didn't chuck the whole thing. Sarah and I loved each other, and we loved each other for twenty-seven years.

"We bought this house in '49. Moved out of the city because the neighborhood was changing. I didn't want to leave the city, but we bought this house with another couple. The woman was a friend of mine. She and her husband lived upstairs; Sarah and I and the child lived down here. I bought them out in '51: borrowed the money from my mother. I learned how to do everything after that— plumbing, electrical work. We didn't have money to pay anyone.

There's no mortgage on this place now. I can live here comfortably.

"The fifties were good years. Financially difficult, but good. We sent the child to boarding school—high school. She was having academic problems. It was the first time we'd ever been alone. Just the two of us here together seemed like a renewal—things were never better. We were close, we could be uninhibited—they were good years. Whatever difficulties we'd ever had seemed to be resolved."

"Was Sarah ill before she died, Mary?"

"I find it difficult to talk about, even after all these years," she says with a sigh. "I suppose I had a lot of warning, but I wasn't prepared. She'd been tired, not feeling well. She was in bed all day. That night she had chest pains. I called a doctor, an old man down the street who made house calls. He wanted her to go to the hospital and have an EKG. She got very upset, refused to leave the house. She said she'd go in the morning. She must've felt she was dying and didn't want to leave the house.

"I sat with her and we talked. You know, we talked about the first time we were together. We talked about a lot of memories—we'd been together a lot of years. We talked about how much we'd loved each other. She told me I looked pale, I should eat something. I came out here. She yelled my name, but when I ran into the room, she was in the throes of death. She died the way she wanted to die—with me and in her home.

"I went to stay with my sister and her husband for a while. After about a month I came back here. Our tenants upstairs didn't even know Sarah had died. And when I told them she had, they thought my sister had died.

"We hadn't been friendly with anyone in the neighborhood, not even the neighbors next door. So when I came back here, I was really alone. I couldn't think of one good reason to go on living. It was as if I'd died too. Nothing I'd cared about before even interested me: music, books—nothing. I brooded.

"Finally, I decided to go into therapy because I wasn't getting over it. It helped, really did. Then I got into painting, writing. Writing was a way I could record our life together. I'd work all day, come home, and compulsively write or paint all night. I terribly abused my health after Sarah died. I didn't eat, and I was smoking three packs of cigarettes a day. I hardly ever slept because I had to get it all down on paper, I had to get it out. It was no surprise to me when I got a heart attack in 1967.

"After I got home from the hospital, one day I impulsively

bought myself a puppy. Then I bought another puppy. But after eighteen months, the first one was killed by a car. Seemed that nothing I cared about could survive. But my life was changed by these dogs. I had something alive in the house when I came home at night. I stopped writing and painting so compulsively. Later I went back to school in the evenings."

"And what about now, Mary? Did you think about selling the house?"

"People told me to sell the house after Sarah had died. I didn't want to. The memories are good here—we were closer and happier here than we'd ever been. In a way, I feel her presence here."

"Mary, you and Sarah spent all your time together. You didn't have that many friends. Did that make adjusting to losing her harder?"

"The only time we weren't together was when we were working. Home, we were together. I couldn't have been any different than I was. I will say it makes starting a new relationship very hard. In the late sixties I got involved with another woman. She was divorced, had an older son. I was afraid for her and for him that somebody would find out—you know, on the job or something. It was her first relationship. I didn't want to get involved with anyone again. So when it was over, it didn't bother me that much. I don't know. I guess I didn't love her."

"How do you feel now about the deceptive life you lived with Sarah for so many years?"

"I'm not upset about it. It was the times we lived in—I would've lost my job. You couldn't be open. It was something we never discussed. It was the right thing to do at that time."

"Would you be interested in another committed relationship at this point in your life?"

"Yes, I certainly would. Two years ago, I met a woman at a party. Nothing developed with that, but I became interested in what I looked like. I lost weight. I got interested in myself again. Basically, I'm a monogamous person, and I'd like another relationship. It's always a possibility. I don't want to live with anyone again, don't think I could tolerate the overintimacy. I would like a sex life, compatibility, companionship. I'd like someone I could go around with so I could feel part of something. After Sarah's death, the word *we* was like a bullet hitting me everytime I heard it—the thought that it was no longer *we,* it was *I.* We loved each other. When she died, I felt as if I'd been kicked out of her life by her death."

JAMES *and* MARK

"Please excuse me if I seem a little bit confused," says James. "But driving over here I was going over the past, trying to remember things I wanted to tell you. It's almost eight years ago, but it's very painful. I don't want to talk to you, but I have to.

"We'd spent a beautiful New Year's weekend with friends and relatives at the house. We had an apartment here in the city, but the house was really our home. It was oceanfront property, and we'd built and designed it together. Mark was planning to retire early, and I would've quit my job. We were going to spend the winters in Florida and the rest of the year living in our home on the ocean.

"I'm sorry—I'm rambling. The week after New Year's, we came back to the city. Mark went to visit his sister. She called me the next morning and said he was dead. He died of a heart attack. He was only forty-two. We'd been together fifteen years, but we still had our whole life ahead of us.

"I was in a terrible emotional state. Mark's sister handled the wake and the funeral. I wasn't even consulted. My mother lived here in the city with Mark and me—the three of us had a good life together. But she and I weren't even allowed to ride in the family funeral cars. I resented all of it. Mark and I had lived together as two married people. His sister decided he would be buried in the family plot. We'd always said we wanted to be buried near our home on the ocean. But I had no say in any of it—he's buried here in the city. I was so grief-stricken. There's a little cove near the house—we always used to walk there together. Please don't think I'm crazy, but I went up there and brought back some sand and salt water. I sprinkled them over Mark's grave. What I was trying to tell him was, even though he couldn't be home with me, I could bring a little bit of the sand and the ocean to him."

"What happened after the funeral, James?"

"Well, I was in a terrible emotional state. But after the funeral, I was also terrified. During the wake, Mark's sister had told me we'd discuss the house and its contents after the funeral. If we hadn't had a will, she would've taken everything away from me. Even after I told her about the will, I knew she was checking things out legally—she was planning to take me to court. All I could think of was, 'I've lost him and now she's going to take everything else away, too.' It was my house because Mark and I worked hard to put everything into it. The house is in another state, and I spoke to our lawyer there. He told me not to worry—our will covered the land, the house, and all the contents. He told me not to talk to her and, if she continued to bother me, to just refer her to him. She's a very materialistic woman. Even though Mark had left her a sizable estate, she wanted everything. She'd always objected to me. She resented me because she wanted to see Mark married."

"What about emotional support? Was anyone there to help you get through this?"

"My two brothers and their wives were very responsive. I could've never gone through it without them. I believe my mother and my family knew about Mark and me, but no one ever said anything. And when Mark died, they didn't even say then that they knew; but they did know what my loss was.

"I stayed with one of my brothers during the wake. I was in another room and I could hear my sister-in-law talking to my nieces and nephews. The children couldn't understand why I was so upset. I heard her tell them, 'It's the same as it would be for me if Daddy died—I'd be as upset as Uncle James.'

"They helped me emotionally, but they also helped me settle a lot of the financial affairs. You see, it took both of our incomes, Mark's and mine, to pay the mortgage on the house. Neither of us had any life insurance. So when he died, I couldn't afford the mortgage payments alone. Even though I didn't lose the house to Mark's sister, I was afraid I was going to lose it to the bank. We'd applied for mortgage insurance when we first built the house in the early sixties, but we were turned down because we were two unrelated males. My brother and sister-in-law came to the bank with me. The bank officer was very nice. Mark and I had been accepted in the community, we were respected and liked. The bank worked out a second mortgage. I remortgaged the house to get the payments down to an amount I could afford alone. That's what I did to keep the house. But even now I can only use it during the winter, because I have to rent it in the summer to keep up with the expenses."

"Tell me about your life with Mark, James."

"Mark was the only man I was ever involved with. I came out with him when I was seventeen; he was twenty-seven at the time. We had a great life together, and we were very devoted to each other. We had a strong home life. Even having my mother with us was fine—we were happy together. As far as socializing, we entertained straight friends and family. We only had two gay friends, and they were overseas at the time of Mark's death."

"How did you adjust after Mark's death?"

"When you have such a beautiful thing and it's so quickly cut off, it leaves you feeling dead and empty. I floundered. I became extremely lonely. I still had my mother with me, and I guess she helped me keep it somewhat together. She was even helping me out financially. She's come to the house with me sometimes on weekends. I had this old convertible. We'd put the top down and the two of us would sing out loud all the way to the house. I remember our favorite duo used to be, 'I Left My Heart in San Francisco.' We'd sing our hearts out. But then my mother died. Within a year, Mark, my mother, and my sister all died.

"I was destroyed and I don't even know if I have it fully together even now. I'd built my world around Mark and my mother. I didn't need anybody else. But then my whole world collapsed. My body was still going, but I think I was dead. I was conscious of everything that was going on around me. Like if I saw a red light, I'd stop. If I saw a green light, I'd go. But mentally, I was out of it—the whole world had ended for me.

"I tried going to the gay bars several times but it turned me off. Mark and I weren't accustomed to going to the bars, and I wasn't comfortable. I couldn't meet anyone there—it was a different lifestyle. And I couldn't go to the bars because I felt guilty. I felt guilty because I was betraying Mark by going to the bars even though he was dead. It was also my extreme Roman Catholic upbringing that made me feel guilty about picking someone up. The bars weren't the real world for me. I'd known a different kind of life with Mark: we'd had a home, family, and friends. I just couldn't cut it in the bars.

"I think gay people have to prepare themselves for the eventuality of death. It happens to us just like it happens to straight people. I didn't have any gay friends, and now I'm more aware of the importance of that. If I'd had gay friends at the time of Mark's death, there would've been people for me to relate to."

"What about now, James? What about the future?"

"I'd like to meet someone with whom I could have a relationship similar to the one I had with Mark. I'm looking for love; for a person I'd be compatible with. A person who likes the simple things in life: a home, walks by the ocean. I'm looking for someone I can be devoted to, someone to work with.

"I think I'll be able to find this person now because I'm finally getting my head on straight. I realize now my relationship with Mark was a beautiful part of my life. But it's behind me now and I have to go forward."

BILL *and* CHARLES

"It all happened very suddenly; he hadn't been ill. It was Mother's Day weekend of '76. We'd brought my mother here to our country home for the weekend. Charles was working in the garden with her. I was watching him watering the flowers. When I turned around again, he was lying on the ground. And that was the end—heart failure. He was fifty-five. It was a shock, and yet I was happy he'd died the way he did—he was doing what he liked to do. I'm sure if he had a choice, he would have chosen to die as he did—no prolonged illness, no agony. It was a peaceful death.

"I called his brother and he and his wife came right away. I relied a lot on them. They handled all the arrangements for having his body moved to the city; they took care of the funeral. They were just beautiful, and they gave me a lot of consolation."

"Did Charles's brother and family know you and Charles were a homosexual couple?"

"I'm sure they knew we were gay, but nothing was ever said. Charles and I had been together for twenty years, and I was better accepted into his family than I was into my own. I was part of his family, and I had no trouble with them at the time of his death. There was no contesting of property ownership. Our country home was in both our names, and there was no will. His brother helped me work with a lawyer, and everything was taken care of. There were no large sums of money to speak of. We did have a joint account, which, through his brother's handling, was cleared and I received the money. I'd bought a car, but it was in Charles's name. There was no problem with that either."

"How did you adjust to Charles's death, Bill?"

"I was in the state of shock for a while. The funeral and the details of death distract you. I never had time to think during those days. I can't remember getting hysterical during the wake. Things went smoothly. I guess I was very bewildered, but I received a lot of support from our close friends—they seemed to rally round me. They came to the wake and stayed with me.

"After the funeral, though, I felt very alone and very confused. All of a sudden I was very lonesome. I felt that I was all by myself, that I had no one to talk to. Charles was gone—I had no one to make plans with, no one to consult or to ask questions. I took a week off from work, but then I was glad to get back.

"But thank God for close friends. I managed to get out and have some interests. I wasn't into self-pity, I was just very sad. I wasn't allowed to stay home—friends insisted that I be with them. I was able to get out and do things and not sit home in remorse. I'll say it again. Thank God for close friends because, three years later, I think I'm doing very well. I've gotten accustomed to living by myself, being my own person again. Of course, there's always the phone and people I can call. It's not the same as having a partner, but I do have hopes that someday something of that nature will happen to me again. At this point in my life, I'm just going along."

"Tell me about Charles."

"When I first met him, he was thirty-five. He was an interior decorator with a clientele of sorts. Later he went into sales: rugs, wallpaper. He was tall and handsome. Of course, he changed through the years as we all do. We aged together and neither of us complained. Charles was very jovial, and he loved to tell dirty jokes. He loved to entertain and he loved to dance. We had a lot of good times together. Our life was full and healthy: we were for each other. It was a good relationship; he was considerate of me as I was considerate of him.

"During our first five years together, he was still living at home because he was taking care of and supporting both his mother and his grandmother. Later, when they'd both died, we began to live together."

"Did you consider your relationship with Charles a marriage?"

"Yes, I considered it a marriage—it was a marriage between two people. It was two people looking after each other no matter what, through sickness and in health. It was an honest relationship."

"Was it a monogamous marriage, Bill?"

"Yes, sexual fidelity was important to us. It was the way we wanted it—it was our life together. In the beginning our sex life was fantastic. But later on it slowed down to, let's say, a more natural pace. I think that's normal. About six or eight months before his death, our sex life was placid. But it was something we both accepted.

"I'm a very straitlaced and loyal person. I didn't have sexual relationships with anyone else during my life with Charles. I looked around—you always look around. But I was very satisfied with what I had—in fact, maybe too satisfied. I don't believe Charles had had any outside sexual relations during our years together. We were very happy and we had quite a bit in common. We liked the same sort of people, we enjoyed traveling together. We were here in our country home every weekend."

"What sort of plans had you and Charles made for the future?"

"If Charles had lived, we would've been living here in the country now. Our goal was to come out here and retire, to become full-time members of this community. I've got a good retirement plan. I would've retired early and forced him to retire. We would've managed.

"Charles's death was so bewildering to me because we'd so closely planned what we were going to do. It wasn't that I was afraid of the future without him. I know life has to go on. But without him I procrastinate now more than I used to. I've lost my ambition to do things. With Charles I had enthusiasm. I don't have the 'push' we shared. We used to do things around the house together—it was our home, it settled and sealed our relationship.

"Our retirement plans were 'our' plans. With Charles gone, the plans don't mean that much to me. Because of our closeness, the plans were very exciting and meaningful for us. We were planning an addition on the house, a larger dining room. We were planning to sell the house in the city, and once we were established out here, we wanted to be able to travel. We'd once taken a five-week driving trip across the States, and we were looking forward to doing more traveling like that. We'd had such a ball on that trip we wanted to do it again.

"After his death, these plans never meant that much. They've gone by the wayside—I live from day to day. I don't plan too much for the future. I'm sixty-four and I'm even undecided about whether or not to retire in a year."

"I'm thirty-five. I'm committed to a woman in what I hope will be a lifelong relationship. You're not that much younger than my own father, Bill. What advice can you give me?"

"I've become very matter-of-fact. Call me a realist or a fatalist. But I would have to say be very thankful for the times you have together because they'll probably never be repeated. Be thankful to God because you'll have memories to live with and to be content with. If in the future you lose this woman you love, and if you meet another woman, it would be another type of relationship. It, too, will bring its joys and excitement. It's a shock, but you've got to be realistic: you've got to be big enough to face death and go on.

"I can't recapture what I had, I don't expect to. I'd like to have a companion, but I don't know if I've looked too hard to find one. Even if I met someone, I don't know if I'd be able to adjust. I have no remorse and no regrets. I still have our home, even though I'm here alone. It's something that Charles and I wanted, something we did together. I find a lot of consolation being here. It's our achievement—we both worked hard for it. I'm only sorry he's not here to enjoy it as I do. But this home is part of Charles, and it's a part of myself."

ADELA *and* DIANE

"Diane and I met when we were both twenty-four," Adela reminisces. "It was September 1954. I'd dropped out of college and was working in the city and living at home. Diane was studying to be an actress, and she had her own apartment in the city. We began seeing each other. I started staying overnight. Eventually, we began living together. She was into writing. We used to have these poetry readings at the apartment. I went back to school in the evenings and was working full time during the day. She had various jobs in theater and in television. At that point in my life, I wasn't attracted to men and I wasn't attracted to women—I was attracted to Diane. See, when I was coming up in the forties and fifties, nice middle-class Jewish girls didn't grow up to be lesbians. Diane and I weren't 'out'—not the way we consider being 'out' today. We didn't hide our relationship, but we didn't broadcast it to anyone. We lived together, we did things together, we shared our life with close friends."

"Adela, what do you think held the relationship together for twenty-two years?"

"Well, Diane and I had many similarities in our backgrounds. We'd both lost our fathers when we were fourteen. We each had one sister. But when I think about it, we started out neurotically. We were two people who fed each other. I wanted somebody to tell me what to do and so I picked a loving mother. Diane wanted someone who'd take care of her, who'd be good and kind. But as we each grew, the relationship changed. It became a relationship of mutual love and mutual respect.

"But we did have our problems. We split up for ten months in 1964. We continued to live together in this apartment, but not as lovers. Diane was so upset by my not wanting to be involved with her as a lover, she began seeing a psychiatrist. She ended up with a lesbian 'shrink' who hadn't resolved her own problems. Anyway, Diane began having an affair with her. When I realized what was going on, I became extremely jealous. Then it dawned on me that I was jealous because I loved her, and my saying I no longer wanted to be involved with her was ridiculous. We came together again and we were never apart until the end.

"It was so unfortunate that she became ill because by that time we were two people who loved each other in a very healthy way. We'd gotten through all the neurotic aspects of our relationship. We were both people who were standing on our own two feet and enjoying each other as people. There was more love and more thoughtfulness between us than many of the heterosexual couples we knew."

"When did Diane become ill?"

"In May of 1972. We'd bought a little country home in the woods in 1971, and we were supposed to go out there for the weekend. On Friday she asked me if I'd mind not leaving the city that weekend. She told me on Saturday that her doctor had found a cyst on her breast and he was going to remove it on Monday. So we spent the weekend in the apartment wallpapering the kitchen and the bathroom.

"Of course, I was at the hospital on Monday. After the results of the biopsy, the doctor told me it was cancer and he'd have to remove her breast. By that time Diane had a very good job with one of the television networks, and she didn't want anyone at work to know. After her operation, she was very self-conscious. We had to work through a lot of that and I had to reassure her that one breast doesn't make a person.

"She recovered and went back to work. In November the cancer recurred and she began chemotherapy and radiation treatments. By the summer of '73, she was having these terrible pains in her back. We were told swimming was the best thing for someone who'd lost a breast, so we built a swimming pool at our country home. She couldn't even make it around the pool—the cancer had spread to her bones. Shortly after, she went in for surgery again. It was at that point that she stopped working full time. The network kept her on full salary and she ran her office from our apartment."

"Adela, did Diane know she was dying?"

"She asked the doctor point-blank. But even before she asked him, I think we both knew. He told her, 'Knowing what we do about this disease—yes, you will die of it. But our job is to keep you functioning and mobile as long as possible.' She was able to work for a good eighteen months more beyond that point. She needed help dressing and moving around but she did work. It was a slow process of deterioration. She was dying for four years."

"Did you and Diane ever openly discuss her dying?"

"Yes, we openly discussed it. At one point she wrote out instructions for me for her funeral. She was very creative, and writing about her funeral, I suppose, helped her. Dying isn't something you discuss all the time—it's something you know. But you can't deal with it every day. You have to put it aside or else you go crazy."

"How did you survive through all of this, Adela?"

"It was difficult. And, of course, as she became weaker and more immobilized, it became even more difficult. I continued with my own life. I was working during the day and teaching at night. Thank God, I was in therapy through this. My analyst insisted that I continue with my work. He felt it was important for both of us. And so I'd leave her and feel guilty when I did. Understand, there were stages. For a while, I'd dress her in the morning and then she'd be able to get herself around during the day. Then she fell and broke her hip, and there was really nothing they could do for her. I think the day the wheelchair arrived at the apartment was probably one of the hardest days. Even with that, she continued to have business meetings at the apartment.

"And we did have a lot of help from our friends. If I couldn't take her to the doctor because I was working, there was always a friend to take her. We were still able to go to our country home on weekends, and I always had help getting her in the car.

"In June of 1976, we moved her to our country home. I had to work the month, and the man she worked for spent two weeks taking care of her there. And then the families took over, and they were with me until the end."

"What families, Adela?"

"On the country road where our home was, there were five families—two gay families, including us, and three straight families. We'd always been close, but Diane's illness made them larger than life. No matter what hour of the day or night, they were there when they were needed to do whatever they could. No one ever sat down and spelled out the relationship—that we were a lesbian couple was never discussed. It was taken for granted.

"All the families celebrated Diane's forty-sixth birthday together with her on June nineteenth. One of the women made a cake. They were there with me—helping me feed her, helping me wash her.

Every night three of us would stand on one side of the bed, three of us on the other; we'd lift her on a tight sheet so we could change the bed. I was surrounded by people who cared and who would not leave me alone.

"Even during the last days, when I'd hired nurses, the families still stayed with us. On Sunday her temperature hit 106 degrees. Frank and Ron, the homosexual couple, told me they were going to take me for a walk on the beach. The three of us walked by the ocean for a while, and then we went back to the house. I stood by the bed watching her and they all stood with me. There seemed to be a longer and longer time between her inhaling and exhaling. Finally, she inhaled and never exhaled. You know, everyone broke down except me—I just stood there. During the four years, I'd trained myself not to cry. Even when she cried, I wouldn't. I knew I had to be strong, and I knew it wouldn't have been good for her if she saw me crying. So in the moments right after she died, I couldn't cry. And I haven't really cried it out yet."

"And where are you now, Adela?"

"I'm still lonely. But I enjoy my life, my friends, and my work. I was bound to Diane by love and by loyalty. I now have a greater sense of self than I had before, a greater sense of my own personal accomplishments. I want to be in love with someone and I want someone to be in love with me. It may never happen."

"Why is it that *now* you have a greater sense of self and your own accomplishments?"

"I've come a long way since Diane's death. When she died, I didn't want to live anymore. I would've traded places with her any day—I felt that she could do so much more than I could. You have to mourn and you have to grieve. Now I believe that each person must be a person within themselves. Then you seek out someone to love. Diane was my whole being—she was the center of my life.

"People should make a life for themselves within their relationships. Each one of us has our own special wants, needs, and interests. Two people can't be the same, can't be together all the time. Our relationship improved tremendously when we began to understand each other's needs. It was just fate. There was cancer in her family and she used to say she'd never live past forty-five—and she did, but just by one year."

NORMAN *and* JOSEPH

"We'd just retired and moved to the country—we thought we'd finally made it." Norman sighs. "We had so many plans. Between both our pensions, we would've been living in luxury after a lifetime of struggling. I wanted us to enjoy the leisure time we'd worked hard for."

"Norman, tell me about your life with Joseph."

"Joseph and I met each other in 1949. He was forty-four and I was twenty-nine. He worked for the railroad; I was a teacher. We had very little when we started out. We worked and we saved. We had a nice apartment, and then we were able to buy a car. In 1958, we bought a little cabin. We worked on it for fifteen years until, little by little each year, we had built it into a year-round house. It was our retirement dream—it was our home.

"During our twenty-seven years together, we were always involved with both our families. We went to all family occasions together. If they knew we were a homosexual couple, they never said anything to us. My mother also had us for dinner. We visited my brothers and sisters and their families. I think they knew, but they never pointed any fingers at us.

"We had a very beautiful relationship. I think it was better than some of the straight relationships in my own family. We had a sexual relationship until he became ill. It was a close, loving relationship. We never went out on each other; we were always there for each other. I doubt if I could ever duplicate the relationship I had with Joseph."

"What were the circumstances of Joseph's death?"

"He developed cancer in January 1975. He was operated on, and the doctors said he was fine. He felt great, and he went back to work. We took a cruise, and we went to London. And then we retired. He became ill again and was operated on in July of '76. The doctor told me the cancer had spread—there was no hope. It was just a matter of months. When we made the decision to retire, I knew he was sick. I didn't expect him to pass away as quickly as he did. I thought we'd at least have a year together.

"He'd say, 'Norman, why am I so sick?' It used to tear my insides out. I bathed him, took care of him. He kept telling me he didn't know how to thank me. I'd say, 'There's no reason to thank me— that's why I'm here.' Knowing he was dying, watching him waste away—it was terrible. He was always a very active man and it was so hard to watch him sitting and sleeping—it just wasn't him.

"I was glad he was still alive even though I knew he was sick and dying. I wanted him as long as I could have him. During those months of watching him die, I couldn't think of what life was going to be like without him. We'd made so many plans for retirement. I would just look at him and it was eating my insides apart.

"In September we'd been together twenty-seven years. I didn't want it to end—I wanted it to go on and on. But I knew it was coming. Once he went into the hospital in October, he went very fast. I was with him one day at the hospital, we were talking. He told me to leave. 'Go visit your brother,' he said, 'I'll see you tomorrow at two.' When I got to the hospital the next day, they told me he'd passed away."

"Did Joseph know he was dying, Norman?"

"He never admitted he was dying, but I think he knew. We'd rented an apartment in Florida for the winter, and he told me he didn't think he was going to make it. And then, about two days before his death, he insisted on being cremated when he died. And so we had a lawyer change his will. And, of course, I respected his wishes."

"How did you react after his death?"

"Even though I knew it was coming, there was such a terrible void in my life. I knew I had to snap out of it because life does go on. I had to get out, visit people. I kept myself busy doing things so I wouldn't be depressed. I went ahead—alone—to the apartment we'd rented in Florida. And that helped—we had friends there; it was different surroundings. I had to help myself. I kept trying to push my way out of the depression. I never got into drinking or pills. Joseph was gone—that was reality, and I knew I had to face it. After twenty-seven years, you simply don't forget someone. I was alone and I hated being without Joseph."

"Did you get any support from family or friends after Joseph's death?"

"My brother died two months after Joseph, and so my sister-in-law and I had a lot of suffering in common. But I think it was my sister who seemed to feel so much more for me. Of course, she was closer to Joseph than any other member of my family. My sister knew I'd lost someone important. She responded to what the loss really was. She'd have me over for dinner; we'd talk. But then she died ten months after Joseph. As to the other members of my family, it was like 'Norman lost his friend, I'm sure he'll get along.' These were people whom I thought were my friends, but they had that same attitude.

"Joseph and I'd had a lot of friends, but so many of them let me down. They all wrote notes saying, 'If you need me, call.' But they weren't there when I needed them. There are one or two friends who did spend some time with me, who talked to me."

"Norman, what did you need from other people?"

"I needed someone to sit and talk to in the evening, maybe have a cup of coffee together. It would've helped me tremendously because I was so much in need of someone to talk to. I needed someone who could understand that I'd lost Joseph. Ours was a union like any other marriage. We shared everything: happinesses, sorrows, ups and downs. We shared building ourselves to where we were when he died. There was a straight couple who used to invite me over for dinner once a month. They'd talk to me about Joseph's death and about my own situation. It doesn't have to be gay people—it has to be someone who is understanding of what the relationship really was. I needed people to talk to who'd understand I'd lost Joseph—I'd lost my lifelong partner."

"Did you have financial problems as a result of Joseph's death?"

"No, not really. He had a five-thousand-dollar insurance policy. Of course, I have the house. Luckily, I had some money saved, and I do get a good pension. I've been working in Florida during the winter months, and that helps a lot. Joseph hated to think of death—he wouldn't even discuss getting more life insurance."

"Where are you now, Norman?"

"Jack came into my life about a year after Joseph's death. He helped me a great deal with getting out of my depression. It was rough trying to establish another relationship. In the beginning I didn't want to settle down. However, once we both knew what we wanted, we could get it together."

"Norman, what does 'In sickness and in health' mean?"

"It means the same thing to me as it would mean in any straight marriage. It meant no matter how sick Joseph was, I was there when he needed me. He became very ill and I stood by him—that's what it means. It's no different from a marriage between a man and a woman. Joseph and I were one. We lived it—in sickness and in health—and death did part us."

10

SAVE *OUR* CHILDREN
Gay Youth Speaks Out

ANGEL *and* TIMOTHY

In talking with Angel and Timothy, I ask them if they believe their homosexuality will affect their career choices or their job security.

"Not really," says Timothy, "I think homosexuality is being better accepted by the public. We're young yet, and we're not really into careers. But I do think by the time we're established it might be less threatening because people will be even more accepting then than they are now."

"I'm out at the office," adds Angel. "I've become close with some of the people I work with. There's this woman—we're friends. We'd talk about personal things, and I used to lie. Finally, I told her I was gay. And it was okay—now we talk freely and openly. Then I just started to talk to other people I work with and I wasn't afraid anymore because these people seemed to be understanding and accepting."

"What do you think has changed the situation somewhat?"

"More people keep coming out," answers Timothy. "And straight people never thought these people they've known were gay. The more straight people realize their friends and the people they work with are gay, the more they'll take a second look at the whole gay issue. I've noticed it with my straight friends—kids my own age. Their views are changing, maybe broadening. They're more interested in the gay issue, and they're not as much into just stereotyping gays."

"Angel, you realized you were gay when you were quite young. What kind of support did you need when you first acknowledged your homosexuality?"

"Oh, wow, someone to talk to. I was so scared, so confused. I didn't understand what was happening to me. If I'd had somebody

214

my own age, maybe a little older—fourteen, fifteen—it would've helped a lot. Somebody who understands the situation, understands being gay. You need somebody you can look up to, somebody who's got their own act together. I guess it really doesn't have to be a gay person—somebody you can respect and talk to. If you've got confidence in this person, maybe they can help you have confidence in yourself. They can help you see it's not such a bad thing."

"Tim," I say, "you've been out of high school five years. Angel, you've been out two years. What was the attitude toward homosexuality when you were in high school?"

"It was just a word teachers skipped over very quickly," says Timothy.

Angel laughs. "I'm laughing but it wasn't funny at the time. I was in health class. The teacher asked one boy what he'd do if he found out his kid was gay. The kid said, 'Nothing.' The teacher said, 'If it was my kid, I'd throw him out.' And that was the end of the discussion. You know how that makes a gay kid feel who's sitting there listening to something like that? Tim and I know kids who are still in high school. It's the same as when we were there—homosexuality is a negative. You're a faggot and that's it."

"How do you think it should be handled by teachers?"

"I think it should be openly discussed," answers Timothy. "Kids ask questions about straight sex in health class. But no kid is going to ask any questions about being gay. They're too scared to ask because everyone will think they want to know because they're gay. No kid can handle being called a faggot in high school. So if there are any gay kids in a class, they're not going to ask questions. The teachers have to discuss the topic—they can't wait for the kids to ask questions about it."

"I think teachers have a responsibility to show all aspects of life," adds Angel. "They should talk about homosexuality for what it is— a normal part of life. These teachers don't know how many gay kids are sitting there in their classrooms. They should discuss the topic in a very neutral way—not positive, not negative—just another part of life. It's got to be openly discussed. When they say bad things about it, they don't know what they're doing to the gay kid who might be sitting there."

"Let's change our direction a bit," I say. "Do you think teenagers—say, under eighteen—should tell their parents they're gay?"

"That really depends on the parents," explains Angel. "It depends on the relationship they've got with their parents. You've got to look at the educational background of your parents, their ethnic and religious background."

"I agree with Angel one hundred percent," adds Timothy. "It really depends on the relationship you have with your parents. And the kids themselves are the best judges of that. In most cases, I don't think it's a good idea. I think it's very rare to find accepting parents. It's a hard thing for the average parent to deal with."

"Timothy, why did you tell your parents?"

"See, in the beginning I thought I had to hide. I had to build this wall between them and me for self-preservation. I withdrew from them and they kept asking me why. Finally, I went out with my Dad one night and I got him a little bit drunk and then I told him. I was just sick of lying to them all the time—that's why I told them. I guess I figured, okay, if they reject you, they reject you. But I knew I had to take my chances and tell them the truth. I couldn't stand what was happening to the three of us because I was hiding my life from them, lying to them."

"Angel, what about your parents?"

"Well, like I told you—my mother started lighting candles when they found out I was gay. And then she was sprinkling this potion around the house. My father is a quiet man. He doesn't mix too much with us kids. When he first found out, he was very upset. My mother told me he was crying a lot. He lost a lot of weight, and he got even more quiet than he was before. But then he seemed to get over it. I went to see them just last week, and he said something to my mother which really surprised me. He said, 'We can't complain about our children, they turned out to be decent people after all.' He was talking to her about me and he said, 'It's not something we should be ashamed of.' I couldn't believe I was hearing my father say that."

"What advice would you offer to parents when they find out their child is gay?"

"I'd tell them to keep calm," answers Timothy seriously, "I'd tell them not to have a fit because that's the worst thing that can happen to the kid. Let's say it's a teenage boy. I'd tell the parents not to ask him if he's sure. Because the kid probably isn't sure and when the parents ask if he's sure, they're just adding to the confusion. And the other really big thing I'd want to tell parents is not to blame themselves. Parents get on this 'blaming themselves' trip, and it's really not their fault.

"Parents shouldn't be scared, either. See, parents get upset because as soon as the kid says he's gay, the parents think he's going to spend the rest of his life in kinky sex and drugs. Well, it isn't like that. The parents are buying the media stereotype of gays. They're afraid because they don't want their kid to lead that kind of life. Well, just because the kid is gay doesn't mean he's going to have a terrible life. The same goes for girls. It's still your daughter—the girl you raised. Just because she's gay doesn't mean she's going to spend the rest of her life hanging out in bars.

"You know, after I told my parents," Timothy continues, "my mother just cried. Everytime she looked at me, she'd start to cry. We didn't even have to be talking about it or anything—she just cried. She felt sorry for me—she really felt sorry for me. She was so worried because she felt the life I was planning to lead wouldn't be any good. She was caught up in the stereotype—you know, pornography, the whole scene. My father thought I was on some sort of binge, that I didn't know what I was doing. My mother's concern was, 'My God, how are you going to handle it?' I tried to help her, but I don't know if I did.

"Now that I think back about telling my own parents, well, the worst thing the parent can say is, 'You don't know what you're doing.' That's a bad scene because that just makes the kid feel worse, even less self-confident. Of course he doesn't know what he's doing; of course he's confused. But as soon as a parent says, 'You don't know what you're doing,' the kid feels put down, his self-image gets worse. And he's already having problems with his self-image because he thinks he's bad now that he knows he's gay. Why can't parents say, 'Hey, I know you're confused. So am I. Why don't we try to work out our confusion together?' Why can't parents say that? Why can't they admit they're confused too? At least then the kid won't feel so alone."

"When some parents realize their children are gay," I explain, "they're upset because they feel they're going to be deprived of grandchildren. What would you say to a parent like this?"

"That's a hard one." Timothy shakes his head. "That's more or less what happened with my own mother. I don't know—maybe I'd say, 'Is this your own need—to have a grandchild? Isn't it selfish?' When parents say that, it's like they're ignoring the generation in between. Like there's them, and then there's a grandchild. But what about their child who's the generation in between them and their grandchild? Their child has a right to his own life."

"You're telling me all the things parents shouldn't do. What should they do?"

"They should think about it," continues Timothy, "just think about it awhile before they get crazy. Think about why being gay is supposed to be so bad. Think about that everything is the same, nothing has changed—this is the same kid they loved, the same kid they raised."

"Say if it's a girl," adds Angel, "the parents should look at her and ask themselves if she's a good person. Are they happy with the way she's grown up? Is she an honest and responsible kid? If they can answer yes to all of that, then they should ask themselves why her being gay is so terrible. Boy or girl, I think if the kid is confused, the parents should try to share that confusion. Parents should try to work with the kid, talk with the kid."

"What can gay teenagers do to help their parents?"

"Respect their parents' rules," answers Angel. "If they want you in at a certain time, be in at a certain time. You would've been respecting their rules if you were straight, so you should be respecting them if you're gay. And don't go around being overly gay—act the way you always acted around them. Try to behave— don't make it worse. Don't get yourself in trouble. And like keep it a family matter—between you and your parents. Don't go telling your aunts and uncles, your grandparents. And cool it in the neighborhood."

"Hey, look," adds Timothy, "just because a kid realizes he's gay, he doesn't have to go shouting it from the rooftops. This goes for girls, too. You don't have to go making a big Broadway production out of it, but you shouldn't condemn yourself either. You just roll with it and accept it as part of your life."

"I guess we've got to understand our parents come from another generation," Angel continues. "When they were being raised, gays didn't exist—or at least they didn't know about it. If they knew about it, well, they were raised to believe it was the work of the devil. I think the most important thing is to let your parents know you still love them. Nothing has changed just because you're gay."

"There's an expression," I tell them. "We should allow straight people as much time to accept our being gay as it took us to accept our own gayness, as it took us to accept ourselves. What do you think about that as far as parents go?"

"Yeah," says Angel, smiling. "It took me seven years to accept myself. I was ten years old when I realized I was a homosexual. But I was seventeen when I accepted it. I can see what you're saying. I guess we've got to be fair and give the other person a chance. I guess some things take time to understand. Up to now, I complained about my parents not handling it very well. I guess if it took me seven years to accept myself, maybe I've got to give them at least seven years to get it together—to really accept me."

"What do you think, Timothy?"

"Well, I don't think we can just thrust our parents into the eighties or into the Gay Liberation Movement. I guess we've got to be patient and understanding. It's two different worlds. Maybe if we're cool, we can bring the two worlds together. Yeah, I guess it goes both ways: if we want our parents to be patient and understand us, we've got to give them a break and think about where they're coming from. Fair's fair, huh? Maybe if we realize that, both sides will be able to meet somewhere in the middle."

JEANNE

Jeanne, twenty-two, arrives thirty minutes late for her interview. "Sorry I'm late, but I've got to run my seven miles a day. Had to do that before I did this. Before we start this," she continues, "I got to tell you I don't like the word *marriage*. I've been in a relationship with another woman for five years, and the word *marriage* just doesn't apply. I call it my relationship and that's the word I'll use. Okay?"

"Okay," I say, "use any word you want. Tell me about your relationship. Tell me about your life."

"My life?" She laughs. "Changes, changes—my whole life's been changes. A lot of different relationships, a lot of different lifestyles. I was thirteen when I realized I was gay. Got involved with a young lady. A lot of changes, though, because I was still seeing young men. Then I got into heroin for two years. I went into a therapeutic community for drug addicts when I was fifteen. And that's when I really went through a lot of changes. I decided who I was and what I wanted: I was gay and I didn't want these drug crazies in my life anymore. When I was seventeen, I met Barbara. And even there there's been a lot of changes."

"Jeanne," I say, laughing, "we're not more than three minutes into this tape and suddenly I feel a hell of a lot younger than you. Tell me about your relationship with Barbara. How do you live it out?"

"Well," she explains, "it's an equal relationship—we share

everything. We do everything as one—there's none of this 'yours' or 'mine' business. We share all the bills and all the responsibilities of living together. We share all our feelings and all our loving. It's beautiful and I'd like it to last as long as possible. I'm doing everything in my power to keep it together."

"Jeanne, do you see it as a permanent relationship? When you and Barbara got together, did you believe then it would last until old age?"

"Yes, I believe we have a permanent relationship. And yes, I've always thought it'd last until old age. I'm pretty comfortable and secure with the whole thing. Now I want to see us expand the relationship."

"When you say 'expand the relationship,' what do you mean?"

"Well, a relationship can pretty much head in one direction— you're just living together day by day. And I don't want that. There are new things I want to do, there are new experiences I want to have. Barbara feels the same way. What's new is getting to know your partner more and more. Getting to know all about her personality—her fears and her insecurities. And she gets to know you more and more. That's what expanding means to me—you just keep going. There's so much to life and I want our relationship to expand so we get more and more of life.

"Both of us are concerned about our careers, so we're both expanding and trying to do what we want to do. Barbara is thirty, and she's looking at other things now. Whichever way either of us goes, we're going to deal with it together. See, changes—it's all changes and they just keep happening. I have to be able to understand and accept what she wants to do. And she has to be able to understand what I want to do. And in my process of trying to understand her, I'm going to be changing too."

"Is sexual fidelity important in the relationship you and Barbara have?"

"Yes, it is. At the beginning of our relationship, we said we were going to be faithful. Even though we said it, I did a lot of running— one-night stands. But they didn't lead anywhere—it wasn't what I really wanted. What I really wanted was a relationship, and I have that with Barbara. It gets down to sharing, and now I know I want to share myself emotionally and sexually with just one person. And I'm selfish—I don't want the woman I'm sharing my whole self with to be sharing any part of herself with anybody else."

"Do you think there are differences between gay and straight relationships, Jeanne?"

"More similarities than there are differences. Love is the big similarity. It doesn't matter who's loving who—two men, two women, a man and a woman. They love and they share their love."

"What's love, Jeanne?"

"It's such a big word. Love is a lot of different things. It's giving and sharing. It's opening yourself up to someone else and going through all the motions of loving whether it's good times or bad times. Gay people, straight people, men, women—we all love. Maybe it's expressed differently, but we all love."

"What do you think are some of the other similarities?"

"Sharing goals, sharing responsibilities. Living together and trying to make it work is the same for everyone. Even this role business—gays and straights are both into roles. People get into these roles—a husband is boss; a lesbian 'fem' is supposed to do this or that. Somebody decides they want to be a bull dike. The roles come from society. And it doesn't matter whether you're gay or straight—people take on roles. These roles are passed down from one generation to the next. Roles are here and they are with us—we got to change that."

"Do you believe that gay people are capable of permanent relationships, Jeanne?"

"Hey, baby, I'm gay and I've got a permanent relationship—that makes me very capable. I believe gay men and women can have primary, or permanent, relationships. We love just as well as anyone else. We hurt just as much as anyone else. And our lives are as meaningful as anyone else's life. If we mistreat our loved ones, it's the same as anyone else. If we abuse love, we're no different than the straight person who is abusing love or abusing loved ones."

"Jeanne, if you could have a gay adult role model, what type of person would you be looking for?"

"I'm pretty strong. I'd want someone who's as strong as me or stronger. I'd want someone who's secure, someone I can learn from. Nowadays there's nobody out there you can look to. You've got to grow on your own, find your own way. If you've got expectations for yourself, you've got to do it on your own. An older gay person can teach you about life. See, if you'll listen, an older gay person can point you in the right direction. An older gay person has been through a lot—gay relationships, heterosexual relationships. But it would have to be an older gay person who's got it together, who's settled and positive about life and about being gay. Someone who's together, because I've met some older gays who are still pretty messed up. I also think it could be an older straight person—doesn't matter if the person isn't gay. All that matters is they understand you and accept you as the person you are. Someone older can help you see what you're going through because they've been there themselves. They can work with you. Talk to you about jobs and careers."

"Have you ever felt less of a woman because you're a lesbian, Jeanne?"

"No, I don't feel less of a woman. I'm more of a woman. And being a woman is the greatest thing in the world. I can do all the things I want to do and still be a woman. I can run seven miles a day, come home and put on a dress and be a woman. Or come home and put on jeans and a T-shirt and still be a woman. I can love a woman and still be a woman. I don't feel any less of a woman because I'm a lesbian. It doesn't matter to me. What does matter to me is being myself."

"Where do you stand on God and religion?"

"I believe in God. I had a religious upbringing but I don't go to church anymore. You see, I do pray but I don't have to go into church to do it. I believe God is there and He's protecting me. God accepts me as I am. He just wants people to be themselves. I think He wants us to enjoy the time we have and not do things in craziness. I think God wants us to live life to whatever fulfillment we can reach. God doesn't want us to hurt ourselves or to hurt anybody else. He just wants us to be who we are."

"Jeanne, you say you believe God wants us to be who we are. Would sin, then, be a situation where we're not being who we are? You're a lesbian—would it be a sin for you to pretend you're a heterosexual?"

"Yes, it would. It would be wrong for me to try to do that because I would be taking myself through changes unnecessarily. It'd be like putting myself in a negative environment. Making myself choose something I didn't want to choose, and doing it because I felt I had to. I lived that way for the first thirteen years of my life before I knew I was gay. But now, knowing I'm gay, I'm out of the closet and into the streets. That's the way people should be all the time. Just be themselves—that's all God's asking of us."

"Jeanne, you've got everything going against you—you're not only an ex-addict, but you're a lesbian. And you're not only a lesbian, but you're a black lesbian. Name a prejudice and you've got it going against you. Where do you get your will from?"

"Let me tell you something. I was in a drug rehab program for two years. They did such numbers on me, and I survived that. It was hell and I went through a lot. I learned a lot and it made me more secure as a woman. Being gay was the icing on the cake, because then I knew who I was and where I was going. I knew I had a lot to learn—I was going to become someone. I was going to be somebody and do something with my life. I made up my mind I was going somewhere positive—I wasn't going to be stagnating. I was getting rid of all the negatives in my life. I wasn't going to spend my life dealing in drugs and crazies. I wanted to do something and I wanted to go somewhere positive. And I'm doing it.

"There are obstacles for me because of who I am, because of my lifestyle. I know it. I'm feeling it already on my job. Whatever feelings people have about me, they're going to have to learn to deal with those feelings. They're going to have to learn to accept me because I ain't going away.

"Whatever obstacles are out there, I'll take them on head-on. I believe in everything I'm doing, and I know there are so many more things I want to do. I believe in myself and nothing will stop me from doing what I want to do. I'm going to make something of my life, and if any obstacles get in my way—I'll go right through them."

AMY *and* JUDY

Amy and Judy walk in for their interview looking like they have been subpoenaed by Hoover's FBI. Both young women sit with their knees together and their hands on their laps. They do not look at each other, and they barely look at me. When I ask if the tape recorder is a problem, both of them say it is not.

"Well," I say, smiling, "why don't we just talk awhile. We'll get into more specific questions after you tell me a little bit about yourselves."

"What about ourselves?" Amy questions.

"Talk about you, where you're coming from and where you're going? Hey, nobody says you have to do this. If you don't want to, it's okay—no problem."

"No," Amy answers, "we want to do it. We know what you're doing. It's important that kids like us help out. Well," she continues, grinning, "you already know my name is Amy. I'm eighteen years old. I guess I realized I was gay when I was in elementary school. When I got into junior high, it became more real. I started having sex with other women, started having relationships. I started reading anything I could find to figure out what I was about. I've known all my life that I liked girls—had crushes on them and all that. So it wasn't a problem for me, and I wondered about that and read all I could. My parents are in their mid-forties. They're very liberal. They never raised me to be a bigot or a racist. I think that's probably why I could accept being gay. I met other gay girls in junior high and high school, and talking to them helped me a lot."

"Judy, you with us?" I ask, teasing her. "Your turn."

"I'm not holding that microphone," Judy protests.

"You don't have to," I answer. "It'll pick up your nervous stomach from five feet away."

"I'm Judy, but you know that. I started to become aware of my attraction for girls when I was in kindergarten. Both my parents were born in China and they're very traditional, so sex was never discussed in the family. When I turned twelve, I started coming out to the people around me—other kids in school. I went to an all-girls high school so it was much easier for me. A lot of kids in school knew I was gay but it was all right—no one bothered me."

"Okay," I say, "let's get into some heavy stuff. You two have been together in what you describe as a committed relationship for eight months. Is it a marriage?"

"It depends on what you mean by marriage," Amy answers. "If you mean marriage as a commitment to each other, then it's a marriage. When I say I'm committed to Judy, it means I will love and take care of her. It's a one-person thing. She's the person I want to love and she's the person I want to love me. We're going to live together as a couple. We'd like to get married, but because we're gay we can't do that."

"To me," Judy continues, "being committed to Amy means I try to understand her, help her with her problems. She understands me and helps me. We're two people who've made a commitment to making our relationship last. And we're both willing to put all our efforts into making that happen. We want our relationship to succeed."

"What makes a relationship a success, Judy?"

"It's a success," Judy answers, "if there's understanding, if we both get a lot of support from each other, if we're willing to make sacrifices for each other."

"Amy," I ask, "do you think your relationship with Judy is going to be a long-term, permanent relationship?"

"Yes, I do." She smiles. "It'll be as permanent as it can be. If something happens and we can't get along, that's it. But we do have a commitment to each other, which means if something happens you just don't walk out. We try to understand each other, try not to turn our backs on any of our problems, try to work them out."

"What are some of the problems you're having now?"

"Communication is a big one for us," Amy explains. "We sometimes misunderstand each other. And then we just have to keep talking. Transportation is a big problem because we're both still living at home with our families. And then there's jobs and money. We both just got out of high school and we're trying to get it together financially so we can live together."

"Okay," I say, "you're both eighteen, just starting out. Do you think the problems you're having would be any different if you were a straight couple?"

"No," Amy answers. "I think most of the problems are the same—money, jobs—and we don't have any experience at doing anything. We want to get an apartment together but we want to live decently. You've got to have jobs before you can do that."

"What are some of the differences between you and a straight couple your age, Amy?"

"Parental support is the big difference. Our parents are not going to let us live together and sleep together. They'd probably do anything they could to stop our relationship. We don't have anyone to look up to—not anyone we can be honest with, anyway. There's no one we can ask questions about things like jobs and apartments. And there's no one to help us with certain problems that maybe we can't solve between the two of us. Even if there was somebody around to tell us how to better handle money."

"Let's go in another direction. Judy, do you think sexual fidelity is important in a relationship?"

"Sexual fidelity is important in this relationship," she says, laughing. "I can't say that for all the other relationships I've had with women. But for this one, yes."

"Why for this one?" I ask. "What makes this one different?"

"Well, when I first met Amy, sexual fidelity was one of the terms she handed me. I went along with it, I guess. But now that we've been together for eight months relating to each other—well, it seems the bond between us is just growing daily. It doesn't interest me to go out and find that kind of emotional bond with someone else."

"Wait a minute, Judy, you just switched gears on me. We were talking about sexual fidelity and then you started using the expression 'emotional bond.' What are you talking about?"

"When I say 'emotional bond'," Judy explains, "I mean a lot of support and understanding for each other. Both Amy and I have dated men. I don't 'know' if it's different because we're two women. But I 'feel' it's different between two women. Our lovemaking is more refined—it's softer, it's not aggressive. For Amy and I, it's like sex and emotions enhance each other. It's a kind of cycle that keeps repeating itself. When there is a lot of good feeling between us, it tends to make sex better. When sex is better, there's a lot of good feeling. Sex and loving and loving and sex—for us, they're both a result of each other."

"Why is sexual fidelity important to you, Amy?"

"Basically," she says, blushing, "I guess I'm just monogamous. What I wanted was a marriage, and I told Judy that was what I wanted. See, if I were sleeping with other people, my emotions would be branching out to those other people. If I slept with someone, my emotions would be in it. I wouldn't do it just for sex. So that would kind of split my relationship with Judy because I'd be splitting my emotional life."

"Amy, when you look ahead, what are your hopes for you and Judy?"

"I guess I always want the peacefulness we have when we're together. I feel secure with Judy, and I want that for always. I'd like to see us have a nice circle of friends. And I want us to have fun. I'd love to live in the woods, somewhere remote."

"And you, Judy, what do you hope for?"

"I want us to be together. We have a lot of love for each other and I want us to always have that."

"Do you see yourself growing old with Amy?"

"Yes." Judy laughs. "I see the two of us sitting in rocking chairs."

"Amy, would you like to know older lesbian couples? And if you knew some, what do you think you could learn from them?"

"It would comfort me to see older women who've been able to make their relationships last. But I don't know any older lesbians. Our families are probably the biggest problem that Judy and I have. So if I knew older lesbians, I'd ask them how they worked things out with their families. Our families want us to get married and have kids, but we love each other and we want to live together. Maybe older lesbians could help us work that all out."

"Judy, do you feel any less of a woman because you're a lesbian?"

"No," Judy answers adamantly, "not at all. I'm more of a woman with other women. You can have a more equal relationship with another woman than you could ever have with a man. 'Equal' is important to me because I'm willing to give a lot, and I ask for a lot. In a relationship with a man, he's the domineering one. The man lays the groundwork and puts down the terms—it's not an equal relationship, and that's what I want."

"Do you feel less of a woman, Amy?"

"Not at all. I'm just as feminine and as masculine now as I was when I was going out with guys."

"What's your greatest fear, Amy?"

"Being caught in a sexual act by our parents. I guess I don't want them to actually 'see' that Judy and I are lesbians. I think it would hurt our parents and I don't want them to be hurt."

"What's your greatest fear, Judy?"

"To be alone without anyone. To be alone without companionship, without having someone there—someone I can depend on."

"Now you two are probably going to jump all over me with the next question but . . . you're both eighteen—do you think you're old enough to make a commitment and enter into a monogamous relationship?"

"I had my first real relationship with another girl when I was thirteen," Judy answers. "And I had other relationships after that. I feel I want to settle down now with the person I'm with, and that's Amy."

"What about you, Amy? Do you think you're old enough to settle down with one person?"

"I can't say for sure. How do you measure whether the experiences you have had make you ready to settle down? Age doesn't mean anything to me. I've had relationships with other women. I had a serious relationship with a man, became pregnant, and had an abortion. I'm comfortable with Judy. I love her. I want us to be able to live together and make it together. Judy and me for many years of laughing and crying and everything else that goes into a relationship."

"Okay," I say, "we've changed the perspective from age to experience. Do you think you've had enough experience to settle down, Judy?"

"The feedback I get from Amy says I'm experienced enough for her. And that's all that counts."

MICHAEL

Michael, seventeen, is a soft-spoken young man. With dark hair and dark eyes, he boasts to me that the mustache he is sporting is his first. "I realized I was gay when I was fourteen," he tells me. "I tried to fight it by going out with girls. But it wasn't until this year that I met other gay kids—it's made it a lot easier for me. I used to get depressed because I didn't have anyone to talk to. But now, I'm a lot happier even though I still have conflicts."

"Michael," I ask, "tell me what it was like before you started meeting gay people your own age."

"It was terrible, that's what it was like. I was all alone. I'd go out with straight kids who'd make cracks about queers and I knew they were talking about me, only they didn't know it. I couldn't stand the queer jokes. It bothered me that I couldn't say anything. I'd have to laugh at the jokes but it was laughing at myself for being what I am. I got into drinking and drugs for a while, but it didn't last that long."

"Why did you get into drinking and drugs?"

"Well"—he sighs—"I guess I was trying to escape, I'd have gay thoughts and I'd try to block them. I felt guilty about being gay because I was raised in a strict Catholic family. I couldn't meet kids my own age to talk to, so I'd get high and go out and meet older guys someplace. But then you end up just having sex, and I still didn't have anyone to talk to. I felt lonely and out of place because I knew I was different than my friends, and I didn't have any friends who were like me. I knew if I told my friends it would be the end of the relationship I had. I got heavy into Christianity for a while because I thought it would help me get rid of my gay thoughts. But it didn't, and I just got guiltier."

"Sounds like you were terribly isolated, Michael. What happened that made the difference?"

"I got a part-time job after school when I turned sixteen and I started meeting people. I met this girl and we became friends and I told her. And it was okay, and now we're very close. I always enjoyed the friendships I had with girls, but it wasn't that special kind of fulfillment I wanted. I wanted to meet guys my own age. I wanted somebody I could talk to who could relate to me. I tried to force myself into the straight scene, but it didn't work. I had a lot of guilt about being deceitful, pretending I was straight."

"Michael, what about your parents? Do they know you're gay?"

"No, my family doesn't know. I still lie and tell my mother I'm going out with girls. It bothers me but I've got to do it. My parents have been separated for years and I live with my mother. My father would probably yell his brains out. My mother would be upset. But I don't think she'd throw me out or cut me off like other parents do to their gay kids. My mother wouldn't do that to me. We have a relationship. I think she'd try to understand. I think she'd want me to go for some psychological counseling so I'd be straight. I don't think she'd accept it because she was brought up in a different way—but she wouldn't throw me out."

"What are the conflicts about being gay?"

"They're not so much conflicts about being gay—they're sexual conflicts. I think I'm happy being gay—it's religion that's causing the conflicts. It's having sex with another person that's the religious conflict. And then Christianity says homosexuality is a sin. I don't see anything wrong in having sex before you're married. But gays can't marry so then I can't have sexual relations. That's the big problem, and I'm confused. I'm at a point where I can accept different interpretations of the Bible. I'm getting better about homosexuality being a sin. So maybe it's not a sin for me to be a homosexual. But I can't get married and sex outside of marriage is a sin. I don't know."

"Why is religion so important to you, Michael?"

"I've got a strong belief in the hereafter and I believe everyone is going to be paid for their deeds. My conscience tells me the Bible is right, and I just can't ignore it. But it's not religion. A spiritual life is important to me because I think it affects your physical life and your mental well-being.

"I want a spiritual life, I want God to be the center of a lot of things in my life. I used to pray to God to make me straight. Now I pray to God to show me a way so I can accept the two things—my gayness and my religion. I want to live a life for God and still live a gay lifestyle. I just want to love a person, and if the person happens to be of the same sex, I can't believe God wouldn't accept it. He created both of us—me and the man I would love. It'd be hard to meet a man and have us love each other and then tell him I couldn't have sex with him because of my religion. How can you carry on a relationship like that? Either way, with a girl or a guy, I'd still have the conflict—sex is a sin unless you're married; I'm a homosexual and I can't marry."

"When you talk about a relationship, Michael, are you talking about a permanent relationship?"

"Yes, I'd like to settle down. I don't like flying from one guy to the next or from one girl to the next. I'd like to be secure with one person, have a place and live together."

"As a homosexual, do you believe it's possible for you to have a permanent relationship?"

"Yes, I believe it's possible. There's the gay myth and all the business about it being impossible for gays to have relationships. But I think if you have the right two people it can work. It's the same for a straight relationship. Gay or straight, if two people love each other they're going to stay together and try to make it work."

"If you had such a relationship, would you consider it a marriage? And I'm not talking about churches and religions."

"Yes, I'd consider it a marriage. If we'd openly committed ourselves to each other, to not be with other people, to love one another and stick together—yes, I'd consider it a marriage. If our intention was to stay together, that would be a marriage to me. If you love one another and commit yourself to each other, that's a marriage. A piece of paper saying we were married wouldn't be important to me."

"What about sexual fidelity? Would that be important to you?"

"Yes, it would. Right now my freedom is important to me. But as I get older, my freedom won't be so important. Freedom isn't that important if you love someone and you're in a stable relationship. If you really love someone, why would you need anyone else? I think when I settle down I'd want a bonded relationship where we were sexually faithful to each other."

"Michael, have you ever felt less of a man because you're a homosexual?"

"I did, but not anymore. It doesn't make a difference to me now. You see so many men who are supposed to be strong male figures— real men and all that. They have so many weaknesses, their strength is just a superficial image. Inside they're not so strong. To me, it's more important to be more of a person or have a strong personality. Person qualities, not male qualities. Before I had to prove I was a man so people wouldn't know I was gay. Now I don't look at it as something that's wrong with me as a man. My conflict is the religious conflict: I'm not the full man I'm supposed to be according to God. My insides have started to tell me being a homosexual isn't bad. And I'm trying to reach a happy medium with the religious aspect."

"Michael, what do you think gay teenagers like yourself need?"

"We need a sense of being accepted, of not being an outsider or weird or abnormal. We need to be able to accept gayness as normal behavior for ourselves. We need a better understanding of our own gayness. We need to be able to have relationships with kids our own age, not older men who just use you and mess you up. We need relationships—not sex. And we need to meet other gay kids our own age so we can talk, openly discuss our positive and negative feelings about being gay.

"We need more programs that reach out to gay kids. Programs where we could go and meet other kids, where there'd be counselors to talk to us. Gay groups for kids are important because we're so isolated and alone. We're trapped by ourselves. If there were more programs where kids could go for help, they wouldn't feel so ashamed. There should be ads in the newspaper and on television for places where you can go to meet other gay kids. All you see in the newspapers are ads for bathhouses. It's raunchy and we don't want that. It's just like the straight pornography that straight kids get mixed up in. It would also help if you knew older gay people. You know, gay role models."

"Why would older gay role models be important?"

"It'd be someone you could look up to, someone who could give you confidence in yourself. Straight kids look at the superstars, people on TV, their parents. It's rough for a gay kid. You don't see things the way your parents do. Everything you think is opposite from the way they think because you're gay. If you know a stable gay adult who has a good relationship, you could look at him and know that it's possible for you to grow up and have a good life, too. Older gay people can give you hope that maybe someday you can be a couple with another man or woman. You wouldn't feel so weird if you saw gay adults. The more gay adults you see the better. You feel all alone because you're the one kid in your family who's gay, and you think because everyone else in your family is straight, they'd never understand what you were going through. It would be great to have a gay adult to look up to and talk to.

"I think television programs should show better images of gays and gay couples. Then the kids wouldn't think being gay means being far out. TV should show a normal image of gays. I believe normal gays are out there. But all you see on TV are the weirdo gays."

"What about the parents of gays—what do they need?"

"I'd like to see parents more educated about being gay so when a kid comes home and says he's gay they don't blow up and throw him out."

"Do you know kids who've been thrown out by their parents?"

"I know one kid who got thrown out, and then he came back. But when he came back, it wasn't the same anymore. He used to be close to his parents, but now that they know he's gay, they don't talk to him anymore. Another kid's father is a cop and he used to beat the kid up and ridicule him in front of the whole family. Another friend of mine—he's fifteen—he got into prostitution when his parents threw him out. They never even tried to find him. Once he called and they hung up on him.

"The parents are the ones that need help. Even if they think being gay is wrong, they should try to help the kid, not throw him out. I know this kid, he's sixteen and he's from a small town. Bunch of men in his town raped him. Nobody did anything because they said he was 'just a fag.' No one would help him—people laughed it off. So he ran away and he's been just moving from town to town."

"Michael, you're giving me a headache. Let's try to go a little deeper. What happens to gay teenagers when their parents reject them?"

"If your parents reject you because you're gay it causes more self-hate. It's being rejected by somebody you love, and somebody who's supposed to love you. It makes you feel worthless. It's worse if you've been close with your parents because you feel like garbage if they cut you off. I'd get torn up if my mother rejected me—it'd destroy me. If she loved me all my life, how could she drop me like I never existed? That would hurt a lot."

"What advice would you offer to the parents of gays?"

"The most important thing is to see if the kid is happy. Parents have to understand it and try to figure out *why* the kid thinks he's gay. The kid may just be rebelling or maybe the kid isn't sure. Work with the kid. If the kid is sure he's gay and he's happy with it, the parents have to try to understand it. Maybe the parents can't accept it because of the way they were raised or because of the things they believe. But try to understand the kid as your child. Don't let his gayness get in the way of your love for him as your child."

"What advice would you offer gay teenagers about their parents?"

"The kid has to go easy breaking it to his parents. You can't bring a lover home right after you tell them. If the kid is easy about it, the parents should try to understand and talk it out. A lot of parents won't talk. They've got an opinion on it, and that's it. Parents are closed because of society and because of religious values. All of that has been drilled into their heads. Some parents may have even had gay thoughts themselves and they're guilty about it—that's why they're so strongly against it.

"I can't understand how parents can love a kid all his life, raise the kid and have the kid loving them—then to reject the kid because he's gay is really cruel. A lot of parents reject the kid because they feel it's their fault that the kid is gay, that they did something wrong. What I don't understand is, if parents love their child, doesn't it hurt them to reject the child they love? Parents reject the kid because they can't cope with it. But while they're pushing gay out of their minds, they're also pushing their own child out of their minds."

"Michael, what do you think about gay foster parents for gay kids?"

"I know some kids who are much happier with their gay foster parents because they finally feel accepted. I know a lot of religious organizatons are trying to stop it. But what are you going to do with these kids? First their parents throw them out, and then they go to a straight foster care family where they're ridiculed by the other kids. Then they end up getting thrown out of these straight foster care families. They're constantly going from one place to another. If they can get into a home with gay foster parents, they'll be accepted and finally be able to feel good about themselves. A gay foster parent is the perfect role model because it's a situation where they can grow up learning to accept themselves.

"Gay kids can grow up with their natural parents if their parents understand them and don't torture them because they're gay. But for all the kids whose parents don't accept them, I think it's horrible not to allow gay people to bring up these kids. Everybody worries about the gay foster parents sexually abusing these kids— the same thing can happen with a kid's real mother or father or a straight foster parent."

"What is a parent, Michael?"

"A parent is a person who's there when you need them. A parent is someone you can talk to. Somebody who loves you and who you love. A parent is a person who cares for you until you're old enough to care for yourself. And it doesn't matter to me if you have one or two parents—just as long as the parent loves you and accepts you as you are. That's what's most important to me. A parent—one person gay or straight who loves you and accepts you.

"I don't think a parent has to be someone who gave birth to you. Plenty of people adopt kids and raise them as their own. You can love someone who isn't your natural parent. Biology isn't as important as love. Sometimes I think if my mother remarried I could see myself loving my stepfather even if he wasn't my natural father. If he was a person I could look up to, I'd respect him and love him if he accepted me as I am.

"You know, there are a lot of kids who've known their natural parents and it's been a bad experience. Any kid who feels loved by a parent figure isn't going to care if it's his natural parent. You can love someone a lot if they accept you and love you as you are."

JENNY

If I had seriously tried to find a Jenny, I would never have been able to find her. If I had put out "feelers" for an articulate, bright, self-identified thirteen-year-old lesbian, people would have thought me mad. But I found Jenny—or rather, she found me. We sat on the front steps of a city brownstone one sunny Saturday afternoon. I interviewed *her* most of the time—she interviewed *me* some of the time. Here I will exercise my author's prerogative. I am not editing this interview. Instead, I will present it as it went down on tape.

• • •

"Jenny, let's talk some more about what we were discussing before. You were telling me you've had a six-year relationship with another girl."

"It wasn't until I was eleven years old that I realized it was a gay relationship. At that time, I'd been having this ongoing relationship for six years. One of my other friends saw my girl friend and I together and she said we were 'gay.' I asked her what that meant and she explained it to me. I totally went into shock because I realized the attitudes people had about being gay. I kind of just forgot about it, but then it started coming up again—the feelings I have toward other women. I realized it's something you're not going to fight. I thought, If you feel more comfortable this way, accept it. So I did."

"Tell me about your relationship with this other girl. Let's call her Pam."

"Okay, Pam—that's a nice name. We became friends when I was five and she was eight. She sort of instituted what you'd call a relationship. Every time I went to her house, we had sex. It kind of fitted into a game we used to play."

"What was the game, Jenny?"

"She used to be my roommate. I'd go out and come back as her boyfriend. We'd have sex, then I'd leave and come back in as her roommate. Then I'd go home."

"When you say you had sex, what are you talking about?"

"Oh, basically kissing and fondling. No oral sex. Nothing involved that could really mentally involve one person with another. It was what *we considered* serious at that point in time."

"Where is Pam now? What happened to your relationship?"

"Well, after she turned fourteen, she decided to start going out with boys and forget all about me. It hurt me when I found out. It's strange. It hurt me because I really liked her. I loved her. Call it eleven-year-old love, but I guess it exists. It hurt me very much to have a person reject me like that after six years of sharing myself with her. It's a kind of involved feeling for an eleven-year-old, but I felt like that."

"All of this happened to you two years ago, when you were eleven. Did you tell anybody?"

"No, not right away. I recently told one of my best friends. She accepted it, and she accepted the fact that I'm going to feel like this toward women for the rest of my life. And I told another friend, but she didn't accept it at all. She went spreading it around the school."

"Jenny, are you looking for another girl friend now?"

"Straight society says you should have a boyfriend. Maybe I feel I 'should have' a girl friend. But I think I'd 'really like' a girl friend at this point in my life. I'd like to share a lot of things with her—like school and home. I also need someone I can have a sexual relationship with. And that sort of gets me into a problem. I've been thinking about getting sexually involved with someone. For a while, I forgot I was a lesbian and started getting involved with boys. I've had three boyfriends and they were all typically straight men—they got their sex, which is what they wanted, and then they left. My last boyfriend was a different situation. He's younger than I am so I was the one who kind of deserted him.

"Looking for a girl friend isn't the basic point of my life right now. I have school and I have my friends to think about. But when I do think about sharing some of myself with someone, I go around looking for a person I can love. Yes, I do."

"What is love, Jenny? What's a commitment?"

"Love is sharing yourself with a person. It's sharing your feelings and your hopes. It's being nice to each other, and it's being friends. Love is a feeling. Telling the other person how you feel about what they're doing, or how you feel when they get hurt. *Love* is a word that means a whole bunch of things. A commitment is a vow and a pledge. It's a promise to be with another person whenever she needs you and whenever she wants you. And that's the promise that the other person makes to you in return."

"Okay, you're thirteen now. Say when you're a young adult, do you see yourself settling down with another woman in a marriage? Do you see that as real for you?"

"Yes, I do. My mother implies that you should settle down with someone. She thinks a man; I think a woman. But it's the same. I still have the idea I should settle down. I think I'd want to because I'm a very emotional person. I just can't go from one girl friend to another. It's too impersonal for me."

"When you say 'settling down,' what do you mean?"

"I mean sharing an apartment or a house with a woman. Living with her and loving her. That's my basic definition of settling down with a person."

"If you were settled down with someone, Jenny, would sexual fidelity be important to you?"

"It would be very important to me. Like I said, I'm not the kind of person who can jump from one person to another. I'm hoping to find a person who's the same as I am because I'd get hurt easily by someone who jumps around."

"Why would sexual infidelity hurt you? What does that represent to you?"

"It represents using a person for sexual pleasure and then just leaving the person alone by themselves. That scares me because this world says you always have to be with someone every minute of every day. I've started thinking like that. I feel that if the person just leaves you alone, then I guess I get afraid of it."

"You'd want somebody that would be totally with you?"

"Yes, totally, when I wanted her to be. When I needed to be alone, I'd like her to leave me alone. I'd feel the same way with her; when she needed time by herself I'd leave her alone."

"Jenny, can you describe the kind of woman you'd like to settle down with someday?"

"I'd like her to be intelligent, to be very emotional. I'd like her to be tall. Someone who's interested in what I'm interested in. Someone who makes thirty thousand dollars a year." She laughs. "No, seriously, that's a good old society implant there! I'd need someone like me. When I look at a dike, I can't accept her as anyone who can share something with me. I'd feel she was too masculine, out to show the world she's masculine. I need someone who's toned down but not overly feminine. I need someone like me for me to have any feelings for her. I'd like to be very comfortable with the person I love. I think most people would. Role-playing is good for people if it adds something to their relationship. But for me personally, I wouldn't get anything out of it. It would be too false for me."

"Jenny, do you feel, because you're a lesbian, the world is telling you you're not going to succeed, not going to have a happy life?"

"I don't think so. Believe it or not, so far I'm getting along very well with my sexuality. I can accept it. I don't have the kind of friends who'd taunt me for the rest of my life. Nobody's saying, 'Hey, lesbo.' And the job I've picked for myself doesn't have anything to do with sexuality. Journalism is an open thing. I don't need to be feminine. So I feel fine. I don't think the world is saying I can't succeed or I can't have a happy life. I know I *will* no matter what the world says."

"Are you aware of the general feelings of society about gay people?"

"From my mother, yes. My mother is very unaccepting of gay people. That's why I'm afraid to talk to her about it."

"Do you think your mother might feel that way because deep down she knows you're a lesbian?"

"Yes. When I was younger and having my relationship with my girl friend, my mother knew about it. She told me, even before we broke up, that she never wanted me to do anything like that again. That it's dirty and it's wrong. So her antigay feelings could stem from her thinking I'm a lesbian."

"What did you think when your mother told you your relationship wasn't right—that it was dirty?"

"I think it was unfair of her to say those things to me. A person has a right to love whomever they want no matter what the person's sex is. I'm still a human being and I can still love. My mother doesn't realize that there are some people in this world who don't love anyone. And I feel that to be able to love is one of the most important things for a human being."

"Is it important for you to show people who you really are?"

"Yes, it is. If I have to hide, I freak out. I just can't control myself by hiding. I have to be able to open up to everyone no matter what they think."

"Would it be helpful to you to know older lesbians like myself—women you could talk to?"

"I think it would be helpful. You're someone I can talk to and I can show you who I really am. My Freudian symbolism is coming back to me about mother images, but forget it, it's completely off the wall. Talking to older women would be helpful because they've gone through what I'm going through now. They could share their experience with me. And for someone to know what I'm doing now would be comforting. It'd be comforting to know there are other people like me who've gone through what I've gone through. I'd ask an older woman if she's happy being the way she is. I'd ask her if she has someone she loves. I'd ask her if she'd ever been truly hurt by someone."

"Do you think you're going to be hurt more as a person because you're a lesbian?"

"Yes and no. Yes, because maybe people are going to reject me, and rejection is something I can't handle. And, no, because I figure I'll grow accustomed to rejection after a while. Unfortunately, it'll probably ruin some of my personality, but I'll get accustomed to it."

"Jenny, what do you mean when you say it'll probably ruin part of your personality?"

"My personality is to be open, and rejection will probably teach me not to be open. I'll know that if I'm open I'm going to get hurt, so I'll just keep to myself. I'd hate doing that because I'm open. Part of my personality will be completely hidden from people I don't know too well—you know, people I'd like to be friends with. There are certain people I'm afraid of even though I'd like to be friends with them. I'm afraid of them because I think they'll turn on me because I'm a lesbian."

"What does it mean to be a lesbian, Jenny?"

"It means to be a human being first, and next a person, and next a woman who loves other women. Human beings always come first in terms of my defining anyone. So I feel a lesbian is a human being who loves other women."

"You don't see any problem with that, do you?"

"Not at all. My parents' attitudes seem to have gone right over my head. I learned on my own—and very early—to love another woman isn't bad no matter what they say. I still think it's all right. It's a person's right to love another person."

"Jenny, do you think there's a difference between emotional preference and sexual preference?"

"Sexual preference is physical. Emotional preference is looking at the person's personality—her likes and dislikes. I feel there's a difference between them, but when you're choosing a mate they go hand in hand. A gay man isn't going to go out and choose a straight woman because she has the same emotional preference he does—they both happen to emotionally prefer men. This man and this woman might be attracted to each other as friends. But I do feel that some of my friendships with girls do have a small sexual input. I guess I just haven't accepted the fact that there's a separation. Unfortunately, that gets me into trouble once in a while. My straight girl friends want to be my friends emotionally, but they don't want anything to do with me sexually. But when I try to show my affection, they just back off."

"You mean they're afraid?"

"Very. They don't know enough about it so they get scared. If they knew more about homosexuality, they'd be able to accept my affection. They'd be able to show affection for me and know that it wasn't wrong."

"Are you separating affection from sex?"

"Big mistake, Jenny! Nice going, Mary. I shouldn't have separated affection from sex. A friend's affection for a friend, a lover's affection for a lover—they're basically the same but technically different. Sexual affection is a little bit more involved than affection between two friends."

"Jenny, what is homosexuality?"

"Homosexuality is just a preference. It's not going to interfere with a person's mentality. True, gay is a way of life, but we're still human beings. A lot of people think that gays aren't human beings. We are—we're just the same as anyone else. It's just that our sexual preference is different, that's all."

"What do you want out of life, Jenny?"

"A four-year college scholarship. Someone I can love. Friends I can trust. Parents who accept me as I am. And two cats—I love cats."

"Do you think you're any less of a woman because you're a lesbian?"

"Oh, definitely not. From a lesbian's point of view, most of what I've read says it makes you more of a woman. Getting married and pregnant isn't a woman's only prerogative. A woman's prerogative is to be what she is—to love another person and just be human. I can't accept all these stereotypes for girls. I wouldn't accept them if

I was straight. You shouldn't be forced into all these things just because you're a girl."

"What's your greatest fear?"

"Being alone. I don't want to be alone. Loneliness is my biggest fear."

"Do you think you'll be more subject to loneliness because you're a lesbian?"

"Yes, I do. It's harder to find people like me. Straight people don't have to hide the fact that they're heterosexuals. It's easier for straights to find people. It's harder for homosexuals to find people. You never know who is or who isn't gay. You end up being very careful, and in being careful you end up very lonely. What you think is, Am I going to find a straight person and mistake her for gay? Then you're going to get hurt and get yourself in a whole big mess."

"Jenny, where do you stand on religion? What do you think about God?"

"My feelings about God and religion collide. I feel that God doesn't discriminate against a person because she loves a person of the same sex. God is definitely here and He loves us no matter what we are. I've drawn away from the church—I don't think of its restrictions anymore. I've forgotten about religion. I practice my own philosophy of life: there is a God, He is there, but He doesn't make all the decisions. We're human, we're the people who make our own destiny. God's there"—she laughs—"as the universal binding force. You like that one!"

"How will you make your own destiny as a lesbian?"

"I will find my own lover. I will find my own job. I'll do everything for myself. Making a destiny for myself means planning my own future. I'm starting right now. I'm going to be a journalist. I know I'll do it, I know I'll be all right."

"You told me before that you've dated boys. Did you have sexual intercourse with these boys?"

"No, no. Religion still has its reins on me!"

"Well, if sexual intercourse with boys is heavy, what's the equivalent heavy with another girl?"

"Cunnilingus, I think. I don't know. It just seems that something that serious would be on the same level as sexual intercourse."

"Would you practice cunnilingus with another woman?"

"At my age! But then when I think about it, I guess it would depend on how much I wanted to get involved with her. I would if I thought we were still going to be going out together a year later."

"Now what does that have to do with religious restrictions on sex?"

"My religion says you don't have sexual intercourse until you're married, and cunnilingus is absolutely out of the question."

"Where does that leave you, Jenny?"

"That leaves me a heretic!"

"Are you saying that certain sexual acts have a dimension of seriousness attached to them? Is there an emotional seriousness attached to sex?"

"Definitely, I was raised like that. It's always been my personal feeling that if you have sex with a person, you're emotionally involved with that person. I've always connected sex with an emotional and mental involvement. If I was practicing oral love with a woman it'd mean I was emotionally involved with her."

"Do you think you could get that emotionally involved now with a girl?"

"Not with a person my own age. But with an older girl—maybe fifteen or sixteen—yes. I've always liked older friends, and I think I'd be interested in an older woman anywhere from sixteen to twenty-five. Anyone over twenty-five years old would be inaccessible to me and not interested in me."

"What do you expect of me as a gay adult in representing what you've had to say?"

"I hope you'll look at it in terms of what I'm going through and identify with it. It's a very painful time because kids like me are stuck between things. Most gay kids have a negative image of themselves. If you write a positive book, it could give kids a better image of themselves. It could make them feel better about who they are and what they are."

"Jenny, I'm almost out of tape and I could talk to you all weekend."

"I'm getting kind of nervous, Mary. It's almost five o'clock and I have to go all the way home. It's a thirty-five minute ride."

"Come on," I say, "let's go."

We begin to walk to look for a bus, and as we walk we continue talking. I tell Jenny I had lived as a "closeted" gay for seven years. She finds that astonishing until I tell her that just three weeks before, I had interviewed a woman who had lived in a "closet" for almost thirty years.

"I don't know, Jenny," I say, smiling, "I had her a couple of weeks ago. I have you today. Maybe I'm somewhere in between you and her. She's in her sixties, I'm thirty-five, and you're thirteen. I feel like I'm the missing link caught somewhere in between. Like she's the past, I'm the present, and you're the future."

Jenny and I stand on a corner and we can see her bus approaching from several blocks away.

"That's my bus, I'll have to run to the next corner," she says.

I extend my hand to her to say goodbye. She stares at my hand for a second, and then she is hugging me, tighter than I have ever been hugged by any thirteen-year-old.

"Mary," she says, still holding me, "if you write this book, it's going to be so exciting and so hopeful. It'll help kids like me."

As suddenly as she had hugged me is as suddenly as she lets me go and runs for her bus. I watch her racing for the corner, her long hair flying, her sneakers kicking the air. Jenny is a pair of jeans chasing a bus down any avenue in any city. I stand there watching the bus she has caught pull away from the curb. "Bye, Jenny, womanchild in the not-so-promised land. Maybe, after all, life *will* be better for you."

EPILOGUE

As a minority group, homosexuals and lesbians *are* the "gay issue." But as people, we are more important than the issue. Everywhere I went in the course of doing this book I heard the issue of gay rights discussed. I saw pain and I saw rage.

But everywhere I went I saw hope *exclusive* of the issue. I met lesbian and homosexual couples who are shaping their lives and creating their own futures. I met gay men and gay women who are working together to reach out to *our* young and *our* elderly. As a minority group, we are building and strengthening ourselves from within by recognizing and responding to the needs of *our* people—by recognizing and responding to the needs of each other. How we are perceived by a heterosexual society is irrelevant. What is important is how we perceive ourselves as individuals and how we perceive ourselves collectively as an emerging minority group.

I believe that together we must continue to establish our own identity exclusive of the issue. Because we cannot wait for the gay issue to be resolved. As persons, we must live our lives—because our lives are more important than the issue. As we continue to free ourselves of the standards and values of a heterosexual society, we will further actualize our own values as people. And not only do we have values, but we have values of which we can be proud. We need not emulate heterosexual marriages or heterosexual lifestyles. Perhaps the integrity, the lifestyles, and the values of the gay people I have met in the writing of this book should be emulated by a heterosexual society.

For me personally, the most hope-filled experience was talking with the youngsters I interviewed for this book. They well understand the political issues for gays. But they do not understand why they should hide, why they should accept less, why they should be rejected by people they love. They simply do not understand. And therein is the hope because they are a new breed of gay. Because

243

they do not understand the attacks against their dignity and their value as persons, they will be less likely to accept those attacks and less likely to believe they are not as good and as decent as anyone else. Hopefully, all the youngsters—Timothy, Angel, Jeanne, Amy, Judy, Michael, and Jenny—will not do to themselves what I did to myself, what so many of us have done to ourselves.

Considering my upbringing and the influences of society on my life, it would be unreasonable of me to believe that I can have a happy and full life as a lesbian. It would also be unreasonable of me to expect a predominantly heterosexual world to respect my values and my commitment to the woman I love.

However, I have made a personal commitment to persist in being unreasonable. Because to be reasonable is to accept the dictates of a society that is asking me to hate myself, to live as an emotional cripple, to accept second-class status in every aspect of my life, and to pay taxes to support a system of government that denies me my civil rights.

I am comfortable being unreasonable. And, actually, my unreasonableness is not only altruistic, it is also patriotic. If I were to be reasonable, I would be denying society the opportunity to grow and accept *all* people regardless of their ethnic background, race, religion, sex, or sexual orientation. If I were to more reasonably conduct my life and accept my plight, I would be depriving society of the opportunity to adapt to me. And it is important to the health of a society that it adapt to all realities—I'm here, I'm gay, and I ain't going away.

APPENDIX

ADELA OLIVER, PH.D.

Adela Oliver, a licensed psychologist, is responsible for the design of the "Speak Out" questionnaire. Dr. Oliver field-tested a pilot sample of "Speak Out" and later developed a computer program and coding system for the returns on the questionnaire. Dr. Oliver, a graduate of Yeshiva University, is a practicing psychologist and is currently employed as a behavioral science management consultant working with major corporations throughout the country. President of the Metropolitan New York Association for Applied Psychology, Dr. Oliver has a broad background in research, counseling, questionnaire design, and attitude surveys.

SPEAK OUT

Several months ago, Crown Publishers asked me if I would be interested in writing a book on permanent gay relationships—both female and male. "You mean gay marriages." I said. They seemed confused. "Well," I explained, "what makes a straight marriage any different from a permanent gay relationship? The essence of permanent relationships is the same for both gay and straight couples." The discussions that ensued became the basis for a book that I will write and Crown will publish.

The objective of the book: to serve as a vehicle through which gay people can explore the lifestyles of gay couples; to review financial problems unique to gay couples and suggest approaches to such issues as mortgages, insurance, joint ownership of property; to introduce role models of gay couples to gay young adults.

I believe there are millions of other gay people like myself who live happy and full lives with the partner of their choice. I am therefore reaching out to the gay community across the country for its assistance—your assistance—in expressing a total lifestyle.

Please complete and return this questionnaire by April 23. If you can, make copies of it and distribute it among your friends. I hope my book can say that there are thousands of gay couples who are or have been involved in meaningful relationships, and who feel their marriages/relationships are as valid as those which have been sanctioned by the church or state.

I need your help to say it. Thanks for speaking out.

Mary Mendola

March 1979

246

The QUESTIONNAIRE

The American Heritage Dictionary defines marriage as the legal union of a man and a woman. However, that same dictionary defines the verb *to marry* as entering into a close marriage, uniting or forming a union. In the second reference, there is no distinction made as to the sexes or the legality of the act. For the purposes of this questionnaire, the term *marriage/relationship* applies exclusively to gay couples: two men or two women committed to a permanent or ongoing relationship with each other.

INSTRUCTIONS

This questionnaire has fill-in questions plus multiple-choice items. The latter consists of a series of statements and questions; each is followed by several numbered choices. Read each question carefully, decide which of the choices most nearly indicates your answer, and circle the number next to that answer. Please be frank so that the information I receive from you is meaningful. When you complete the questionnaire, simply enclose it in the attached postage-paid envelope and return it.

Your privacy in participating in this survey will be respected. You yourself determine the confidentiality of the questionnaire: you are being asked to give neither your name nor your address. If you wish to attach additional comments, and they are welcome, you need not sign your name.

1. What is your definition of a gay marriage/relationship? _____
   _____
   _____
   _____
   _____

2. Your sex is:
   1 Female   2 Male

3. Based on your own definition, you are presently:
   1—Permanently committed (married)
   2—Living with someone
   3—Separated from your partner (divorced)
   4—Widowed
   5—Single

If, according to your own definition, you were previously involved in a gay marriage/relationship, but are now living alone, answer the following questions based on your previous relationship.

If you are presently single and have never lived with someone, you need not answer the following questions. However, please answer question 18 and do complete the background information on the back page. Thank you for your thoughts in question one.

4A Do either you or your partner have children?
   1 Yes   2 No

4B The children are:
   1—Yours
   2—Your partner's
   3—You each have children

4C Please list age and sex of children: _____
_____

4D The children live:
   1—With you and your partner most of the time
   2—With you and your partner less than half the time
   3—Do not live with you but visit in your home
   4—Do not live with you, and visit only outside your home
   5—Do not see you at all

5. Do you feel that the presence of children in a marriage/relationship creates stability?
   1—Yes
   2—No
   3—No opinion

6. How long did you and your partner know each other before you began to live together?
   1—less than 3 months
   2—3 months but less than 6
   3—6 months but less than one year
   4—one year or longer

7. Did the decision to live together just evolve, or did it include an agreement:
   1—To live together on a trial basis
   2—To live together permanently
   3—It just evolved

8. Do you and your partner:

1—Have sex exclusively with each other
2—Have sex mostly with each other, but have occasional outside sexual affairs
3—Have sex both together and outside your relationship on a regular basis
4—Live together without a sexual relationship and each of you is free to have sex outside the marriage

9. If your parents are aware of your marriage/relationship, do they:
   1—Accept it (eg: invite you and your partner to family functions)
   2—Treat your relationship as simply two friends living together with no commitment
   3—Refuse to see you and your partner together under any circumstances
   4—Are not aware

10. If your brother(s) and/or sister(s) are aware of your marriage/relationship, do they:
    1—Accept it (eg: invite you and your partner to family functions)
    2—Treat it as simply two friends living together with no commitment
    3—Refuse to see you and your partner together under any circumstances
    4—Are not aware

11. There are many sources of conflict in a marriage/relationship. Check as many areas as are applicable where you and your partner have conflicts.
    1—Job/Career responsibilities
    2—In-law problems
    3—Problems with children
    4—Financial problems
    5—Sexual problems
    6—Communication problems
    7—Other _____
    (Please specify)

12. Do you believe, or hope, that you and your partner will grow into old age together?
    1 Yes   2 No

13. If you had a choice, would you choose to be:

1—Married in a civil ceremony
2—Married in a religious ceremony
3—I do not choose to be married in any type of ceremony

14. Check as many choices as are applicable. If your neighbors are aware of your marriage/relationship, do they
    1—Accept it (eg: treat you and your partner as a couple)
    2—Treat it as simply two friends living together with no commitment
    3—Deny or ignore it (eg: invite only one or the other of you to social functions)
    4—Refuse to have anything to do with you because they know you are gay
    5—We do not socialize with our neighbors by choice
    6—Our neighbors are not aware that we are a gay couple
    7—We are careful to make certain our neighbors do not know we are a gay couple
    8—We do not care whether or not our neighbors know we are a gay couple

15. Where did you meet your partner?
    1—Through business
    2—At a gay organization
    3—Through friends
    4—At school
    5—At a religious organization
    6—At a bar
    7—Through family
    8—Other _____
       (Please specify)

16. If you were having marital/relationship problems, you would consider discussing them with (check as many as applicable)
    1—A brother or sister
    2—Parent(s)
    3—Gay friends
    4—Straight friends
    5—Clergy
    6—Psychotherapist (psychiatrist, psychologist, social worker)
    7—Other _____
       (Please specify)

17. You and your partner socialize with:
   1—Gay people exclusively
   2—Mostly gay people
   3—Mostly straight people
   4—Straight and gay people
   5—Only straight people

18. I am comfortable with the use of the word "marriage" as applied to permanent gay relationships.
   1 Yes   2 No

19. Do you and your partner have a financial partnership, planning your spending as a couple?
   1 Yes   2 No

20. Do you and your partner pool all or part of your individual paychecks to cover essential living expenses?
   1—We pool part of our paychecks
   2—We pool our total paychecks
   3—No, we don't pool our money on a regular basis
   4—Not applicable: only one of us works

21. Is your house or apartment:
   1—Rented
   2—Owned by you
   3—Owned by your partner
   4—Jointly owned

22. Do you and your partner jointly own any of the following? (Check as many as are applicable)
   1—A business
   2—A country home
   3—Land
   4—Household furnishings
   5—Car(s)
   6—None of the above
   7—Other _____
   (Please specify)

23. Do either you or your partner own life insurance naming the other as beneficiary?
   1 Yes   2 No

24. Do either you or your partner have a will bequeathing to the other either all or part of monies, properties, etc?
   1 Yes   2 No

25. Do either you or your partner have a retirement plan?
    1 Yes   2 No

26. Health insurance (check as many as are applicable)
    1—I have health insurance
    2—I do not have health insurance
    3—My partner has health insurance
    4—My partner does not have health insurance

27. Are you active in any of the following organizations? (Check as many as applicable.)
    1—Religious
    2—Charitable
    3—Political
    4—Citizens/Committee
    5—PTA or similar
    6—Scouting
    7—Little League
    8—Big Brother/Sister
    9—Other _____
                            (Please specify)

BACKGROUND INFORMATION

The information below allows the comparison of responses of different groups of people on specific topics.

28. My partner and I have been (or if you based your answers on a previous relationship *were)* living together:
    1—Less than one year
    2—One year but less than two
    3—Two or more years but less than 5
    4—Five or more years but less than 10
    5—Ten or more years

29. Based on your own definition of a marriage/relationship, how many times have you been married?
    1—Never
    2—Once
    3—Twice
    4—Three or more times

30. My partner and I live in:
    1—The suburbs
    2—A rural area
    3—A city

31. Please list the state you live in:
    _____

32. My occupation is:
    _____

33. My partner's occupation is:
    _____

34. Age

	SELF	PARTNER
18-24—	1	1
25-29—	2	2
30-34—	3	3
35-39—	4	4
40-49—	5	5
50 or over—	6	6

35. We are:

	SELF	PARTNER
American Indian	1	1
Black	2	2
Caucasian (White)	3	3
Hispanic	4	4
Oriental	5	5

36. My partner filled out a separate questionnaire:
    1 Yes   2 No

37. What do you feel are the *differences* between a gay marriage/
    relationship and a straight marriage/relationship?
    _____
    _____
    _____
    _____

38. What do you feel are the *similarities* between a gay marriage/
    relationship and a straight marriage/relationship?
    _____
    _____
    _____
    _____

39. What do you consider to be most important in a marriage/relationship?

_____

_____

_____

_____

Thank you for sharing your thoughts with me.

RESULTS of the "SPEAK OUT" QUESTIONNAIRE

1. What is your definition of a gay marriage/relationship?

	TOTAL percent	FEMALE percent	MALE percent
Commitment	53	55	52
Companionship	19	19	19
Interpersonal relationship	12	11	13
Self-actualization	12	11	13

2. Your sex is:

	percent
1—Female	56
2—Male	44

3. Based on your own definition, you are presently:

	TOTAL percent	FEMALE percent	MALE percent
1—Permanently committed (married)	67	70	63
2—Living with someone	11	13	9
3—Separated from your partner (divorced)	11	10	13
4—Widowed	1	0	1
5—Single	10	7	14

4A Do either you or your partner have children?

	TOTAL percent	FEMALE percent	MALE percent
1 Yes	21	25	17
2 No	79	75	83

4B The children are:

	TOTAL percent	FEMALE percent	MALE percent
1—Yours	43	39	50
2—Your partner's	40	42	37
3—You each have children	17	19	13

4C Please list age and sex of children:

	TOTAL percent	FEMALE percent	MALE percent
One	38	36	43
Two	30	23	43
Three	12	17	4
Four	10	15	0
Five	7	7	7
Six	1	0	4
Seven	0	0	0
Eight	1	2	0

4D The children live:

	TOTAL percent	FEMALE percent	MALE percent
1—With you and your partner most of the time	38	58	3
2—With you and your partner less than half the time	1	0	3
3—Do not live with you but visit in your home	44	39	53
4—Do not live with you, and visit only outside your home	4	2	7
5—Do not see you at all	13	2	33

5. Do you feel that the presence of children in a marriage/relationship creates stability?

	TOTAL percent	FEMALE percent	MALE percent
1—Yes	21	22	20
2—No	51	57	43
3—No opinion	28	21	38

6. How long did you and your partner know each other before you began to live together?

	TOTAL	FEMALE	MALE
	percent	*percent*	*percent*
1—less than 3 months	19	17	24
2—3 months but less than 6	24	22	27
3—6 months but less than one year	21	20	23
4—one year or longer	35	42	26

7. Did the decision to live together just evolve, or did it include an agreement:

	TOTAL	FEMALE	MALE
	percent	*percent*	*percent*
1—To live together on a trial basis	12	15	8
2—To live together permanently	32	34	29
3—It just evolved	56	51	63

8. Do you and your partner:

	TOTAL	FEMALE	MALE
	percent	*percent*	*percent*
1—Have sex exclusively with each other	64	83	37
2—Have sex mostly with each other, but have occasional outside sexual affairs	29	14	49
3—Have sex both together and outside your relationship on a regular basis	4	1	8
4—Live together without a sexual relationship and each of you is free to have sex outside the marriage	3	2	6

9. If your parents are aware of your marriage/relationship, do they:

	TOTAL	FEMALE	MALE
	percent	*percent*	*percent*
1—Accept it (eg: invite you and your partner to family functions)	40	37	44

2—Treat your relationship as simply two friends living together with no commitment	21	18	25
3—Refuse to see you and your partner together under any circumstances	3	3	2
4—Are not aware	35	41	29

10. If your brother(s) and/or sister(s) are aware of your marriage/ relationship, do they:

	TOTAL	FEMALE	MALE
	percent	*percent*	*percent*
1—Accept it (eg: invite you and your partner to family functions)	53	54	52
2—Treat it as simply two friends living together with no commitment	16	12	22
3—Refuse to see you and your partner together under any circumstances	1	1	2
4—Are not aware	29	31	24

11. There are many sources of conflict in a marriage/relationship. Check as many areas as are applicable where you and your partner have conflicts.

	TOTAL	FEMALE	MALE
	percent	*percent*	*percent*
1—Job/Career responsibilities	32	49	51
2—In-law problems	14	59	41
3—Problems with children	8	79	21
4—Financial problems	31	52	48
5—Sexual problems	32	57	43
6—Communication problems	45	51	49
7—Other _____ (Please specify)	10	64	36
Role identification/adjustment problems	2	71	29
Daily adjustment problems	9	51	49
Religious conflicts	1	60	40
Jealousy	3	91	9

258   *Appendix*

12. Do you believe, or hope, that you and your partner will grow
into old age together?

	TOTAL percent	FEMALE percent	MALE percent
1 Yes	95	98	90
2 No	5	2	10

13. If you had a choice, would you choose to be:

	TOTAL percent	FEMALE percent	MALE percent
1—Married in a civil ceremony	9	11	7
2—Married in a religious ceremony	33	30	39
3—I do not choose to be married in any type of ceremony	55	58	52

14. Check as many choices as are applicable. If your neighbors are
aware of your marriage/relationship, do they

	TOTAL percent	FEMALE percent	MALE percent
1—Accept it (eg: treat you and your partner as a couple)	26	49	51
2—Treat it as simply two friends living together with no commitment	31	56	44
3—Deny or ignore it (eg: invite only one or the other of you to social functions)	3	27	73
4—Refuse to have anything to do with you because they know you are gay	1	33	67
5—We do not socialize with our neighbors by choice	29	58	42
6—Our neighbors are not aware that we are a gay couple	30	77	23
7—We are careful to make certain our neighbors do not know we are a gay couple	12	77	23

8—We do not care whether or not our neighbors know we are a gay couple	48	53	47

15. Where did you meet your partner?

	TOTAL *percent*	FEMALE *percent*	MALE *percent*
1—Through business	13	19	5
2—At a gay organization	6	5	7
3—Through friends	21	24	18
4—At school	13	18	6
5—At a religious organization	9	5	15
6—At a bar	18	11	27
7—Through family	1	2	1
8—Other _____ (Please specify)	11	11	11
Other gay establishments (baths, bookstores, restaurants, etc.)	6	3	9
By mail (newspaper/magazine ad)	0	0	1
Professional associations	1	2	0

16. If you were having marital/relationship problems, you would consider discussing them with (check as many as applicable)

	TOTAL *percent*	FEMALE *percent*	MALE *percent*
1—A brother or sister	14	58	42
2—Parent(s)	8	41	59
3—Gay friends	85	56	44
4—Straight friends	35	61	39
5—Clergy	23	34	66
6—Psychotherapist (psychiatrist, psychologist, social worker)	53	66	34

17. You and your partner socialize with:

	TOTAL *percent*	FEMALE *percent*	MALE *percent*
1—Gay people exclusively	2	1	2
2—Mostly gay people	37	37	36
3—Mostly straight people	3	6	1
4—Straight and gay people	58	55	61
5—Only straight people	0	0	0

18. I am comfortable with the use of the word "marriage" as applied to permanent gay relationships

	TOTAL percent	FEMALE percent	MALE percent
1 Yes	56	56	56
2 No	44	44	44

19. Do you and your partner have a financial partnership, planning your spending as a couple?

	TOTAL percent	FEMALE percent	MALE percent
1 Yes	71	72	70
2 No	29	28	30

20. Do you and your partner pool all or part of your individual paychecks to cover essential living expenses?

	TOTAL percent	FEMALE percent	MALE percent
1—We pool part of our paychecks	41	44	36
2—We pool our total paychecks	29	29	28
3—No, we don't pool our money on a regular basis	25	22	30
4—Not applicable: only one of us works	5	5	5

21. Is your house or apartment:

	TOTAL percent	FEMALE percent	MALE percent
1—Rented	51	48	54
2—Owned by you	15	12	18
3—Owned by your partner	11	9	13
4—Jointly owned	24	31	15

22. Do you and your partner jointly own any of the following? (Check as many as are applicable)

	TOTAL percent	FEMALE percent	MALE percent
1—A business	8	64	36
2—A country home	7	57	43
3—Land	8	59	41
4—Household furnishings	59	62	38

	TOTAL	FEMALE	MALE
5—Car(s) or motorcycles	26	61	39
6—None of the above	28	48	52
7—Other _____ (Please specify)	5	84	16
Pets	2	80	20
Savings Accounts/Investments	4	68	32

23. Do either you or your partner own life insurance naming the other as beneficiary?

	TOTAL	FEMALE	MALE
	percent	*percent*	*percent*
1 Yes	56	60	51
2 No	44	40	49

24. Do either you or your partner have a will bequeathing to the other either all or part of monies, properties, etc.?

	TOTAL	FEMALE	MALE
	percent	*percent*	*percent*
1 Yes	45	46	44
2 No	54	54	55

25. Do either you or your partner have a retirement plan?

	TOTAL	FEMALE	MALE
	percent	*percent*	*percent*
1 Yes	73	72	76
2 No	27	28	24

26. Health insurance (check as many as are applicable)

	TOTAL	FEMALE	MALE
	percent	*percent*	*percent*
1—I have health insurance	87	57	43
2—I do not have health insurance	8	53	47
3—My partner has health insurance	78	58	42
4—My partner does not have health insurance	9	57	43

27. Are you active in any of the following organizations? (Check as many as applicable.)

	TOTAL	FEMALE	MALE
	percent	*percent*	*percent*
1—Religious	47	43	57
2—Charitable	16	37	63

3—Political	26	62	38
4—Citizens/Committee	14	47	53
5—PTA or similar	3	75	25
6—Scouting	2	83	17
7—Little League	1	50	50
8—Big Brother/Sister	2	57	43
9—Other _____ (Please specify)	6	61	39
Professional organizations	13	67	33
Gay service organizations	9	59	41
Community health/welfare/ service organizations	5	70	30
College or educational organizations	1	33	67
Women's organizations (NOW, etc.)	4	100	0

28. My partner and I have been (or if you based your answers on a previous relationship *were*) living together:

	TOTAL	FEMALE	MALE
	percent	*percent*	*percent*
1—Less than one year	19	19	19
2—One year but less than two	16	16	15
3—Two or more years but less than 5	29	29	29
4—Five or more years but less than 10	19	20	19
5—Ten or more years	17	17	18

29. Based on your own definition of a marriage/relationship, how many times have you been married?

	TOTAL	FEMALE	MALE
	percent	*percent*	*percent*
1—Never	11	10	12
2—Once	47	47	46
3—Twice	31	31	31
4—Three or more times	11	12	11

30. My partner and I live in:

	TOTAL percent	FEMALE percent	MALE percent
1—The suburbs	39	46	29
2—A rural area	7	9	4
3—A city	54	45	66

31. Please list the state you live in:

	TOTAL percent	FEMALE percent	MALE percent
New England	12	14	9
Middle Atlantic	38	31	47
North Central	16	11	22
South	10	12	8
Mountain	3	3	2
Pacific	21	28	13
Canada	1	1	0

32. My occupation is:

	TOTAL percent	FEMALE percent	MALE percent
Officials and managers	12	9	15
Professionals	54	60	46
Technicians	6	6	7
Sales workers	5	4	6
Office and clerical	9	8	11
Craft workers (skilled)	3	2	4
Operatives (semiskilled)	3	3	3
Laborers (unskilled)	1	0	1
Service workers	2	2	2
Students	4	5	2
Clergy	1	1	2

33. My partner's occupation is:

	TOTAL percent	FEMALE percent	MALE percent
Officials and managers	11	8	13
Professionals	55	61	48
Technicians	7	7	8

Sales workers	3	2	5
Office and clerical	8	6	11
Craft workers (skilled)	3	3	4
Operatives (semiskilled)	1	1	2
Laborers (unskilled)	1	1	0
Service workers	4	4	4
Students	5	7	3
Clergy	1	0	2

34. Age

Self

	TOTAL percent	FEMALE percent	MALE percent
18-24	10	10	10
25-29	17	16	19
30-34	23	21	26
35-39	19	21	18
40-49	21	24	17
50 or over	10	8	12

Partner

	TOTAL percent	FEMALE percent	MALE percent
18-24	11	11	11
25-29	18	16	21
30-34	23	20	26
35-39	21	23	17
40-49	20	24	16
50 or over	7	6	9

35. We are:

Self

	TOTAL percent	FEMALE percent	MALE percent
American Indian	1	0	1
Black	2	1	3
Caucasian (White)	95	95	94
Hispanic	2	3	2
Oriental	1	1	0

Partner	TOTAL percent	FEMALE percent	MALE percent
American Indian	0	0	0
Black	3	2	5
Caucasian (White)	92	94	90
Hispanic	3	3	3
Oriental	1	1	2

36. My partner filled out a separate questionnaire:

	TOTAL percent	FEMALE percent	. MALE percent
1 Yes	61	69	51
2 No	39	31	49

37. What do you feel are the *differences* between a gay marriage/ relationship and a straight marriage/relationship?

	TOTAL percent	FEMALE percent	MALE percent
Societal approval	47	47	47
Economic relationship	16	17	15
Interpersonal relationship	14	16	11
Parent/Family	10	6	15

38. What do you feel are the *similarities* between a gay marriage/ relationship and a straight marriage/relationship?

	TOTAL percent	FEMALE percent	MALE percent
Commitment	41	40	42
Companionship	19	17	22
Interpersonal relationship	18	20	16
Self-actualization	7	8	6

39. What do you consider to be most important in a marriage/ relationship?

	TOTAL percent	FEMALE percent	MALE percent
Interpersonal relationship	49	52	44
Commitment	26	23	31
Companionship	12	12	12
Self-actualization	12	12	13

INDEX